# NIKLAS LUHMANN'S MODERNITY

*Cultural Memory*
*in*
*the*
*Present*

*Mieke Bal and Hent de Vries, Editors*

# NIKLAS LUHMANN'S MODERNITY

*The Paradoxes of Differentiation*

*William Rasch*

STANFORD UNIVERSITY PRESS

STANFORD, CALIFORNIA

2000

Stanford University Press
Stanford, California

Printed in the United States of America

Library of Congress Cataloging-in-Publication Data

Rasch, William
    Niklas Luhmann's modernity : the paradoxes of differentiation /
William Rasch.
        p.    cm. — (Cultural memory in the present)
    Includes bibliographical references and index.
    ISBN 0-8047-3991-9 (alk. paper) — ISBN 0-8047-3992-7
(paper : alk. paper)
        1. Luhmann, Niklas.    2. Sociology.    3. Differentiation
(Sociology)    I. Title.    II. Series.
HM479.L84 R37    2000
306—dc21                                        00-057327

  ∞  This book is printed on acid-free, archival quality paper.

Original printing 2000
Last figure below indicates year of this printing:
09  08  07  06  05  04  03  02  01  00

Typeset by James P. Brommer in 11/13.5 Garamond

# Acknowledgments

Revised versions of the following essays appear in this volume as Chapters 1 through 7:

"Theories of Complexity, Complexities of Theory: Habermas, Luhmann, and the Study of Social Systems." *German Studies Review* 14 (1991): 65–83.

"Injecting Noise into the System: Hermeneutics and the Necessity of Misunderstanding." *SubStance: A Review of Theory and Literary Criticism* 21 (1992): 61–76.

"Luhmann's *Widerlegung des Idealismus?*: Constructivism as a Two-Front War." *Soziale Systeme* 4, no. 1 (1998): 151–59.

"In Search of the Lyotard Archipelago, Or: How to Live with Paradox and Learn to Like It." *New German Critique* 61 (Winter 1994): 55–75.

"The Limit of Modernity: Luhmann and Lyotard on Exclusion." *Soziale Systeme* 3, no. 2 (1997): 257–69.

"Immanent Systems, Transcendental Temptations, and the Limits of Ethics." *Cultural Critique* 30 (Spring 1995): 193–221. Published by the University of Minnesota Press.

"Locating the Political: Schmitt, Mouffe, Luhmann and the Possibility of Pluralism." *International Review of Sociology* 7, no. 1 (March 1997): 103–15. Published by Carfax Publishing, Taylor & Francis Ltd., P.O. Box 25, Abingdon, Oxfordshire, OX14 3UE, UK.

The interview with Katherine Hayles and Niklas Luhmann first appeared as:

"Theory of a Different Order: A Conversation with Katherine Hayles and Niklas Luhmann." *Cultural Critique* 31 (Fall 1995): 7–36. Published by the University of Minnesota Press.

My endeavor to come to terms with the work of Niklas Luhmann began as I worked on my dissertation during the 1980s. My advisor, Jeffrey Peck, was gracious enough to humor my diversion, which, after my dissertation was completed, became an obsession. I am grateful to Peck as well for introducing me to Klaus Wegmann, who provided me with my first comprehensive introduction to Luhmann's work.

Over the years, encouragement has come from numerous sources. I wish to thank members of Indiana University's Science and Literature Affinity Group, especially Richard Nash, Marti Crouch, and Stephen H. Kellert, for many evenings of stimulating conversation. Early encouragement came from John McGowan, despite his profound disagreements with some aspects of my work, and Hans Ulrich Gumbrecht. Paulo Barbesino, Norbert Bolz, Fritz Breithaupt, Urs Stäheli, Salvino Salveggio, Uwe Steiner, Bianca Theisen, and Thomas Wägenbaur have read various essays and offered helpful criticisms. I appreciate Dirk Baecker's invitation to submit work to the German journal *Soziale Systeme*. James Rolleston and Carsten Strathausen offered valuable suggestions for revision of the final manuscript. I am particularly grateful to Katherine Hayles for her support and her willingness to participate in the somewhat unorthodox interview printed in these pages, and to Niklas Luhmann for his patience, good humor, and fascinating conversation.

Without the generous support and tireless efforts of Helen Tartar, of Stanford University Press, this book would never have seen the light of day. Nancy Young may very well be the closest reader this book will ever have. I owe her a debt of gratitude for the clarification of numerous stylistic and conceptual problems.

My chair, Terence Thayer, has been a constant source of encouragement. Financial support has come from the Indiana University Dean of Faculties office.

Donna Przybylowicz and Abdul JanMohamed opened up the pages of *Cultural Critique* to an examination of systems theory, and Peter Uwe Hohendahl and Andreas Huyssen were very interested and active coeditors of a special issue of *New German Critique* on Luhmann. My thanks to them for their help.

My friend and colleague Andreas Michel has always been a knowledgeable and perceptive reader, and to him I owe a special debt of gratitude.

Jonathan Elmer's generosity exceeds the bounds of reason, and his powers of reason are such that I am always enriched by any exchange of ideas with him.

I owe more to Marc Weiner than I can say. He has been a careful critic of nearly all that I have written and a long-standing friend without whom I would not be where I am—literally.

Cary Wolfe has been my "partner in crime," as he likes to call it, on a number of occasions, including the special issues of *Cultural Critique* and the Multidisciplinary Faculty Seminar on systems theory and postmodernity that we codirected. His energy, drive, and no-nonsense work ethic are unmatched. My thanks to him for the "collaborative years."

Eva Knodt was my first partner in crime. She and I invited Luhmann for a two-week stay as a fellow of the Institute for Advanced Study at Indiana University, organized a conference entitled "Systems Theory and Postmodernity," and coedited the *New German Critique* issue. When she gets wind of an idea, she'll track it down to the ends of the universe. Her decision to leave the academy and pursue a real life among the California redwoods was a splendid personal decision but a terrible loss for the profession.

This book is dedicated to my wife, Christine R. Farris—whose own research on the paradoxes of interdisciplinary writing programs and whose fierce observations of the world constantly help me keep my ideas in sharp focus—and to our daughter, Alison Elizabeth Farris Rasch, without whom, why bother.

—W. R.

# Contents

## A Note on Translations

English quotations cited from foreign-language editions are my translations. Quotations cited from published English translations are the work of those translators unless otherwise indicated. Italics in quotations follow the cited sources unless otherwise indicated. Full information on sources is given in Works Cited.

—W.R.

# NIKLAS LUHMANN'S MODERNITY

# Introduction: Paradise Lost, Modernity Regained

> If there is a significant difference between Luhmann's diagnosis of modernity and the contemporary discourse on postmodernism, it would have to be sought, it seems to me, in the theoretical rigor with which Luhmann thinks through and embraces the consequences of modernization—*not* because the society in which we live is the best of all possible worlds, but because an acceptance without nostalgia of the structural limitations of modernity is a precondition, and possibly the only way, of finding creative solutions to its problems.
> —Eva Knodt, foreword to Niklas Luhmann, *Social Systems*

The studies contained in this volume serve as an introduction to the thought of the German social theorist Niklas Luhmann, who died in 1998, leaving behind an enormous body of work that only now is beginning to receive the attention it is due in the Anglophone world. The volume is an introduction, but no primer, no step-by-step explanation of key terms and concepts. Such explanation occurs, to be sure, but only in the context of a larger examination of the nature of modernity as Luhmann envisions it. "Modernity" has become a wide-open term, capable of accommodating multiple and contradictory meanings. For some it is an ongoing project; for others it is history; and for still others it has never happened. For Luhmann, it is the precondition of all our deliberations, the "structure" within which our "semantics" makes sense, even as we think we celebrate (or mourn) its passing. Until we cease being modern (a moment that can only be known, or constructed, in retrospect), all our apocalyptic and utopian longings will serve simply as symptoms of the modern condition. But that, as Luhmann would have quickly pointed out, is the wrong way of phrasing it. Modernity is not a disease for which we seek a cure but rather the question to which we continually devise answers, the insoluble problem for which we find a continuing series of incomplete solutions. Modernity is the structure of contingency that forces selections, which, in turn, force further selections, none able to assert its own necessity. When we grow impatient with the indeterminacy forced upon us and seek solace in community, religion (orthodox or "civic"), consensus, and a universal vision of the good life, we grow impatient with modernity itself.

The image of contemporary society that Luhmann offers has never been particularly popular. As a structure of uncertainty—generally excoriated as late capitalism or simply nihilism—it is not so much the promised exuberance of a eudaemonic postmodernity as it is an echo of the modernity already described by Max Weber. As the proudly skeptical German philosopher Odo Marquard puts it:

What comes after the postmodern? In my opinion, the modern. The formula "postmodernity" is either an anti-modernist or a pluralist slogan. As an anti-modernist motto it is a dangerous illusion, because to do away with the modern world is in no way desirable. As a pluralist one it affirms an old and respectable modernist motif, for the modern world was always and still is rationalization and pluralization. (Marquard 1989, 7)

Rationalization and pluralization are Weberian themes, evoking not only the "disenchanted" world, in which nothing remains mysterious because "one can, in principle, master all things by calculation" (M. Weber 1946, 139), but also the irreconcilable "polytheism" of values and the very splintering of reason itself into a plurality of system rationalities. Could it be, therefore, that after the apogee of the postmodern critique—which is said to reflect the political, social, and technological changes emerging during the second half of the twentieth century—we find ourselves once again in the middle of the coolly calculable modernity that was diagnosed by sociology in its early-twentieth-century infancy? Have we never left it, or are we instead to think that, to adopt Bruno Latour's phrase, "we have never been modern"—until now? Whatever the answer to that question, we can still ask: If this is modernity, do we really want to be here? Marquard apparently thinks that to be elsewhere would be worse. Yet, for most of the twentieth century, our best and our brightest have insistently told us how dissatisfied we must be with what we have. Rationalization and pluralization, we have heard, are really reification and alienation, really social and psychic fragmentation. Rationalization has epistemologically separated us (subjects) from our natural surroundings (objects), while pluralization has voided us of our moral center. With no vision of the whole and our place in it, we have no sure knowledge of how to live. Nihilism and relativism, argue both the Left and the Right, is the inevitable fate of such a meaningless modernity. Rationalization and pluralization have therefore been emphatically rejected, have been sublimated in a variety of historical and political theodicies; and even when grudgingly acknowledged as irreducible and necessary, they have nevertheless been quarantined, kept at a distance from that lifeboat named the Lifeworld, the last remnant of authenticity and free intersubjectivity equipped with a rudder.[1] And yet now—after the postmodern critique has once again questioned the wisdom of a too narrowly defined Enlightenment project, and as we enter another millennium without the benefit of Messianic guidance—it seems that neither our quasi-theological rejections of the world nor our political theodicies and ethical lifeworlds have been able to move us beyond the barren landscape of rationalization and pluralization. If Marquard is right and there is no place like our present homelessness away from home, then it is Luhmann who can best guide us in this ever-expanding wilderness.

What follows in this introduction, therefore, is not so much a conventional explication of the work of Niklas Luhmann as an examination of the structure of modernity that both dictates his observations and emerges as a result of them. In the first section, modernity takes shape as a defiant defense of Kantian antinomies. In the second, it forms itself from the bottom up, as it were, as the empirically determined impossibility of empirical observation. In the third, it asserts itself as the paradoxical necessity of contingency.

## Sublation Canceled

In her masterful assessment of the twentieth-century sociological tradition, *Hegel: Contra Sociology*, Gillian Rose tells a classically Marxian tale about Hegel and the dichotomies of modern society. "Hegel's philosophy," she writes, "has no social import if the absolute cannot be thought." By "absolute" she means "the comprehensive thinking which transcends the dichotomies between concept and intuition, theoretical and practical reason." As yet, however, the absolute "cannot be thought (realized) because these dichotomies and their determination are not transcended" (Rose 1981, 204). The dichotomies in question are Kantian in origin, located *in*

Kant's First Critique (the dichotomy between concept and intuition) and *between* his First (theoretical) and Second (practical) Critiques. Whereas Kant saw these dichotomies as constitutive of reason and thus as nontranscendable, Rose, with Hegel, reads them historically, as correlated with existing social structures (law and property) and thus as transcendable. "The overall intention of Hegel's thought," she therefore concludes, "is to make a different ethical life possible by providing insight into the displacement of actuality in those dominant philosophies which are assimilated to and reinforce bourgeois law and bourgeois property relations." Yet "as long as these relations prevail," this insight, this ability to think the absolute, will remain an impossibility, for under these circumstances, "the absolute can only be thought by an abstract consciousness," a consciousness that will inevitably reinscribe the dichotomies (208). Indeed, "an abstract opposition," Rose maintains, "is a bad infinite which is therefore repeated but never sublated or transcended" (212). A genuine thinking of the absolute, on the other hand, both presupposes and occasions a concrete transformation of the actuality from which the thinking is done: to think the absolute, that is, to overcome the abstraction of the dichotomies, necessitates the overcoming of bourgeois law (the dissociation of the right from the good) and bourgeois property relations, while to overcome *these* requires the ability to think the absolute, a thinking that recognizes their historical contingency.

Overcoming dichotomies means recognizing that they can be overcome; and such recognition presupposes another distinction, between those who accept dichotomies as irrefragably given and those who believe in and desire resolution. As the title of Rose's study indicates, this latter distinction is that between sociology and Hegel. Rose reads modern sociology as a bad infinite based on the neo-Kantian abstract opposition of validity and value (Rose 1981, 1–47, 211–20). If the "structural metacritique of validity (Durkheim)" leads to the absolutizing of the "totally conditioned agent," then the "action-oriented metacritique of values (Weber)" results in the absolutizing of the "unconditioned actor" (212, 214). On the one hand, we have the primacy of theoretical reason, the "structured" realm of necessity that is nature; on the other, the primacy of practical reason, the free, supersensible, self-positing "Ich" that simultaneously posits its conditioned other. The former leads to an "empty" structural sociology, the latter to a "blind" action theory. Social theory—whether we label it "French structuralism" or "German humanism"—becomes, therefore, a de facto justification of the modern order precisely because it lacks reference to "transformative activity," as well as to "property relations, law and the corresponding media of representation" (214). In other words, the same dichotomies that Kant chronicled and Hegel critiqued run through modern social theory as well, because competing schools cannot perceive the unity of their difference—a unity that transcends the conditions that these theories describe and therefore a unity that, if perceived, could alter these conditions. As such, Rose suggests, modern sociology cannot be the place from which transformative thinking of the absolute could occur. Rather, it can only be a historical symptom, since by virtue of its very structure it reflects the abstract antinomies that characterize modernity, antinomies that the thinking of the absolute is designed to transcend. Modernity, on this view, is forever incomplete. It is simply the condition for the possibility of its own transcendence. Accordingly, politics within modernity can only be figured as the politics of modernity's destruction, a kind of chronic, low-grade infection of discontent with the affirmative and an antibiotic affirmation of the critical. It is as if the City of Man, in which we are of necessity condemned to live, perpetually suffers from the knowledge that it is not, though it somehow should be, the City of God. The resultant fever is messianic, for even if the concluding words of Rose's study strike one as ironically Kantian, nevertheless the linking of Hegel's speculative logic with the necessity of social transformation is meant, ultimately, to issue in a desired "comprehension of the conditions for revolutionary practice" (220).

On this view, if theory is to have social import, if it is to have emancipatory and not merely contemplative potential, then reason's dichotomies must be linked with social ones. How this linkage is to be effected depends on the type of import intended. Crudely speaking, the Left, for all its emphasis on the "dialectical" relationship between base and superstructure, has tended to posit a causal relation leading from social contradictions ("bourgeois property relations") to theoretical antinomies; while conservatives (such as the followers of Leo Strauss)[2] generally find fault with decadent, self-contradicting intellectuals who have lost their nerve and become too lazy or fashionable to search for the deeper, more elusive unity of thought. This desired, if difficult to imagine, unity of thought (and of the society that, it is hoped, would occasion it or be occasioned by it) has differing articulations, again depending on the frame of reference. If the Hegelian Left bemoans the rupture separating theoretical from practical reason, a Kantian reification that Rose codes as the difference between Durkheim and Weber, then the Straussian Right mourns the loss of the classical unity of the True, the Good, and the Beautiful (see, e.g., S. Rosen 1969). In both cases, modernity carries the burden of a lack. The missing unity of our differences weighs heavily on the modern soul. Thus, we might say that the unity of *their* difference—that is, the difference between the Left and the Right, between the inequitable base and the cowardly superstructure—is a belief in a perceivable "deep structure," to purloin a phrase from Chomsky, which underlies and causes immediately evident ("empirical") surface phenomena. The ability to perceive this deep structure becomes the ability to read surface complexities symptomatically as manifestations of a rationally comprehensible totality. What appears irrational and randomly contingent on the surface can therefore be seen, it is said, as a necessary consequence of "capitalism" or some other secularized prime mover. Surface events, then, are not what is truly contingent, for they are embedded in a structure that determines their relations as outcomes. Rather, it is the deep structure itself that is thought to be contingent because it is historically, not logically, determined, and thus also historically unstable, decomposable. For theory to have social import—which is to say, for theory to live up to its purported imperative to change and not just understand the world—it must be able to articulate the connection between deep and surface structure in such a way as to make the deep structure eminently alterable. It must grasp the deep structure, in other words, from some perspective that is itself not determined by that structure. To fail to do so would be to fail in one's duty as either a Marxian historical materialist or a Straussian political philosopher.

    The critique of modernity just discussed, at least the critique from the Left, presents itself as a thoroughly *modern* critique, both deriving from the Enlightenment tradition and overcoming its limits. Nonetheless, this critique presupposes a perspective that is not rooted in modernity but rather escapes it, a view, says Seyla Benhabib, from a "space outside the walls of the city" where "normative priorities" can be ordered and the desire for the "wholly other [*das ganz Andere*]" can function as a "regulative principle of hope," without which "not only morality but also radical transformation is unthinkable" (Benhabib 1995, 28, 30). Such a view, reminiscent of a Straussian affirmation of philosophy's mission,[3] ultimately implies a unity of reason, no matter how plural its voices (as Habermas insists),[4] and the comprehensive vision that such a unity provides. What, however, if the absolute can be thought, but the consequences of thinking it are other than what Rose imagines? The Hegel scholar Robert Pippin agrees with Rose on the desirability of being able to think the simultaneity of dichotomies (of being able to think, for instance, the simultaneity of the self-determining and yet determined nature of subjectivity) (Pippin 1989, 272 n. 49). He also maintains, however, that such an ability to think the unity of this particular difference does not necessarily lead to the fullness or satiety usually associated with the absolute. Indeed, an ineradicable Kantian impossibility remains in Pippin's Hegel, for what Rose sees as an inevitable consequence of attempting to think the absolute from within the space of bourgeois society, Pippin seems to see as constitutive of thought itself. In Pippin's reading of Hegel's *Logic*, the Absolute Idea resolves oppositions by "an absolute comprehension of the nature of the incompleteness of thought's determination of itself, of the necessity for reflectively determined Notions, and yet the instability and ultimate inadequacy of those Notions." The incompleteness and inadequacy of thought's reflectively determined notions could be understood as Rose would want it to be understood, that is, historically, as the manifestation of an incomplete and inadequate society. But if "incomplete" now defines the endpoint of thought, that is, the "Absolute Idea," then we are left with the suspicion that this inadequacy cannot be overcome, not even by a radical shifting of social relations. "Incompleteness" would have to be viewed as a terminal condition rather than as pointing to a whole of which an incomplete notion is only a part. Accordingly, what characterizes the absolute, Pippin contends, is the realization of limits, an awareness of "the *eternal* opposition of thought with itself," which he associates with "Kant's view on the inevitability of Reason's self-opposition" (Pippin 1989, 257). The eternal nature of thought's opposition with itself does not argue against social change, but it does give pause and cautions us about what can be achieved by radical social change. If Hegel's philosophy has no social import without the ability to think the absolute, and if, after one's odyssey through Hegel's *Phenomenology* and his *Logic*, one can think the absolute only as the measure of its own impossibility, then one's faith in the efficacy of social change must also be somewhat relativized. Indeed, if we suspect that oppositions, even when historically determined, are "eternal," then the imperative to link philosophical reflection with social action becomes oppressive, because philosophy is thereby commanded to think the social conditions for its own perfection and the intellectual conditions for social perfection, all the while "knowing" that its limits make such a task unrealizable. The resignation of late-twentieth-century thought, its ennui, interrupted only by the desperate self-stimulations of its eternal and groundless moral exhortations, could be taken as a sign of this oppressive guilt.

Therefore, if Pippin's reading is plausible, and Hegel's resolution of dichotomies is vexed with the paradoxical difficulties that constitute and bedevil (modern) thought, then the more credible reading of modern sociology would *not* regard all limits as being transcendable just because they are historically determined. Rather, that reading would emphasize the historically determined nature of attempts to deal with deeply ingrained and untranscendable limits, attempts that may manifest themselves differently in different times but that can result only in limited transformations, not in the transformation of all limits. Such a view would have to recognize the circumscribed and incomplete nature of revolutionary practice itself as a practice *enabled* by the structure of modernity, and not as a practice designed to sublate it (read: destroy it). Accordingly, modernity would confront us once again in all its vast and insurmountable immanence, just as it did the founders of sociology a century ago; and any *Aufhebung* of modernity would truly be its cancellation, with no way of predicting or imagining what the aftermath of such a cancellation would look like.

Ironically, we owe the rediscovery of modernity in its Weberian shape to a purported break with modernity that has enjoyed calling itself postmodern. As Albrecht Wellmer writes in his aptly titled collection of essays, *The Persistence of Modernity*:

If there is something new in postmodernism, it is not the radical critique of modernity, but the redirection of this critique. With postmodernism, ironically enough, it becomes obvious that the critique of the modern, inasmuch as it knows its own parameters, can only aim at expanding the interior space of modernity, not at surpassing it. For it is the very gesture of radical surpassing—romantic utopianism—that postmodernism has called into question. (Wellmer 1991, vii)

Wellmer presents us here with the picture of a resilient and unreconciled modernity as "an unsurpassable horizon" (vii). All attempts to move beyond the modern landscape have proven futile, have, in fact, provided the energy for extending the domain or the "interior space" of what was to be left behind. Postmodernism, then, rather than being hailed as some supersession of modernity, "at its best might be seen as a self-critical—a skeptical, ironic, but nevertheless unrelenting—form of modernism; a modernism beyond utopianism, scientism, and foundationalism; in short, a post*metaphysical* modernism" (vii) that takes as its primary target not modernity itself but modernity's ill-advised projects of self-transcendence. Thus, what has called itself postmodernity seems a thoroughly modern confirmation of the Kantian and Weberian antinomies so sorrowfully mourned by twentieth-century Hegelians. The incommensurability of language games posited by Wittgenstein and celebrated by Jean-François Lyotard, the complementarity of properties postulated by physics, and the differentiation of system rationalities explored by Weber all accept the contingency and partiality of vision so often bemoaned as relativism, positivism, and nihilism throughout this century. If the initial, eighteenth-century differentiation of reason associated with the name of Kant came to be seen as the problem of modernity that supposedly needed overcoming, then the subsequent uncontrolled proliferation of languages, system rationalities, and observer positions would seem to signal unsurpassable modernity's irreversible triumph. If the inability to overcome modernity is postmodernism's triumph, this is because it marks the end of some of modernity's most treasured illusions. In lieu of *Aufhebung,* then, we are left with the task of reconciliation—the reconciliation not of antinomies but of *ourselves* to the *inevitability* of antinomies.

In a clear response to the definition of the postmodern condition as one in which the unifying metanarratives of knowledge and emancipation no longer redeem their claims to validity,[5] Wellmer draws out the consequences of the paradox inherent in the notion of postmodernism. The postmodern critique of modernity cannot, in fact, launch itself from some external, historically advanced position—from some chronologically determined *post*modern position—precisely because such a universal, historical perspective could only come from one of the collapsed metanarratives that postmodernism takes pains to discredit. Thus, if the critique itself is legitimate, then it must be located within the heart of modernity itself. Postmodernism's skeptical, ironic, and unrelenting critique of modernity's more ambitious projects must, in fact, be the quintessential modern gesture, a type of immune system attacking the anxieties that have produced the fevered delusions of foundation and future reconciliation. Postmodernity, were one to retain the word, would then be seen not as the result of the exhaustion of or disillusionment with modernity but rather as a new realization of modernity's self-imposed limits.

Chief among those self-imposed limits is modernity's seeming inability to establish normative standards either for itself or for its self-overcoming. Jürgen Habermas's formulation of Hegel's basic insight regarding modernity's break with any "norms lying outside of itself in the past" is helpful in understanding our dilemma. The problem of modernity's self-legitimation or "self-reassurance" expresses itself as an "anxiety caused by the fact that a modernity without models had to stabilize itself on the basis of the very diremptions [or divisions: *Entzweiungen*] it had wrought" (Habermas 1987b, 16). The question that has to be decided centers on these "diremptions" and how they are to be dealt with. Are they to be thought of as wounds to be healed, fragments to be pieced back together into a new whole, differences to be overcome, transcended, sublated? Or do they instead define the shape of modernity and, in fact, justify it? If, on the one hand, the former is the case, then the modern project becomes the search for the unity of the differences, and a "theory" of modernity must find a way of locating that unity, along with a way of justifying its own location device—that is, its own method. It must find, in other words, the correct hinge or linchpin on which it can hang a truly "post" modernity, one that can overcome its lack. If, on the other hand, the latter alternative seems more plausible, the problem of self-legitimation becomes even more acute. If the modern landscape lacks not only an authoritative and transcendent God but also His transcendental substitutes (reason, nature, the subject, history), then how is moral, legal, or political authority to be achieved where competing spheres of influence and interest doggedly maintain their own autonomy and own claims to authority? Here the challenge to modern theory involves understanding how the improbability of a self-differentiated modernity can continue to survive in the face of its own disjointed and decentered reality, especially since the desire for unity continues to "threaten" it in the hearts and minds of its denizens. The challenge becomes one of understanding how every critique of modernity extends modernity, whether that extension is desired or not.

Given the genealogy presented here—that is, that what Habermas calls the project of modernity is really an escape from it, and what Lyotard calls postmodernity is really the rediscovery of modernity—it is not surprising that Niklas Luhmann, modernity's most meticulous theorist, should "side," as it were, with postmodernity yet reject the melodramatic term as simply expressing the need, as he puts it, to "catch up on the semantic level" (Luhmann 1998, 18). The fabled loss of metanarratives alerts us to the constancy of the modern condition, namely, the inability to occupy a position from which society could be surveyed in one all-encompassing glance. The metanarratives of knowledge and emancipation that Lyotard excoriates must therefore be seen as reaction formations, compensations for the unresolved antinomies and lack of unity that were already perceived in the eighteenth century. What is therefore important, according to Luhmann, "is not the emancipation of reason, but emancipation from reason," an emancipation that "need not be anticipated," because it "has already happened" (Luhmann 1998, 18). Thus the emancipation from reason that Luhmann recommends is really an emancipation from nostalgia and anxiety, because the fall from reason that has already occurred has landed us not in a surreal wonderland of unreason but rather in the midst of a plurality of competing rationalities, "high-energy rationalities," as he says, "that only cover partial phenomena, only orient society's function systems" (25). Luhmann's trajectory of modernity, therefore, is much like the trajectories traced by Weber and Habermas, who chart the unique development of a European or Western rationality. Unlike Habermas, however, Luhmann is not interested in constructing a functional equivalent for the lost unity of reason; he is not interested in so limiting the rules of acceptable discourse that only those who agree are the ones left talking. Rather, in Weberian fashion, he participates in the operations and mitosis-like[6] self-divisions of modern rationality by describing how those operations function.

Descriptions of modern rationality do not come from nowhere; in fact, they come from modern rationality itself. "European rationality," Luhmann writes, "distinguishes itself from other comparable semantics by its use of distinctions" (Luhmann 1998, 23). Clearly, this description of modern rationality is a self-description, a self-distinction by way of difference. Rather like the old joke—"There are two kinds of people, those who think there are two kinds of people and those who don't"—Luhmann's thesis "that the distinction between European and non-European semantics can only be observed and described from the perspective of distinctions-conscious rationality" (23) necessarily comes from within the space that makes distinctions. This is to say that the uniqueness of European rationality is a construct of European rationality and can only be observed from within that construct. The uniqueness of modern rationality is both the result and the self-description of the way it works, a description that is itself an operation of rationality and that can only be made in the same way that rationality makes any other type of knowledge, namely, via distinction. "I would like," Luhmann remarks in the opening passage of his *Observations on Modernity*,

to start my analysis of modernity in contemporary society by making a distinction between social structure and semantics. My preference for such a beginning, a preference that cannot be justified at the outset, is based on a confusing characteristic of this distinction, namely that it is self-contained. It is itself a semantic distinction, just as the distinction between operation and observation, from which it comes, is itself the distinction of an observer. I must leave it with the simple statement that this logical form is the foundation of productive analyses that can resolve their own paradoxes. In addition, this point of departure already contains at its core the entire theory of modernity. This analysis does not begin with the recognition of tried laws of nature, nor with principles of reason, nor with predetermined or incontrovertible facts. It begins with a paradox that can be solved one way or another, provided one is willing to reduce infinite to finite information loads. This analysis therefore claims for itself the characteristics of its object of study: modernity" (Luhmann 1998, 1).

Thus, much like Kant and Weber before him, Luhmann makes a virtue of the limits of reason that centuries-old religious, romantic, and vitalist critiques have insistently pointed out. Reason can make no compelling or binding claim to a vision of the whole, as required, say, by Straussian and Marxian metaphysics, for its very nature is to form reality by way of differentiation. Though it was once thought of as an immanently accessible yet transcendental substitute for divine transcendence, as a watchtower within the world capable of seeing it as if from the outside, reason has now become a victim, as it were, of its own operations. If the modern world is a differentiated world, defined by functions and relations, not essences, then, too, modern reason is a differentiated reason, distinguishing itself from itself, dividing itself into system-specific and function-specific rationalities. Accordingly, modern reason is precisely that—modern—and can no longer lay claim to a position from which it might serve as the means of transcending modernity. By serving as a thoroughly contingent mode of observation, modern rationality replicates modernity and, thus, cannot found a critique that would lead us to the promised land of a utopian postmodernity.

We have therefore arrived back where we started, namely, at modernity's unresolved antinomies caused by the lamented inability to think the absolute, which is to say, the inability to justify reason rationally or even historically—not to mention dialectically. Thinking the rationality of reason has much the same consequence as thinking the structurality of structure, which, as Derrida says, results in a system "in which the central signified, the original or transcendental signified, is never absolutely present outside a system of differences." Thus, "the absence of the transcendental signified extends the domain and the play of signification infinitely" (Derrida 1978, 280). What Derrida articulates as an event within language was traced by Weber as the historical uncoupling of reason from truth. Once faith in reason (specifically, sufficient reason) is lost, once the monotheistic God or one of His many substitutes disappears, reason reveals itself to be an infinite chain of cause and effect with no First Cause or Final Effect, and thus no ultimate, transcendent justification. As a consequence, Weber defined reason pragmatically, as a means/ends relationship, and replaced the vacated position of the transcendent observer with the re-emergence of an immanent polytheism of warring gods who represent competing and incommensurable value-spheres. "So long as life remains immanent and is interpreted in its own terms," Weber writes, "it knows only of an unceasing struggle of these gods with one another. . . . The ultimately possible attitudes toward life are irreconcilable, and hence their struggle can never be brought to a final conclusion" (M. Weber 1946, 152). It is this image that Luhmann develops, without, it should be said, the martial imagery or tragic, individualist pathos. He sees modern society as a complex, internally differentiated system that further subdivides with every new attempt to observe its operations. Whereas for medieval theology the observation of God served as the observation of the observation of totality, giving us at least a mediated vision of the whole, for modernity the loss of this proxy leaves us with a proliferation of observations of observations, none serving a central function. Weber's polytheism of warring gods becomes the plurality of systemic rationalities that construct an observable world by drawing and designating distinctions.

## What Can We Say We See?

The premodern unity of reason fragments into a plurality of rationalities that operate by way of distinction. Rationalities, then, become finely tuned measuring devices, deriving the observable world (physical, psychical, and social) from the "buzzing, booming confusion" in which we find ourselves. If the ideal of the unity of reason sees a world rationally ordered and waiting to be discovered, modern rationality sees as its mission the organization of unorganized complexity. As in the Beginning, the favored organizing principle is observation—not as an empirical process but as a logical operation. The Kantian antinomies remain inescapable. The preceding section dealt with the dichotomy between theory and practice as the difference between epistemology and transformative political activity. Here, the equally problematic Kantian disjuncture between "intuition" and "concept" will be explored by posing the question: What can we say we see? The attempts to answer this seemingly simple yet unresolved question lead us back again to the central problems of modernity introduced above.

Understood epistemologically, the question asks about sense perception, or more precisely, about the relationship between sense perception and language, about whether language contains empirical contents. The question has a distinctly modern, that is to say, a distinctly Cartesian, flavor. It seems to imply a sensing apparatus and objects independent of that apparatus, and then asks how the sensing or measuring instrument can be calibrated so as to register adequately the object at which it is aimed. The question, however, also allows for doubt—another Cartesian spice. Perhaps we can say things we cannot in fact see, or see things we cannot say. Or perhaps all we can say is that we see sense impressions, and that we give particular names to particular sense impressions. Perhaps we see, in other words, what the act of seeing "tells" us, what is presented to cognition by intuition, regardless of whether the apparatus is aimed at anything or not—which is to say that the question of the existence of physical objects may be moot. Versions of this latter proposition have proven to be appealing. The physical object, the *Ding an sich*, has been declared unknowable, nonexistent, or simply a convenient myth, a *deus ex machina* to get us out of jams. In W. V. Quine's elegant rendering, "Physical objects are conceptually imported into the situation as convenient intermediaries—not by definition in terms of experience, but simply as irreducible posits comparable, epistemologically, to the gods of Homer" (Quine 1964, 44).

Quine's answer suggests a revision to our original question. "What can we say we see?" can be done up as: What serves as a guarantee that descriptions stand in a necessary relation to the world they putatively describe? Theoretically, Zeus can be that guarantee, or some Zeus-like substitute— God, for instance, or the transcendental subject—making sure that apparatus, language, and object all match in a snug fit. Traditional empiricism rejects divine intermediaries and replaces them with a unidirectional causal relationship between physical objects and sense data, with the latter regarded as the necessary result of the former. The fit is snug because the instrument is accurate and the recording of data precise. But it is this "dogma" of empiricism—the claim that individual statements can be verified (or falsified) by a simple appeal to empirical evidence—that Quine, following in Pierre Duhem's footsteps, famously wished to refute.[7] As Quine put it, "it is nonsense, and the root of much nonsense, to speak of a linguistic component and a factual component in the truth of any individual statement. Taken collectively, science has its double dependence upon language and experience; but this duality is not significantly traceable into the statements of science taken one by one" (Quine 1964, 42). Science is to be taken (or left) as an indivisible whole. Either one places one's trust in physical theory (and Quine believes there is good reason to so place it, and those reasons are pragmatic) or one does not. The particulars of physical explanation are eminently revisable, but revision is not the direct result of empirical confirmation or refutation of discrete elements of particular theories. Theoretical descriptions of the world, in other words, are overwhelmingly underdetermined by the putative object they describe, because narratives to account for empirical data can be spun in a wide variety of ways. Science, as a system or totality of interlocking descriptions of the physical world, is, then, a nearly closed system, a "man-made fabric which impinges on experience only along the edges" (42). Thus, experience is, paradoxically, not directly registered in the accounts science gives of it. It is as if science were some huge Central Asian empire, governed by a formal and abstract bureaucracy, and protected by an intricate network of outposts at its borders. Reports of disturbances are continually filed by border guards. What could these disturbances be? Natural catastrophes? Supernatural apparitions? Command central prefers to attribute them to marauding bands of nomads, precisely because it feels that it can have a far greater control over the occasional horde of horsemen than it can over the intervention of the gods. So reality becomes an account of recalcitrant and fiercely independent rebels living just beyond the borders. But thanks to the superiority of the well-trained and well-equipped imperial forces, the disturbances caused by these rebels can be easily managed.

    Reality, then, is not a pattern of objects but an account of such a pattern. Put another way, the account of physical objects gives us not a reflection of their configuration in space and time but rather a narrative construction of that configuration. There may be many narratives to choose from, but our criterion is efficacy, not accuracy, and the former does not necessarily presuppose the latter. Again, Quine's language is more elegant than my own: "Our talk of external things, our very notion of things, is just a conceptual apparatus that helps us to foresee and control the triggering of our sensory receptors in the light of previous triggering of our sensory receptors. The triggering, first and last, is all we have to go on" (Quine 1981, 1). On this view, the narrative we devise to describe reality is not a representation, not a duplication of reality in symbolic terms, but rather a vehicle that allows us to navigate. During the course of our navigations, we leave in our wake a navigable world, one that can be navigated not because we charted it beforehand but because we have already navigated it. The world of objects comes into being with its description, not prior to it.

Here, however, we run into unavoidable circularity, a type of self-referential circularity that the realist ontology of preexistent objects is designed to avoid. Quine not only acknowledges this circularity, he enacts it:

In saying this I too am talking of external things, namely, people and their nerve endings. Thus what I am saying applies in particular to what I am saying, and is not meant as skeptical. There is nothing we can be more confident of than external things—some of them anyway—other people, sticks, stones. But there remains the fact—a fact of science itself—that science is a conceptual bridge of our own making, linking sensory stimulation to sensory stimulation; there is no extrasensory perception. (Quine 1981, 1–2)

What I am saying applies to what I am saying. Feared self-referentiality is actually embraced. The narrative that claims that physical objects are cultural posits relies on the evidence provided by such posited objects—that is, "people and their nerve endings." The priority of the object's "objectivity" or its "positedness" is impossible to determine. Does the empirical objectivity of sense receptors determine that all we can say we see is the narrative connection of their firings, or does the priority of narrative determine that what "fires" are "objects" we call sense receptors? And is not the narrative itself a posited physical object, not just sound waves or light or marks on paper, but a series of triggerings and firings of the very sense receptors it posits in order to describe itself? Quine is not interested in unraveling these rival claims to priority by way of a transcendental or first philosophy. Rather, and rather remarkably, for Quine, a logician, the seeming viciousness of this circularity does not vitiate the statement's truth. It confirms it. "Truth is immanent," he writes, "and there is no higher. We must speak from within a theory, albeit any of various" (Quine 1981, 21–22). What is thereby rendered moot is the "transcendental question of the reality of the external world— the question whether or in how far our science measures up to the *Ding an sich*" (22). Thus, Quine's enterprise has nothing to do with denying the validity of talk of external things, and everything to do with the anxiety of whether that talk conforms to the way things "really" are. When truth is rendered immanent, statements produce the conditions for their own possibility. As a social system of such statements, science must internally generate its own validity and construct the objects upon which it relies.

Ian Hacking, working very much within the Duhem-Quine tradition, even gives us an account of how the scientific experiment, that ostensible link between theory and reality, is just such a constructive description of an emerging world. Hacking has advanced the thesis "that as a laboratory science matures, it develops a body of types of theory and types of apparatus and types of analysis that are mutually adjusted to each other. . . . They are self-vindicating in the sense that any test of theory is against apparatus that has evolved in conjunction with it" (Hacking 1992, 30). Hacking wishes to stress that the set of physical instruments (the "instrumentarium" [53]), and the methods of analyzing the data produced by these instruments, do not provide independent confirmations of theory but rather are part of a "closed system"[8] in which "a network of theories, models, approximations, together with understandings of the workings of our instruments and apparatus," mesh (30). He believes his thesis accounts for how "ideas" (theories), "things" (apparatus), and "marks" (methods of notating data) enter into a circular, self-vindicating relationship (51 n. 2). "Thus," Hacking concludes, "there evolves a curious tailor-made fit between our ideas, our apparatus, and our observations. A coherence theory of truth? No, a coherence theory of thought, action, materials, and marks" (58).

Hacking's thesis is no more a skeptical critique of laboratory science than is Quine's; rather it is a phenomenology of how science works. That there is no clear way to refute scientific theories by reference to independent observations of reality, that there is no meta-instrument or metameasurement, no "body of instruments to make common measurements, because the instruments are peculiar to each stable science" (Hacking 1992, 31), in no way invalidates the scientific enterprise. What this lack does seem to do, however, is acknowledge science's immanent nature. In what may be called the lay view of the natural sciences—a view shared, of course, by many working scientists—experiments are said to control hypotheses by checking their claims against reality, against nature. Given this conventional supposition, experiments can give voice, as it were, to the physical constraints of the natural world and thereby serve reality by acting as the medium through which the physical world can determine the contents of theory. But in Hacking's view, experimentation, involving the construction and manipulation of physical apparatus and symbolic notation, does not mediate between theory and reality. On the contrary, experimentation becomes theory's self-regulatory device, enabling greater theoretical complexity and sophistication rather than adequacy or greater accuracy. As a result, theories may contradict but cannot invalidate one another; they simply proliferate, presenting us with multiple self-contained worlds, but not with a single picture of *the* world. As Werner Heisenberg noted in the 1948 essay to which Hacking refers, competing physical theories (and Heisenberg identified four theories vying in the realm of physics at the time) do not disprove one another; rather, they coexist—incommensurably, each valid —"where their concepts can be used" (Heisenberg 1973, 91), that is, where their instruments can produce consistent, analyzable results.

So, our simple question—What can we say we see?—ostensibly about sense perception and language, has transformed itself into a question about the operations of a particular social system: science. And in answer to our revised question, we can say that nothing guarantees the *necessary* relationship of description to thing described, whether that description is historical, experiential, or scientific. Rather, description is contingent in the sense that other plausible descriptions are always possible.[9] If, à la Feuerbach, God did not create man in His image, but rather man created God in his, then likewise, if the object is a "cultural posit," the object is not the cause but the result of the conceptual apparatus called description. Therefore, neither God nor object can be the epistemological elixir, and we are left with merely the descriptive narrative.

Such immanent dissolutions of the transcendental question, however, always call into being the ironic query: Are such denials of the possibility of describing the world the way it really is themselves descriptions of the world the way it really is? If, in other words, we cannot say we see objects, how can we say we cannot see objects, if not from a position that can see—and match—both the world (now, not as container of things but as buzzing, booming confusion) and its descriptions? The answer to such a question probably should not be that we cannot say that we cannot see objects, for to say that, it seems, would just add a layer to our hierarchy of comprehension, and at this point the fear of bad infinity begins to grip our souls. But if we shrink back from the apparent abyss of infinite regress, to where do we shrink? Quine says to the original two statements—"There are objects" and "There are no objects, just descriptions"—and insists that, in their own ways, both are valid.

"Here we have," Quine claims, "two competing conceptual schemes, a phenomenalistic one and a physicalistic one" (Quine 1964, 17). From the perspective of the system of science, the physical account, which posits objects and links them in a causal chain, may be the simplest and most elegant answer to our initial question. We can say we see objects because sense impressions are caused by the firing of receptors, and the firing of receptors must be triggered by externally existing physical objects that conform to the images caused. Moreover, visible objects are composed of invisible objects, which, in turn, are further subdivided, ad infinitum it almost seems. These physical objects, Quine writes, "are postulated entities which round out and simplify our account of the flux of experience, just as the introduction of irrational numbers simplifies laws of arithmetic" (18). However, to other eyes, such a seemingly endless proliferation of objects to explain objects may look like so many turtles standing on the backs of turtles:

From the point of view of the conceptual scheme of the elementary arithmetic of rational numbers alone, the broader arithmetic of rational and irrational numbers would have the status of a convenient myth, simpler than the literal truth (namely, the arithmetic of rationals) and yet containing that literal truth as a scattered part. Similarly, from a phenomenalistic point of view, the conceptual scheme of physical objects is a convenient myth, simpler than the literal truth and yet containing that literal truth as a scattered part. (Quine 1964, 18)

The point Quine makes is that each conceptual scheme "has its advantages," "has its special simplicity," "deserves to be developed," "may be said, indeed, to be more fundamental, though in different senses" (17). Furthermore, each answer to the question of what we can say we see, each theory of what there is, brings with it certain ontological commitments. We can develop criteria for determining what those commitments are, "but the question what ontology actually to adopt still stands open, and the obvious counsel is tolerance and an experimental spirit" (19).

But what is tolerance, and what is an experimental spirit? What they are *not* are definitive criteria separating the necessary from the contingent, the true from the false. They are not Reason as Almighty and irreducible arbiter. They are just two "among our various interests and purposes" (Quine 1964, 19) that guide the choice of frames of reference from which the world is seen. Therefore, though Quine suspends disbelief to produce effects and opts for the physicalist account when it comes to seeing the world from the point of view of science, he sees his seeing of the world from an epistemological perspective, choosing to see the contingency of what science posits as necessary. Whereas the realist ontology of science may fit description and thing in terms of adequacy, Quine chooses to fit description with effect in terms of efficacy, choosing also to allow room for differing versions of what is efficacious, and when and where. How is this possible? From where can this impossible tolerance be maintained?

Let us rephrase our question one last time. "What can we *say* we see?" might mean: Is there one single, accurate description of the world? Encore: Is the/a "correct" description of the world necessary, or necessarily contingent? The law of the excluded middle demands an unequivocal answer: "Yes" (necessary) or "No" (contingent). Quine attempts to occupy that excluded middle ground and answers: "Yo." But one can see that such an answer "sides," so to speak, with the original "No," for in accepting the relative validity of both positions, it denies the exclusivity demanded by the affirmation of necessity. And yet, though this middle position sides with the negative answer by excluding ultimate exclusion, it is not identical to it. In opting for "ontological relativity" (Quine 1969), one does not simply observe contingency as one might observe objects; rather, one presupposes contingency as an irreducible value. Put another way, if one can entertain competing descriptions of the world as incommensurable but equally valid, one does so not from a position that can see the adequacy of each position but rather from a position that posits the necessity of competing contingent descriptions. In a world where descriptions proliferate and faith in the authority of reason has gone the way of faith in the authority of God, contingency becomes the transcendental placeholder. "Modernity" is the name we have given to this necessarily contingent world.

## The Necessity of Contingency

But what do we mean by contingency? The notion of contingency has a long history in modal logic, from Aristotle and medieval controversies about determinism and future contingents to Leibniz and beyond.[10] In contemporary Anglo-American philosophy, the contingency of language—the nonnecessary, arbitrary, or conventional fit between representation and thing represented—has been featured in Richard Rorty's brand of pragmatism.[11] As is well known, Rorty distinguishes between a philosophical tradition (rationalism) that assumes truth is found and a tradition (amalgamating aspects of idealism, historicism, and pragmatism) that asserts truth is made. If the former tradition has given up the strong belief, best articulated by Spinoza, that "the order and connection of ideas is the same as the order and connection of things," it nevertheless continues to insist that the charge of language is to represent adequately the truth that is "out there" and that preexists its linguistic representation. Rorty therefore sees in this modern, rationalist position the continuation of the war of reason versus religion, a war that contests the nature of the grounds (rational versus nonrational) for ultimate explanations; only now it is a war between the truth of science and the metaphor or opinion of culture. Rorty's endeavor is to alter the terms of this antagonism and transform the war into an eternal conversation, since for him, the truth of science is just one metaphor, one cultural artifact, among many, a view that would dissolve the tried and true opposition between grounded (rational) truth and mere (irrational or conventional) opinion. As a champion of the historicist and neopragmatic (some would say neo-Sophist) tradition in philosophy, he maintains the necessity of distinguishing between "the claim that the world is out there and the claim that truth is out there." To say that there is a world out there independent of our mental states makes sense, he claims, but to say that truth is out there does not. To deny this latter claim "is simply to say that where there are no sentences there is no truth, that sentences are elements of human languages, and that human languages are human creations" (Rorty 1989, 4–5). Of interest here is the contention that truth is the function of descriptions, not the function of the world itself. "The world is out there," Rorty acknowledges, "but descriptions of the world are not. Only descriptions of the world can be true or false. The world on its own—unaided by the describing activities of human beings—cannot" (5). As such, the truth of descriptions cannot be checked against the "truth" of reality. Descriptions can only be discussed and debated, refuted and affirmed. Once reference to reality is dropped, rational argumentation is reinterpreted as rhetorical persuasion or system-specific communication.

At this point in the argument, critics usually begin to see the specter of self-referential paradox. Is not the claim that "there is no truth out there" a truth claim about the status of the "out there" that is of the same type and scope as the claim that "there is truth out there"? To avoid the potentially self-refuting nature of such a claim, Rorty insists that his is *not* an epistemological statement but rather a pragmatic move in the philosophical language game dictated by use-value: "To say that we should drop the ideal of truth out there waiting to be discovered is not to say that we have discovered that, out there, there is no truth. It is to say that our purposes would be served best by ceasing to see truth as a deep matter, as a topic of philosophical interest, or 'true' as a term which repays analysis" (Rorty 1989, 8). Here, Rorty takes as his model what he thinks is the nature of poetry. Rather than argue within the framework of a traditional vocabulary that would trap one in traditional paradoxes, one should, he maintains, just "invent" new vocabularies. Whether this maneuver really avoids the problem of justification or merely shifts its grounds is not our concern, for what interests us is the limit we have just reached, the limit where descriptions turn back on themselves in consequential and paradoxical ways. If we are to accept, in broad terms, the notion of contingency outlined by Rorty (and his is merely a clearly stated version of many similar positions currently *en vogue*), with its emphasis on the contents of descriptions and not on the contents of purported referents, and if we are to accept his contention that statements, vocabularies, and language games irreconcilably conflict with each other because of the lack of external or metalevel criteria of judgment, then we will also need to accept, and investigate, the potentially paradoxical aspects of such a description of the modern condition. If, in other words, contingency is said to register a series of losses in which divine, natural, transcendental, and historical/cultural authority give way to a plurality of immanent and necessarily competing perspectives with no ultimate court of appeals, then the dilemma of modernity dictates that no matter what instrument we call upon, whether mathematics, symbolic logic, or natural language, whether hermeneutic, linguistic, or historicist analysis, whether scientific method, intellectual intuition, or aesthetic revelation, the observing "eye" must remain blind to itself. No epistemologically privileged center or margin, no transcendent ground or transcendental watchtower, no transparent meta-language, metanarrative, or metasystem can possibly encompass or compose the unity of the restlessly self-replicating and expanding internal differenti-ation of the space of modernity. Modernity, therefore, remains ultimately inaccessible to itself, or rather, gains access to itself by generating a series of partial and conflicting descriptions that can make no claim to absolute va-lidity, because each description must reckon with the possibility that it, too, could be otherwise than it is. Our legitimacy depends on our ability to pro-vide plausible self-descriptions, yet our first and foremost self-description is the description that says we can always describe ourselves differently. Accordingly, this first description, this "necessity" of contingency, must be-come a matter of conviction. Were we ever to lose our "faith" in contin-gency, we would lose our faith in the legitimacy of modernity. Duly chas-tised by postmodernism to give up its utopic yearnings for a necessary and unalterable self-description, modernity grounds itself as that which cannot definitively ground itself, because every determination of a ground is to be articulated as a contingent actuality within a horizon of actual possibilities. Its grounding myth can be sought neither in the necessity of nature nor in the transcendence of the heavens, but must be found in the series of stories it writes about itself, or, more fundamentally, in the very necessity of having to write stories about itself. Since, with the "loss" of transcendent necessity, these stories cannot present themselves as accurate representations of the physical, social, or historical *Ding an sich*, modernity finds itself grounded in the fact that it could always tell a story about itself other than the one it actually does. In the final analysis, modernity locates its legitimacy in its very lack of ultimate legitimation, in its contingency, and *not* in the various attempts to overcome contingency, attempts that ultimately reveal them-selves to be the desire to destroy modernity.

Rationalist critics of the "necessity of contingency" delight in point-ing out the performative paradox involved.[12] If modernity is described as contingent, and if this description itself is necessarily a part of the moder-nity it describes, then the description must also be contingent. It, too, must be as partial and limited, as subject to change, as the modernity it describes, and thus it can*not* claim to be the last word for quite logically sound reasons. If one can say that the "truth" of historicism is itself his-torically determined and thus not absolutely true (for historicism says that nothing can absolutely transcend the determinations of history), and if one can say that the "truth" of relativism is itself relative and not absolutely true (for all truths, even the truth of relativism, must be relative), then is not the "truth" of modernity's contingency itself contingent, nonnecessary, and subject to change? If the modern order exists within a horizon of possible orders, must not one of those possibilities be a *necessary*, noncontingent order—in short, the *right* order that will "cure" modernity of its ills, contingency among them? If these critics are right, then the mutability or nonnecessity that marks the modern social order could be viewed as a flaw, a lack in need of compensation. The fact that modernity could be ordered otherwise would be seen, on this view, as proof that its present order is derived from faulty or from nonexistent principles, and that therefore no real order exists at all. Consequently, flawed (unjust, inegalitarian, immoral, nihilistic) modernity must be replaced by a morally or ontologically necessary social organization—a *right* order, an order derived from and guaranteed by the one and only universal perspective (the Good, the True, the course of History), a perspective beyond the relativity of perspectives, a perspective that would put relativity itself into perspective. Speaking in a quasi-Hegelian manner, such critics would be tempted to say that contingency (like historicism, like relativism) includes, by way of self-contradiction, its own negation and inexorably transforms itself into its opposite. Thus, the destiny of modernity would be *not* eternal contingency but rather contingency's own self-transcendence into its resplendent other. Modernity, on this view, could be seen only as imperfect, as a project to be completed, and thus "true" modernity could be only what actual modernity has not yet become.

If we deny modernity's self-negation and affirm the oxymoronic *necessity* of contingency, however, then change need never be final, for even if with every change old possibilities disappear, new ones will emerge. If modernity is necessarily contingent and there is no escape from partial and conflicting perspectives, no escape from the vertigo of ever-shifting self-descriptions, then the description of *this* state of affairs is itself necessarily *not* contingent. It cannot be otherwise than it is and remain faithful to the modernity it claims to describe. If the conflict of perspectives is not to be reconciled from a higher-order metaperspective; if, in other words, a universal perspective of the morally Good or ontologically True cannot be occupied; if, rather, such perspectives must compete on the same level as all others, with no hope of logical or divine resolution; then, ironically, the statement that describes this state of affairs must "pose" as a metastatement and "occupy" this impossible metaperspective. To describe adequately the ineluctable necessity of the contingency of modernity, the perspective of the metaperspective has to be filled with the assertion that there is no metaperspective, and, thus, the description of modernity as contingent has to serve as modernity's "transcendental" ground. Contingency, then, cannot be merely the contingent condition of modernity; rather, it is the necessary condition required for modernity's continued existence. Again, one might use a quasi-Hegelian formulation and say that left to its own devices, contingency, in a gesture of *Selbstaufhebung*, would inexorably mutate into noncontingency; therefore, in order to preserve itself, contingency must paradoxically posit itself as necessary.

As should be clear by now, I take this paradox, this contradiction or dilemma, this logical impossibility—call it what you will—to be the marker *not* of modernity's theoretical and moral decadence but of the complex and fragile order modernity has achieved, an order perpetually threatened by eschatological visions of reconciliation, emancipation, and truth. Paradox is the sign under which this new order organizes itself, because it must be an order without an origin. Things can be otherwise than they are only if a structure is preserved that allows change and therefore always views change as inherently unstable. As a consequence of shifting the focus from an overcoming of contingency to the assertion of its necessity, the formerly self-transcending project of modernity transforms itself into one of self-preservation. What is to be preserved is not the content of modernity — whatever, at any given time, that may be—but its principle of organization. As the studies that follow will, I hope, make clear, the description of modernity that accounts for its possibility as a resilient and flexible formal structure is, broadly speaking, the Weberian model, in which the Kantian differentiation of reason stands as the philosophical pattern and symptom of the gradual social and institutional differentiation of value spheres, language games, and social systems. This tradition—evoked in a philosophical register by Lyotard's insistence on incommensurability, and developed most fully and abstractly by Luhmann's description of modern society in terms of autonomous, self-reproducing social systems—calls for a revaluation of those features of modernity that have so often provoked the most visceral complaints. Fragmentation, reification, alienation, and the loss of

nerve of a culture (or an intellectual class) no longer anchored in traditional values are still the terms of choice for those, on both the Left and the
Right, whose discontent with contingent modernity drives their ethical
and political concerns. The affirmation of contingency, on the other hand,
takes what these others have seen as self-alienating fragmentation and
turns it into legitimate and legitimizing self-differentiation. In the final
analysis, the description of modernity as inescapable differentiation forms
the ground, and hence the norm, for disagreements about the contemporary world, because as long as God's throne remains vacant, only differentiation allows for a plurality of observer positions and thus for a plurality
of contingent, fallible, antagonistic perspectives on the present. That is to
say, modernity as differentiation is not the object of some logically, morally,
or historically transcendent critique but rather the ground for what replaces such critique. Perhaps, then, we should stop trying to bury modernity. If praising it seems excessive, we could at least acknowledge that its
divided nature is what enables us even to contemplate alternatives—if not
alternatives *to*, then at least alternatives *within*, the modernity we inhabit.

The seven chapters that follow are slightly revised versions of articles
that were written during the 1990s. Though each chapter can be read profitably on its own, I have written a new series of introductions to clarify
contexts, amplify explanations, and weave together the themes that recur
in different guises throughout. In a sense, the introductions exemplify a
significant Luhmannian trope in that they serve as oblique observations of
the observations that are offered in the individual discussions contained in
each chapter. In addition, I have expanded and updated sources and references, taking recent translations and publications into account.

The aim of the following explorations is twofold. First, they introduce aspects of the work of Niklas Luhmann to an American audience—
particularly his challenging notion of observation and the productive character of paradox, his constructivist epistemology, and his elaboration of
modern society as functionally differentiated. Second, they illuminate and
criticize aspects of the work of thinkers already familiar on the American
scene (e.g., Habermas, Gadamer, Lyotard, Wittgenstein, Derrida) by setting their conceptual schemes in motion with Luhmann's. In the course of
these essays I entice Luhmann to engage in contemporary debates about
theories of complexity and communication, foundationalist and antifoun-

dationalist epistemologies, the relationship of morality to politics, and, above all, the stakes involved in the controversies about modernity and its possible postmodern aftermath. Within these contexts, I examine the hermeneutics of Friedrich Schleiermacher and Friedrich Schlegel; the analyses of information theory by Katherine Hayles and Michel Serres; a variety of feminisms, including the work of Drucilla Cornell and Judith Butler; and the political theories of Chantal Mouffe and Carl Schmitt. Hovering in the background throughout is the spirit of Max Weber, whose fundamental ambivalence about the modernity he described remains a challenge to the modernity resurrected in these pages.

The content of the chapters reflects, one might say, the central Kantian antinomies that Rose identifies as the source of twentieth-century sociology's "misguided" observations of modernity. Roughly speaking, the discussion proceeds from a consideration of Kant's concept/intuition antinomy to his theory/practice one. The first chapter deals with scientific theories of organized complexity as they emerged during the second half of the twentieth century. It relates conflicting assumptions about underlying simplicity to the opposed views on consensus and social integration found in Habermas and Luhmann. The core of the argument considers whether observations of social complexity can be carried out by an underlying normative structure that arrogates to itself a supervisory function. The second chapter moves to the issue of communication, emphasizing the interrelatedness of disorder and order, noise and information. Here the links between eighteenth- and twentieth-century investigations are affirmed. In Chapter 3, I examine contradictory passages in Luhmann's final comprehensive study of society (Luhmann 1997) in order to determine whether the emphasis on reception and observation is not really a closet idealism. The seemingly necessary oscillation between "realist" and "idealist" positions that marks constructivism leads to the an interrogation of the centrality of paradox in Luhmann's work of the 1980s and 1990s. Thus, the following chapter, Chapter 4, compares how Luhmann and Lyotard deal with self-reference and paradox and considers what consequences their respective approaches have for both epistemology (description) and politics (prescription). Chapter 5 continues the discussion of Luhmann and Lyotard, focusing on ways of reading Lyotard's notion of the differend and his rehabilitation of the sublime as meditations on the impossibility of thinking limits, including the very limit of modernity itself. In Chapter 6, the impossibility of thinking, or at least actualizing, a transcendent notion of ethics (Wittgenstein) leads to its "quasi-transcendental" substitute, an endeavor Cornell tries to enact with regard to the question of abortion and women's reproductive rights. The dangers of such "transcendental temptations" are articulated with reference to Luhmann's writings on the necessity of domesticating morality and separating it from politics. Finally, Chapter 7 reads Mouffe reading Schmitt from a systems-theoretical perspective to give an idea of what the limits of the political in the modern world might be.

I have also included, as an appendix, two interviews conducted in September 1994. The first interview is a conversation with Katherine Hayles and Niklas Luhmann about their respective versions and assessments of constructivist epistemology. The second interview, a conversation with Luhmann alone, focuses on his notion of modernity as functional differentiation, the question of morality and politics, and, as he put it, his "addiction" to theory. The former interview was originally published in 1995 and was worked over by both Hayles and Luhmann. The latter interview, unfortunately, was never edited for publication before Luhmann died. I am grateful to Luhmann's daughter, Veronika Luhmann-Schröder, for allowing me to publish it now in this form.

# 1

## Theories of Complexity, Complexities of Theory

When, in the early 1980s, Jürgen Habermas declared war on the "young-conservatism" and the "neo-conservatism" of the postmodernists, it did not take long for the volley to be returned. Jean-François Lyotard, in his ironically titled "Answering the Question: What Is Postmodernism?"[1] famously characterizes Habermas as a closet Hegelian and thus a closet terrorist. Habermas, according to Lyotard, "thinks that if modernity has failed, it is in allowing the totality of life to be splintered into independent specialties which are left to the narrow competence of experts." Accordingly, "what Habermas requires," Lyotard continues, is a way "to bridge the gap between cognitive, ethical, and political discourses, thus opening the way to a unity of experience" within which "all the elements of daily life and of thought would take their places as in an organic whole" (Lyotard 1984, 72). It would be easy to refute Lyotard's claims. In the very essay to which Lyotard responds, Habermas acknowledges the irreversibility of differentiation by identifying the Enlightenment "project of modernity" as an effort to "develop objective science, universal morality and law, and autonomous art, according to their inner logic" (Habermas 1981, 9). That eighteenth-century optimism about progress has been replaced by twentieth-century skepticism and cynicism does not mean, according to Habermas, that the project must be given up. Modernization has its problems, he concedes, but they are correctable without resorting to nostalgic or utopic fantasies. In the opening pages of his *Theory of Communicative Action*, Habermas realizes that "philosophy can no longer refer to the whole of the world, of nature, of history, of society in the sense of a totalizing knowledge" and that "all attempts at discovering ultimate foundations, in which the intentions of First Philosophy live on, have broken down" (Habermas 1984–87, 1: 1, 2). It is for this reason that sociology has taken on the traditionally philosophical question of the unity of reason as a problem regarding the unity of social or system rationalities. Max Weber's differentiation of value spheres and the languages that go with them, Habermas recognizes, was merely a sociological reflection of Kant's differentiation of reason into theoretical, practical, and aesthetic/reflective components; and Kant's distinctions themselves were but "a reaction to the emerging independence of distinct complexes of rationality" that had already become differentiated and institutionalized in the eighteenth century (Habermas 1992, 17). Thus, the "philosophical project of modernity" becomes modernity's attempt "*to create its normativity out of itself*," a "self" that can be defined only by the self-inflicted and unsublatable divisions that modernity has wrought (Habermas 1987b, 7, 16). So it hardly seems plausible to accuse Habermas of trying to reconstruct an "organic whole."

And yet, Lyotard got Habermas dead right! True, no explicit invocation of an organic whole appears anywhere in Habermas's writings. But all his thought tends toward finding a rationally authoritative, functional equivalent for such a desirable unity. The modernization process—the process of rationalization and differentiation of various expert systems that begins with the Enlightenment—cannot be halted or overcome, but it should be "steered," Habermas insists (e.g., Habermas 1981, 13), from some perspective that itself at least partially escapes that process. His career has been a continuous search for ways of accommodating hermeneutic, system-theoretic, and poststructuralist descriptions of modernity, while never giving up the desire of Critical Theory (in its original or traditional manifestation) to judge and "critique" normatively an array of modern deviancies —to wit: reification, alienation, the "colonization of the lifeworld," and all the other ills of the administered society. Whereas "postmodernists" like Lyotard follow Adorno to what seems to be the latter's "logical conclusion," namely, the virtual impossibility of critique, Habermas, even in his latest, most liberal and Kantian phase, adopts Max Horkheimer's project of a critical social theory. Therefore it is paramount for Habermas to locate a position from which such a critique can maintain its normative authority. Indeed, if Richard Wolin is correct that Critical Theory took a "rationalist turn" around 1937, as it attempted "to salvage a normative foundation for theory, critique, and the praxis of an 'imaginary future witness,' in light of the obsolescence of Marx's theory of the proletariat as a 'universal class'" (Wolin 1992, 26, 25), then this rationalist turn itself underwent a "linguistic turn" in Habermas some 30 or more years later. At that time, Habermas abandoned the categories of *Arbeit* (labor) and *Herrschaft* (dominance) for a universal pragmatics and ideal speech situation within the stabilizing context of a lifeworld that, despite *its* rationalization, maintained links with "everyday" practice. Now, at the beginning of a new millennium, we are left with a "discourse principle" (Habermas 1996, 107) that leads to the establishment of universally valid moral and legal norms, which, when resisted, are put into practice with the help of the "gentle compulsion" (Habermas 1997, 133) we have become so accustomed to over the past century. That is, for all his critique of traditional First Philosophy, Habermas's attempt to chastise and supervise the almost tropical growth of modern social subsystems from the vantage of an Archimedean lifeworld or procedural rationality cannot help but earn him the distinction of being Germany's foremost First Philosopher.

But why should Habermas's passionate quest for a normative basis for a just society be equated with "terror" (Lyotard 1984, 81)? Despite his insistence on consensus, it seems inherently unfair to equate Habermas with Robespierre, does it not? Perhaps the following passages from his *Philosophical Discourse of Modernity* will help us understand the fear and loathing Habermas so often provokes. "Communicative reason," he writes, "makes itself felt in the binding force of intersubjective understanding and reciprocal recognition." Intersubjective understanding and reciprocal recognition sound benign, even desirable, and binding force is a social necessity. But what is the nature of this "binding force"? Apparently, it is membership in a universal community, a membership that comes urgently to life when the rules of the community are broken. Evoking Schelling, Habermas states: "The violation of claims to truth, correctness, and sincerity affects the whole permeated by the bond of reason. . . . Any violation of the structures of rational life together, to which all lay claim, affects everyone equally" (Habermas 1987b, 324). He then explicitly refers these structures of rational life to an Old Testament "dialectic of betrayal and avenging force," quoting Klaus Heinrich approvingly:

Keeping the covenant with God is the symbol of fidelity; breaking this covenant is the model of betrayal. . . . Thus, betrayal of another is simultaneously betrayal of oneself; and every protest against betrayal is not just protest in one's own name, but in the name of the other at the same time. . . . The concept of "enlightenment" familiar to us is unthinkable without the concept of a potentially universal confederation against betrayal. (Heinrich, quoted in Habermas 1987b, 325)

Participating in communicative reason, then, requires an irreversible decision. Once one enters the "universal confederation," one can leave only on pain of retribution. Indeed, since the community one communicatively enters is "universal," one can leave only by stepping out of the "universe." To question the rules of the game is not to enter a new game but to exit the world. One becomes an instant outlaw, a betrayer of reason and truth. "This means," Habermas concludes, in less biblical but no less absolute language, "that as a participant in discourses, the individual, with his irreplaceable yes or no, is only fully on his own under the presupposition that he remains bound to a universal community by way of a cooperative quest for truth" (Habermas 1987b, 346–47).

For all the deliberation in Habermas's deliberative democracy, we are left, in the end, with a single voice. As Odo Marquard has perceptively noted, for the second wave of the Frankfurt School—by which he means Karl Otto Apel and Habermas—the plurality of opinions and, for that matter, the plurality of fellow human beings serve only as a starting point. Their communicative reasoning merely reduces the multiplicity of convictions, such that the goal of their discourse—universal consensus—is to have no one thinking differently from anyone else. Thus the plurality of fellow human beings and their opinions becomes superfluous. Marquard sees this as the revenge of solipsism upon a philosophy that claims to overcome "intersubjectively" the solipsism of a subject-centered, transcendental idealism.[2] One could, however, also see it as the manifestation of a fear of complexity and of the contingency that is complexity's corollary. The demand for a rational consensus arises to cope with the loss of more traditional means for ensuring cohesion—God, for instance, as the extramundane simplicity that not only explains but creates the complexity experienced by our limited intelligence; or the transcendental subject, who procedurally, self-reflectively, constructs itself as the ground, thus the unity, of the difference that is the phenomenal world. Habermas of course rejects such transcendent and transcendental guarantors of objectivity, but he does not reject the possibility of reducing the multiplicity of perspectives to a common denominator. The means of such a reduction, however, must be located within language itself: "All languages," he insists, "offer the possibility of distinguishing between what is true and what we hold to be true. The *supposition* of a common objective world is built into the pragmatics of every single linguistic usage" (Habermas 1992, 138). In this way, the "discouragement" that accompanies the "paralyzing experiences with contingency" (141) can be controlled and overcome. On the sea of complexity, we have lost our assurance, but communicative reason—and it seems to have come down to this—still gives us *hope* for a common world, or, dare I say, "a unity of experience."

Niklas Luhmann sees complexity and contingency in less alarmist terms. The distinction complexity/simplicity no longer holds, he claims, because in the modern world (including modern science), the search for an underlying simplicity has become futile. Particles continue to dissolve into conglomerations of subatomic particles, which dissolve into conglomerations of subsubatomic particles, seemingly on into infinity—or at least as far as the current imagination can travel. Complexity, then, becomes not a property of a system but a mode of observation—indeed, *the* mode of observation. The "fragmentation" of modernity has led to a "fragmentation" of observation, which leaves us with no access to a commonly assumed objective world. What we see, in other words, is not a single elephant described variously by different blind men but various elephants made visible by different blind spots; and this modern "loss" of objectivity cannot be compensated for by the "rational" demand to see what we cannot see. While observing, we note that systems contain so many constitutive elements that it becomes impossible to relate each element to every other element. Under the constraint of time, we are forced to make selections, and the selections we make could always have been made otherwise. And we have no recourse to a god or demon who could coordinate all of our choices as if they were merely commensurable parts of a comprehensible whole. This state of affairs need not be seen as a loss—indeed, it may be seen as a gain. Complexity guarantees contingency, which is to say, creates meaning—the difference between potentiality and actuality. We can observe the selections that are made; others can observe ours and we can observe theirs; we can even use schemas like truth/opinion, correctness/error, or affirmation/critique to observe others' other schemas. But we can never prevent others from observing selections otherwise—unless, of course, we operate by way of a "dialectic of betrayal and avenging force" and prevent those who differ, who observe otherwise, from communicatively participating in society.

This chapter, then, explores two different ways a science of complexity could proceed. Complexity could be, on the one hand, the strictly quantifiable property of a system; on the other, a qualitatively determined mode of observation. These preliminary remarks already reveal which social theorist is aligned with which view of complexity. The question remaining at the end is political: Does complexity enable political activity or paralyze it? This question will be pursued in subsequent chapters.

Since the late 1940s, it has become commonplace, at least in certain circles, to see science as evolving from a science of simple systems to a science of complex systems. As Warren Weaver put it in his famous article of 1948, "Science and Complexity," seventeenth-, eighteenth-, and nineteenth-century science solved problems of simplicity, whereas the science of the first half of the twentieth century learned, by means of statistical analysis and probability theory, to deal with problems of disorganized complexity. It was Weaver's contention, then, that the task of the latter half of the twentieth century was to develop means of investigating the dynamics of *organized* complexity, complexity not characterized by random behavior and therefore not explicable by the rules of probability alone. By and large, Weaver's call for a research program into organized complexity has been heeded, especially in those domains where traditional, simple-system science had made little headway—the various biologies, economics, and political and social theories. However, the neat, chronological distinctions he made may be somewhat misleading. Not only, as C. Dyke emphasizes, do the results of the sciences of "organized simplicity and disorganized complexity" remain the "foundations upon which to build" any future "reintegrated approach to explanation" (Dyke 1988, 11), but also, as Ilya Prigogine and Isabelle Stengers contend, the "Laplacean dream" of absolute and Godlike determinism, which has "acted as a regulatory ideal" for the science of simplicity, "seems to reappear in every generation, . . . each time translating the continuity of a style as well as the individuality of its contemporary theoretical and cultural context" (Prigogine and Stengers 1982, 145).

This latter, "ideological" recurrence of the same will be the major study of this chapter, following a preliminary definition of complexity. In that study I argue that Jürgen Habermas's attempt to reconstruct the Enlightenment project of modernity not surprisingly also attempts to reconstruct an essential feature of Enlightenment science, the reductionist effort to explain surface or phenomenal complexity in terms of an underlying, normative simplicity. This strategy can most clearly be seen in his attempt to found his distinction between strategic and communicative action on the "reconstructive science" of a universal pragmatics. His concerns are ultimately political, and laudably so, but his foundationalist approach cannot adequately come to grips with the self-conscious foregrounding and problematization of complexity that marks European modernity. Therefore, in the final section of this chapter, I show how the irreducibility or inescapability of complexity necessarily affects the theoretical investigation of complexity, that is, necessarily affects all theoretical investigations. In the process, an old antagonist of Habermas, Niklas Luhmann, emerges as a spokesperson for the Weaver agenda in the social sciences.

## Complexity, Simplicity, and Observation

At about the same time that Weaver was formulating the future agenda for the science of complexity, the mathematician John von Neumann was delivering lectures on the theory of self-reproducing automata. In these lectures of 1949, he examines an apparent paradox in order to explore a concept for which he says he knows "no adequate name" (Neumann 1966, 78), but which he at first calls complication and later calls complexity. His paradox hinges on two "obvious" facts. First, it is a matter of common knowledge, he states, that artificial automata (a machine tool, say) can produce only elements less complicated than itself, that "generally speaking, an automaton A, which can make an automaton B, must contain a complete description of B and also rules on how to behave while effecting the synthesis. So," he continues, "one gets a very strong impression that complication, or productive potentiality in an organization, is degenerative, that an organization which synthesizes something is necessarily more complicated, or a higher order, than the organization it synthesizes" (79). However, when one looks at the natural world, the opposite condition seems equally obvious. Not only do living organisms produce other organisms exactly like themselves (i.e., with no degeneration of organization), but the history of life on earth shows that "today's organisms are phylogenetically descended from others which were vastly simpler than they are, so much simpler, in fact, that it's inconceivable how any kind of description of the later, complex organism could have existed in the earlier one" (78–79). Von Neumann notes that "by any reasonable theory of probability or thermodynamics," the latter situation—life—is "highly improbable" (78). In other words, given the spontaneous movement from a higher state of order to a lower one, as stated in the second law of thermodynamics, how can a simple structure produce a structure of greater complexity than itself? Von Neumann's answer was to postulate a "complexity barrier," a point past which systems change qualitatively, not just quantitatively. "There is thus," he concludes, "this completely decisive property of complexity, that there exists a critical size below which the process of synthesis is degenerative, but above which the phenomenon of synthesis, if properly arranged, can become explosive, in other words, where syntheses of automata can proceed in such a manner that each automaton will produce other automata which are more complex and of higher potentialities than itself" (80).

These rudimentary observations about the emergence of complexity out of simplicity have led some to define complexity in terms of the complexity barrier or threshold von Neumann postulated. The physicist Heinz Pagels, for instance, sees complexity as a "quantitative measure" located on a continuum "midway between the measure of simple order and complete chaos" (Pagels 1989, 54).[3] Furthermore, since it has been shown that in at least some cases an "underlying simplicity" can generate complexity "according to a set of rules," and that therefore, "at bottom things are very simple" (41), the study of complexity could be bypassed by being reduced to the study of underlying generative simplicity. One could marvel at the generated complexity, but, in effect, one could also simply ignore it. Once underlying simplicity were sufficiently understood, it could serve as the norm by which the various forms of complexity could be judged.

Although von Neumann was no doubt sympathetic to this point of view,[4] he introduced a further complication into his analysis of complexity by relating complexity to *descriptions* of systems, thereby including an element of observation in any possible definition of complexity. Basing his notions on then-recent developments in formal logic, especially on certain theorems of Kurt Gödel, he surmised that with simple systems, a "literary description" is simpler than the system itself, but beyond a certain point of complexity, "the actual object is simpler than the literary description"

(Neumann 1966, 47). To use the classic example of billiard balls,[5] the description of the movement of one or even two balls on the billiard table might very well be simpler than the movements themselves, but to describe the movements of a million balls on an imaginary table big enough to hold them would, presumably, be more complex than the actual activity.[6] In other words, to simulate the complex system, one would first have to reproduce it and then include the additional information that the reproduction is meant to be a description of the former. The implications of these observations on observation need to be examined.

If complex systems qualitatively differ from simple systems, or again, if quantitatively increasing complications in a system can cause a qualitatively describable alteration, then perhaps two separate sciences are necessary to investigate the respective phenomena. Similarly, if the descriptions of simple systems are just as qualitatively different from the descriptions of complex systems as those two classes of systems are different from each other, then the two sciences might differ qualitatively not just in their domains of investigation and in their first principles but also in their languages, whether "literary" or mathematical. The language used to investigate and describe a simple system might be inadequate when confronted with complex behavior. Such a simple language, the language, in fact, of traditional (Newtonian) science, would have to reduce complex phenomena drastically in order to deal with them. The claims to universality that (physics-dominated) science has traditionally made may then disintegrate; traditional, simple-system science may find itself dealing with special, limited cases rather than paradigmatic ones.

It is not surprising that biologists and others in the life sciences are prominent among those who draw this conclusion and question the prevailing philosophy of science derived from the theories and practices of simple-system physics and mechanics. As W. W. Bartley III claims, "the philosophical accounts of physics . . . *do not apply to, are irrelevant to, are not true of, and have no equivalent in* biology"; indeed, "biological theory and fact *conflict with* these philosophical interpretations of science stemming from physics" (Bartley 1987a, 8). Accordingly, it is not surprising that the biologist Robert Rosen has explicitly articulated some of what I have seen implied in the work of von Neumann. Rosen notes that modern science has been dominated by the paradigm of Newtonian physics, even its quantum offshoot, and physics is best described as the science of simple systems.

Two aspects of this science need elaboration. First, Newtonian mechanics is reductionist (R. Rosen 1977, 230; 1985, 420; 1986, 37). It states that systems can be modeled mathematically, and, by the application of universally valid dynamical laws, future states of systems can be accurately predicted. In essence, as Rosen describes it, the reductionism upon which Newtonian science rests assumes that a model of a system, based on a limited subset of elements, can be used to describe all aspects of that system, past, present, and future. The goal of traditional science, Rosen writes, has been to "resolve a given system into a spectrum of subsystems, and to reconstruct the properties of the entire system from those of the subsystems into which it has been resolved" (R. Rosen 1985, 322). This assumption rests upon the notion of a universal perspective from which any system can be observed, a perspective that would give the ability to predict the whole from any representative part.

Second, Newtonian science claims that the language of such a representative description is paradigmatic, and that therefore only one language is appropriate to all science, the language of implication (mathematics and logic), because this language mirrors the physical world of causation (R. Rosen 1986, 37–38). Rosen maintains that this image of science has been so successful in the past because it has restricted itself to the only systems for which this model holds true—simple systems. "At present," he observes, "the fact is that there is still no single inferential chain which leads from anything important in physics to anything important in biology" (R. Rosen 1985, 421). It follows, then (to use the language of traditional science—implication), that the relationship of physics to biology, which has always seen as the relationship of a general theory of material systems to a particular application of that theory to living organisms, will need to be revised in light of a science of complex systems that is yet to be fully realized. Then, Rosen asserts, it will be seen that "it is not biology, but physics, which is too special" (R. Rosen 1985, 424).

The science of complexity, as Rosen would construct it, is related to one further implication of von Neumann's remarks on the descriptions of systems. If one way to recognize the difference between complex and simple systems is to recognize the difference between the relationship of description to complex system and the relationship of description to simple system, then it might not be too far off to view complexity not as an "intrinsic property of a system [or] of a system description" but rather as an observer/

observed relationship involving the choices that an observer of a given system makes, including the choice of what constitutes a system to begin with. A system allows for various "encodings"—representations or models—and is considered by Rosen to be complex "to the extent that it admits nonequivalent encodings; encodings which cannot be transformed or reduced to one another" (R. Rosen 1985, 322). A complex system, then, is one that can be described only by selection, each selection constituting a subsystem with no one subsystem definable strictly in terms of any other subsystem or aggregation of subsystems. But the act of selection also constitutes itself as a part or subsystem of a complex system of choosing, a reflexive mode of investigation that recognizes contingency.[7] Complexity therefore cannot exist apart from investigation but arises "from the number of ways in which we are able to interact with the system" and must be seen as a "function not only of the system's interactive capabilities, but of our own" (322).[8]

We have two diverging views then, or at least two distinct emphases, that lead to diverging modes of investigation. On the one hand, complexity can be related to original simplicity and therefore investigated as an outcome of that simplicity, even predicted and potentially judged by it. This general assumption more closely approximates than breaks with the traditional scientific agenda. On the other hand, the process of observation is seen to contribute to the generation of complexity from simplicity. As a consequence, complexity can never be fully reduced to an underlying simplicity since simplicity, like complexity, is a construct of observation that could always be other than it is. Contingency, the ability to alter perspectives, acts as a reservoir of complexity within all simplicity. In the social sciences, I take Habermas's formulation of a reconstructive science of universal pragmatics to be a preoccupation with the former, reductionist view of complexity, while I take Luhmann's elaboration of a systems-theory approach to hinge on the notion of contingency that comes with observation and therefore to represent the latter, more flexible and less normative approach to the study of social complexity.

## Habermas and Generative Simplicity

The rationalist, modernist, Enlightenment project that is Jürgen Habermas's career can perhaps best be seen as a continuous effort to reconstruct a concept of totality (in his Marxist and materialist phase) or universality (in his newer, Kantian liberal phase) that is not marked, or marred, by a Hegelian philosophy of consciousness.[9] Since the publication, in 1968, of his *Erkenntnis und Interesse* (*Knowledge and Human Interests*), Habermas has taken the customary twentieth-century linguistic turn—the substitution of language for consciousness. This venture has led him to define a new normative totality in terms of communication grounded in an ideal speech situation, the contours of which are said to be inherently structured in language itself. The promised social, legal, and political transformations would now seem to presuppose an epistemological one, or rather, a linguistic one, in which communicative action—the basis for a legitimate public sphere and emancipated society—would flow out of the fully recognized and acknowledged rules of linguistic competence. Hegelian satisfactions of self-consciousness become Habermasian transparencies of language.

Within this context, complexity emerges as emancipatory, but also in need of domestication. On the one hand, for Habermas complexity represents the positive, irreversible pluralism that is the inheritance of Western political thought, the victory of the doctrine of natural law and of parliamentary democracy. Complexity, on this view, allows for the emancipation of thought and action (i.e., linguistic communication) from the false totalities of absolutism and monolithic, dictatorial, instrumental reason. On the other hand, for Habermas complexity is also suspect. If it is not grounded in the simplicity that is its origin, complexity threatens to become not rationally shepherded pluralism but irrational deviation. Legitimate complexity is seen as the surface manifestation of underlying, relatively simple, generative rules; thus if surface complexity cannot in some way be recognized as deriving from deep simplicity, then it must be judged deviant and potentially dangerous to the ideal of communicative action. For Habermas, then, the problem of complexity is a problem of rationality.

Following Max Weber, Habermas sees the project of modernity (beginning more or less with the eighteenth-century Enlightenment) as having differentiated rationality into cognitive-instrumental, moral-practical, and aesthetic-expressive modes, reflected in the social systems of science, morality, and art. Questions of knowledge, justice, and taste have respectively become grounded in categories of truth, normative rightness, and beauty or authenticity (Habermas 1981, 8). These categories, however, are autonomous and coequal, having no base or ground in each other. We are therefore faced with a problem. Rationalization—the differentiation of reason into independent spheres of action—involves a seemingly inevitable relativism prompted by the emergence of mutually unintelligible systems of interpretive behavior. Habermas is leery about succumbing, as he would see it, to a systems-theory view of a horizontal proliferation of functionally differentiated social systems that not only has rationalized all aspects of human life but does not allow for any privileged overview of society as a whole. Yet Habermas has also crusaded long and hard against an artificial reassertion of unity by conventional conservatives who seek to erase difference by invoking the authority of religion, nationalism, and (strategically selected) "traditional" values. Therefore he must reject a nostalgic, artificial totality, but he must also reject the rejection of totality altogether. The rationalism of society, he maintains, has not gone so far as to extinguish all traces of a pretheoretical, prescientific, pre-reflective lifeworld; nor, he believes, does modern functional differentiation render impossible any sort of metasystem or metaperspective or metalanguage that can make sense of the whole. There can be, he claims, a sphere of communicative action, an arena of uncoerced, ideal speech situations that does not seek to erase artificially the existing boundaries between social systems but rather makes the differentiated systems of modern rationalization intelligible to individuals in their prerationalized lifeworlds and provides them with discursively developed norms and common aims. It is the paradoxical project of modernity, in Habermas's view, to increase the complexity of reason and still assure its rational coherence.

Now, when we talk of reason and rationalism, we are already talking of a unity that has become fragmented. The question that confronts Habermas is whether that fragmentation is beyond reasonable control. Traditional, monological rationalism, ironically based on an irrational leap of faith that invests either intellectual intuition or empirical (visual) perception with powers not rationally ascertainable, has as its goal the establishment of incontestable certainty. However, the inability of traditional rationalism to fulfill this postulated need for certainty leads to its dissolution and replacement by a more limited and pluralist notion, perhaps best exemplified in the philosophy of Ludwig Wittgenstein (Bartley 1987b, 206–8). A Wittgensteinian view of rationality would localize it, making it context specific (Bartley 1987b, 208–10). Each of the many forms of rationality is determined by the system or language game of which it is a part, and each is constituted by the community of that particular game and the rules tacitly agreed upon. Each community identifies itself in terms of an implicit or explicit consensus, for all participants must recognize themselves in the community and assent to its activities. This form of consensually defined rationality, however, also demarcates the boundaries of each community and thereby becomes as much an exclusionary as an inclusionary device. The authority of local reason does not reach beyond the community that it constitutes and that constitutes it, but neither does it allow the disruptive intrusion of other authorities. Judgments about the truth of other forms of rationality are, by definition, impossible. Reason is domestically supreme but finds itself impotent once it strays from home.

The proliferation of language games and its limitation of rational authority parallels the proliferation of functionally differentiated and jealously autonomous social systems. Habermas seeks to subordinate these systems and these games of rationality to a realm of nondistorted speech, a sort of metalanguage game or ideal speech situation in which discourse, abstracted from the needs and actions of daily life, serves only to ground cognitive assertions through agreed-upon modes of argumentation. The structure of this form of communication constrains participants from exchanging information, influencing actions, or communicating experience. They are limited to seeking arguments and offering justifications for them (Habermas 1973, 25; Habermas 1984–87, 1: 99–101; Thompson 1982, 119). Against unbridled relativism, Habermas asserts that there is a creature called the better argument. Yet, unlike the absolute dictates of traditional rationalism, the better argument is determined through communal consensus, but a consensus that has more than limited, contextual authority. Discursively achieved consensus, in Habermas's view, would not only redeem the validity claims of propositional truth and the performative correctness of any given utterance, but would also serve as a formal model of noncoercive argumentation by which knowledge can reflect a rational common will abstracted from private interest.

Since reason is defined by Habermas as a consensus that can arise only out of what he calls discourse, that is, the metalanguage game or ideal speech situation that meets the above criteria, then reason cannot serve as the ground of discourse, at least not initially. But if discourse is to be used as a norm with which we can identify and judge strategic, merely persuasive and expressive and therefore deviant communication, then the construction of this metalanguage game must qualitatively differ from the construction of language games in which local and relativistically neutralized reason holds sway. Such a metalanguage game, in other words, must be grounded in a way that the language games it oversees are not, and the tool Habermas uses to establish this ground is the traditional Frankfurt School concept of critical reflection. However, his numerous debates with friend and foe have altered the notion of reflection in a way that allows Habermas to base normative discourse in the very structure of language itself. Reflection, in the form of reconstruction, has become the reductionist move that allows Habermas to ground complexity in, and judge complexity by, underlying simplicity.

Criticisms of his *Knowledge and Human Interests* forced Habermas to differentiate between two types of reflection: reconstruction and critique (Thompson 1982, 118). Self-reflection as reconstruction, as Habermas writes in the 1973 postscript to that work, refers to "the reflection upon the conditions of potential abilities of a knowing, speaking and acting subject as such" (Habermas 1987a, 377). Such a procedure makes explicit the tacit rules that govern competent performance. Self-reflection as critique, on the other hand, has as its goal not the conscious manifestation of a structured reality naively but reliably presupposed by action, but rather the "critical dissolution of subjectively constituted pseudo-objectivity" (Habermas 1987a, 377). Whereas "reconstructions explicate correct know how, i.e. the intuitive knowledge we acquire when we possess rule-competence, without," Habermas emphasizes, "involving practical consequences," critique is an illusion-shattering process. It makes "unconscious elements conscious" in order to change the "determinants of false consciousness" (Habermas 1987a, 378).[10] Though these two forms of reflection are distinguishable, it is evident that they are necessarily intertwined. Critique cannot exist without reconstruction, for the reconstructed norm serves as a basis for the activity of disillusionment, in that the realm of nondistorted speech needs to be explicitly discerned in order for distortions to be recognized as distortions. "The logic of a self-reflection . . . can be called 'dialectical,'" Habermas notes, "if it is the task of dialectics to reconstruct that which has been repressed from the historical traces of repressed dialogues," since "the structure of distorted communication is not ultimate; it has its basis in the logic of undistorted language communication" (Habermas 1973, 16–17).

In recent times, the most obvious example of a reconstructive science of the type Habermas champions is Noam Chomsky's generative grammar (Habermas 1987a, 377). Chomsky's "Cartesian" view of language is grounded in a basic and important insight: simplicity not only can replicate itself but can also spontaneously generate great complexity. Language competence is "a system of generative processes" and not just, as Chomsky accuses Saussure of believing, "a systematic inventory of items" (Chomsky 1965, 4). The complexity that is language is a matter not merely of accumulation but of "creativity." From a finite set of relatively simple rules, Chomsky claims, language "provides the means for expressing indefinitely many thoughts and for reacting appropriately in an indefinite range of new situations" (6). The study of language, then, is the study not of its surface manifestation but of the generative processes that underlie surface performance. "Linguistic theory," he writes, "is concerned primarily with an ideal speaker-listener, in a completely homogeneous speech-community, who knows its language perfectly and is unaffected by such grammatically irrelevant conditions as memory limitations, distractions, shifts of attention and interest, and errors (random or characteristic) in applying his knowledge of the language in actual performance" (3). Linguistics deals with the "complex" phenomenon of language in the way that traditional science deals with such phenomena, namely, by abstracting a set of rules or laws that allow for the accurate prediction of actual, empirical events. Chomsky therefore makes a "fundamental distinction between *competence* (the speaker-hearer's knowledge of his language) and *performance* (the actual use of language in concrete situations)" (4). Ideally, performance perfectly reflects what the reconstructed rules of linguistic competence dictate, and when it deviates from normatively derived predictions, it is consigned to the irrelevant realm of performative error. With the essence of language identified as its deep structure, the surface varieties of performance are seen as merely symptomatic. What happens in performance results from prior determinations and in no way constitutes language itself.

Habermas takes great pains to weaken "essentialist claims" (Habermas 1979, 16–20) of Chomsky's rationalist linguistics, but it does serve Habermas as a model of what a reconstructive science should look like, and Chomsky's competence/performance distinction also provides Habermas with the logical basis for a reconstructive universal pragmatics that would allow for the sure distinction between communicative and merely strategic action.[11] Just as the role of reconstructive linguistics is to explicate the rules by which a competent speaker forms grammatical sentences, so the role of speech-act theory, in Habermas's view, is to elucidate the rules by which sentences are transformed into speech acts (Habermas 1979, 26). This second transformation presupposes the first, since Habermas believes "that a speaker, in transposing a well-formed sentence into an act oriented to reaching understanding, merely actualizes what is inherent in the sentence structures" (27). He of course cannot identify grammatical competency with communicative competency; that would rob the latter concept of its normative value by equating communicative action with grammatical correctness. But he does locate in the underlying formal structures of language the conditions for the possibility of undistorted speech. By making these conditions explicit through the reconstruction of the implied rules that govern communicative performance, he can erect a hall of justice through which all communication must pass and be judged.

In his concern with legitimate rationality and a legitimate, normative, politically emancipatory totality, Habermas has enlisted the aid of reconstructive science to intensify his investigation of the underlying simplicity that is said to determine complex behavior. What is studied are ideal, closed systems that are thought to be perfectly predictive models. Discrepancies between what competence predicts and what performance produces are seen as the deviant results of outside interference on the part of the surface-level performer who is in need of corrective self-critique. The marvel of complexity is that it can be generated by underlying simplicity. The fear of complexity is caused by what complexity might do if it is not controlled by controllable simplicity. However, if Weaver's challenge is to be taken seriously, the obsession with simplicity has to give way to the investigation of complexity as well as to the appreciation of the complexity of investigation. What escapes the net of preestablished norms is not necessarily the result of external disturbance. Complex systems can be determined, and yet, contrary to traditional scientific definitions of determinism, not every aspect of its behavior can be foreseen or, for that matter, understood.[12] In fact, the distinction between norm and deviation, order and disorder, is no longer clear, since disorder can be seen as a constituent of all complex order, making it difficult to assume that unpredictability is equivalent to deviation, or that comprehension of the underlying rules of communicative performance can be complete and can fully explain that performance.

## Luhmann and the Irreducibility of Complexity

The observation Habermas incorporates in his reconstructive social science is that of a parole officer who makes sure his newly freed charge does not stray from the straight and narrow, that is, from the determined and predictable. But the observer-observed relationship Rosen outlines is meant not to control complexity but rather to give rise to complexity in the first place. It is constitutive. Yet, as described by Rosen, it is also problematic because the observer is identified, by implication at least, as an observing consciousness, as the scientific investigator. It must be remembered that all observational operations can be performed equally well on the observer; that is, the observer, too, can be observed. But to escape the infinite chain of successive observing consciousnesses (the infinite chain of self-reflection that is the paradigm of the philosophy of consciousness) evidently created by Rosen's model, the observational process must become mutually constitutive. The observed must also be able to constitute the observer.

Luhmann's basic definition of complexity involves the standard notion of a quantitatively defined threshold above which it is not possible for an observer to relate all of a system's elements to each other (Luhmann 1995b, 24; 1970–95, 5: 62). The problem with such a definition, of course, is that it makes complexity simply a quantitatively measurable property of a system and makes observation a passive process of registering and recording. Luhmann, however, attempts to obviate these difficulties by way of his definition of the crucial term "element," and by the way the notion of observation is enfolded into the notion of selection.

Observation, for Luhmann, is simply the ability to make distinctions.[13] To distinguish foreground from background, system from environment, is to constitute such entities. Yet the observation performed by a psychic system (an observing self) is merely one of many possible forms of observation and is not to be seen as paradigmatic. On a higher level of abstraction, observation can be seen as a moment of self-production through constitutive selection, and not a God-like act of creation by an outside observer.[14] The elements of a system are not ontic substances, but arise, as elements of the system, only when that system selects them to be its elements, its ultimate, constitutive, nondecomposable unities (Luhmann 1995b, 20–23). Systems constitute themselves by constituting the elements that constitute them, that is, by selecting them, forming them as elements in the act of distinguishing them from a background. A system's "basic elements are not stable units (like cells or atoms or individuals) but events that vanish as soon as they appear" (Luhmann 1990b, 83). Complexity, in turn, is seen as an observer's inability to define completely all these elements' connections and interactions. Observation is constitutive, but not all-seeing or all-knowing. Within the matrix of observation as selection there is no totalizing perspective or omniscient selector. Each act of observation is embedded in what it observes. Selection becomes not only construction but exclusion. The act of choosing can see only the outlines of what it chooses as it chooses it; it can recognize itself as an act of choosing only when what it chooses emerges as chosen. Each choice, therefore, precludes any number of other possible choices, choices that can no longer be seen as choices once a choice has been made.[15]

The language used to describe such a process can of course be irritating, but it demonstrates not only the relational nature of complexity but also the difficulties language has in indicating a reflexive process without stabilizing it into a reflected object. The claim that the above assertion makes —that there can be no final, all-encompassing overview of a complex system—is contradicted by the form that that assertion takes. The statement itself is an all-encompassing claim about complex systems, maintaining, in a seemingly authoritative manner, that all-encompassing claims about complex systems cannot be made. It is as if some observer has jumped over the metalevel of objective (neutral, total) perspective to a metametalevel from which it is possible to see that no metalevel exists. An observing system observes itself failing to observe itself fully. There is always a blind spot, and each illumination of a previous blind spot creates a new one. The system acknowledges this and thereby gives the paradoxical impression of having at last fully observed itself as a system that cannot be fully observed.

Yet self-referential paradoxes, like the one above, are unavoidable, Luhmann contends, because of the demolition of the ontological basis of science. He attributes—paradoxically so, it must be said—the de-ontologizing of science to precisely what allowed science, in the form of Newtonian mechanics, to arise in the first place, namely to mathematics. The "mathematization" of the natural sciences, he claims, has taught us that any component can be decomposed and further decomposed on into infinity (Luhmann 1995b, 2), making the search for the ultimate particle, the ultimate component of Being, a search with no end, or at any rate a seemingly infinite series of provisional ends. Reductionism, in the sense of reducing reality to ultimate particles as well as seeing ultimate particles, or simple systems,[16] as representatives of wholes, is therefore no longer possible (Luhmann 1995b, 26–27). Instead, contemporary theoretical work must redefine what one does when one does science in general. More and more sciences—whether natural, humanistic, social, or mathematical—are claiming that what a science studies are not autonomous, isolated domains but reflexive relations, not reality in its pristine and disinfected preexistence but the constitution of reality on the level of complexity.

But if the investigation of reality has also become the investigation of the investigator's construction of reality, then the process of scientific or theoretical observation must include an element of self-observation. As Dyke puts it: "Not only are the phenomena to be studied complex, but scientific practice itself is a phenomenon of organized complexity. The complexity of investigation must be studied along with the complexities investigated" (Dyke 1988, 5). In a similar vein, Luhmann notes that it has become a requirement of all theories that claim universality to include themselves as part of what they describe (Luhmann 1995b, 481). But this greatly complicates the process of observation by obscuring the separation of observer and observed, just as the inclusion of observation in the definition of complexity has obscured the separation of simple and complex systems. If realms of entities no longer exist as objects of study,[17] then scientific disciplines can no longer be defined by set domains of objects that it is their task to observe. Thus, no discipline can define for itself a final resting place by claiming ultimate or total knowledge of a field, since any given field is forever being reconstituted by the very act of study that seeks to gain knowledge of it.

Luhmann therefore draws the conclusion that a discipline can be defined not by what it studies but by the constitutive question it asks, and that question, Kantian in form, creates its field of study by positing a given, the improbability of which it is assigned to investigate. The social scientist asks, "How is social order possible?"[18] The form of the question, according to Luhmann, is naive, not skeptical, so that it may point to the real world, which has concretized possibilities (Luhmann 1981, 202–3). In other words, it suppresses the moment of skepticism in order to constitute an entity, called social order, capable of being investigated. At the same time, it expresses a moment of wonder. It is framed as a question of the form "How is ――――― order possible?" precisely to presuppose the obvious, in order to register the "miraculous" nature of the obvious. It acknowledges the necessity—and in this way it marks its own historicity—of explaining how, in the face of the universal degeneration of order (entropy), complex order is not only possible but also able to increase in complexity.

But the disciplinary question does more than just register the complexity it studies; it implicates itself in that complexity in order to allow for its own continued existence. A discipline's constitutive question, according to Luhmann, formulates both a problem that is always already solved ("ein immer schon gelöstes Problem") and paradoxically at the same time an insoluble problem ("und das mag zunächst paradox erscheinen, ein unlösbares Problem"). For in its nature as theory and as a scientific research program, the disciplinary question formulates not a task that can be methodologically or practically solved but rather a problem that must remain a problem, or be able to reproblematize itself, in the face of each and every solution. A discipline, any system, that could adequately and finally answer the question it poses for itself would cease to exist (Luhmann 1981, 203).

It is perhaps in this way that Luhmann can best be distinguished from Habermas. The whole movement of Habermas's thought tends to some final resting place, prescriptively in the form of consensus as the legitimate basis for social order, and methodologically in the form of a normative underlying simple structure that is said to dictate the proper shape of surface complexity. But for Luhmann, complexity does not register the limits of human knowledge as if those limits could be overcome or compensated for by the reconstruction of some universal rule-making process. Rather, complexity, defined as the paradoxical task of solving a solved problem that cannot be solved, or that can be solved only provisionally, or that can be solved only by creating new problems, is the necessary ingredient for human intellectual endeavors. Complexity always remains complex and serves as a self-replenishing reservoir of possibilities (Luhmann 1981, 203–4). Simply put, complexity is limited understanding. It is the absence of information that makes full comprehension of a system impossible (Luhmann 1995b, 27–28; 1990b, 81). But the absence of information is absolutely unavoidable and paradoxically essential for the further evolution of complexity.

What does this all mean for a notion of understanding based, as is Habermas's, on a normatively constructed consensus? Even if it were true that in "everyday life we start from a background consensus," and even if it were true that once this consensus has been doubted, communicative action ceases and something radically other, something Habermas calls strategic action, takes over (Habermas 1979, 3–4), would it be possible, or even wise, to attempt to ground the means for reaching this consensus linguistically? If the surface structure or manifestation of language is a complex system, then the deep structure might best be seen as a simple structure modeling actual complexity. The emergence of deviation, then, would be inevitable, uncorrectable, even required for the continued existence of the complex system. "Error," to cite the work of Robert Rosen again, "is the result of replacing simplicity by complexity," since error registers the "uncontrollable deviations between the behavior of an abstract functional model, and the behavior of a real system, with interactive capabilities not present in the model" (R. Rosen 1977, 231). Deviation is in reality a result of what defines complexity—the observer/observed relationship. Every observation is a contingent selection. An observer builds a model, writes a history, constructs a narrative of a complex system in order to understand it better. From such a model or narrative the observer makes predictions, but expectations inevitably are frustrated because surface-level conditions engender behavior "not comprehended in a simple model of that system" (231). Those errors, those deviations from what was predicted or expected, define the complex system as something other than what the abstract simple system used to represent it says it should be. Without this capacity for deviation, a complex system would be effectively reduced to the simple system that models it. The difference between model and system, between simple system and complex system, would disappear, and the complex system would cease to exist. What are seen as deviations, from the point of view of a simple system, result from a complex system's greater interactive capabilities not modeled, and not able to be modeled, by any subset of that system.

Dealing with error, then, becomes a political or rhetorical (not scientifically linguistic) activity that can have no recourse to some deep levels of controlling simplicity. Habermas's model of communicative action, which attempts to identify and deal with error even before it happens, might then be seen as a prescriptive model designed to *restrict* communicative action. What if, for instance, a member of society disagrees with the notion that consensus can be attained only by way of what Habermas calls discourse? What if such a member insists that other techniques of persuasion besides rational argumentation are appropriate in such a discourse? Or that communicative action is merely the resuscitation of the "Platonic" rhetorical strategy of repressing other rhetorical strategies in the name of reason or truth? By definition, that recalcitrant member would have to give up the deviant view of discourse or be excluded from the process that arrives at consensus. Has that member consented to this exclusion? Has that member even been heard by the community that is excluding him or her? If not, then can it not be said that the Laplacean dream of underlying simplicity manifests itself, at least on occasion, in the form of an unbearable nightmare?

With that in mind, one final paradox needs to be mentioned. Although Habermas is the self-identified leftist and social critic, and although Habermas sees in Luhmann and in systems theory a form of functionalist conservatism, it may very well be to Luhmann that future radical theorists will have to turn. Social and political theorists who are socially and politically committed need not continue to take theoretical concern with complexity as a sign of apathy, resignation, or conformism. As Harlan Wilson notes, the "invocation of 'complexity' for the purpose of devaluing general political and social theory and of creating suspicion of all varieties of general political theory in contemporary political studies is to be resisted." It is true that the increased consciousness of complexity brings with it the realization that "total comprehension" and "absence of distortion" are unattainable, but, Wilson continues, "when that has been admitted, it remains that only general theoretical reflection, together with a sense of history, enables us to think through the meaning of our complex social world in a systematic way" (Wilson 1975, 331). The only caveat is that such "thinking through" will have to be done on the level of complexity itself and will have to recognize that theories of social complexity are part of the social complexity they investigate. In this way, the ability to respond to social complexity in a complex manner will continue to evolve along with the social complexity that theory tries to understand.

## 2

# Injecting Noise into the System

In the previous chapter, complexity, contingency, and information were discussed in near-equivalent terms. Contingency is, quite simply, the fact that things could be otherwise than they are; and things can be otherwise than they are because "things" are the result of selection. This the theory, or definition, of complexity tells us. Yet, Luhmann also informs us, selectivity is equally the means by which information is generated. Thus, what in the "hard" sciences is studied mathematically as complexity is studied in the humanities or the "soft" sciences linguistically as "meaning." "Meaning," Luhmann therefore concludes, "is not an image or a model of complexity used by conscious or social systems, but simply a *new and powerful form of coping with complexity under the unavoidable condition of enforced selectivity*" (Luhmann 1990b, 84). Since, however, "enforced selectivity" is the hallmark of complexity itself, "meaning" is nothing but complexity "choosing" or "referring to" itself. What might this "mean"?

As we have already noted, complexity comes about by way of observation, but we need to examine further what observation consists in. For Luhmann, observation is an operation that creates information by making distinctions—between element and relation, for instance. Observation, in this technical sense, is not (or not simply) a matter of ocular perception but a "logical" process. Elements of a system, whether endowed with consciousness or not, can observe in that they operate by distinctions (or can be seen to operate by distinctions) and thus can "choose" between the alternatives those distinctions establish. A complex system is defined as a finite (if large) set of elements that can establish a mathematically calculable but never totally determined set of relations between elements. (In Kantian terms, one might think of complex systems as mathematically sublime in that their complexity exceeds the power of the imagination to encompass them in a single glance, so to speak.) For an element to link onto another element, it must be able to distinguish among various elements and "choose" one over the others—and this "choice" must be made in time. Thus element $A$ must link onto element $X$ now, and not later, or element $Y$ later, and not now. This distinction and choice between $X$ and $Y$, between now and later, is not (or need not be) made consciously but simply becomes visible to yet another observer (which could be element $A$, if it is capable of self-observation) when the linkage is accomplished. What results is an actuality (element $A$ links now onto element $X$) that precludes the potentialities not chosen (element $A$ links later onto element $Y$). What is not chosen may be chosen later, but the element that then chooses will be an element with a different history, an element $A$ that has already linked onto element $X$ during a certain past time.

In this description of the operations of element $A$, we have already introduced another level of observation in addition to the one engaged in by the element itself. On the basal level, element $A$ simply links, and the distinction and choices that are necessary for this linkage are simply "carried along" implicitly. It is an external observer (which can also be element $A$ itself, using a different set of distinctions from the one it uses in its basal operation) that notes what distinctions are used, what actualities realized, and what potentialities left behind. By utilizing distinctions other than the ones originally used, we distinguish the actual choice made from the potential ones not made and thus generate information about the system. This information, of course, is also contingent; it is also based on choice and exclusion; it also operates by way of enforced selectivity under time constraints; and thus it also partakes of the structure of complexity. In complexly observing complexity, we make meaning.

Other observers could observe the contingent nature of our observations, just as we observed the contingent nature of element $A$'s observations, and those other observers could generate other information than the information we generated. We designate this chain of information generation with the word "communication." When we observe observations, we make two sets of distinctions visible: the distinctions we attribute to element *A* (which allow it to make its necessary linkages), and the distinctions we used in order to see the distinctions that element *A* used. An external observer (which could be us) can use yet another distinction to observe the difference between our distinctions and those we attribute to element *A* in order to generate further information. Thus we alter the traditional information-theory model of knowledge by attributing a constitutive, not passive, role to the receiver of information. The sender does not transfer information; the receiver generates it by distinguishing between the information that the *sender* originally generated and the means by which he generated it. If there is a "transfer," then it is this *difference* that is transferred—though, in actuality, this difference is constituted by its reception. "Meaning allows no other choice than to choose," Luhmann concludes. "Communication grasps *something* out of the actual referential horizon that it itself constitutes and leaves *other things* aside" (Luhmann 1995b, 140). It is for this reason, then, that in his adaptation of Claude Shannon's information theory, Luhmann emphasizes the distinction between information and utterance, and calls the addressee of a message "ego" and the utterer "alter," clearly highlighting the primacy of reception (142, 141). "The metaphor of transmission is unusable," he therefore suggests, because it "locates what is essential about communication in the act of transmission, in the utterance. It directs attention and demands for skillfulness onto the one who makes the utterance. But the utterance is nothing more than a selection proposal, a suggestion. Communication emerges only to the extent that this suggestion is picked up, that its stimulation is processed" (139).[1]

Traditional toilers in the field of information theory (e.g., Dretske 1981) will find this Husserlian emphasis on constitutive choice within a horizon of possibilities that reveals itself only during the act of choosing both irritating and "counterintuitive," as writers in the hard sciences like to say when they rely on undemonstrable "common sense." But humanist "softies" have long since focused their attention on the activity of the "audience" over that of the "producers." The eighteenth-century war against rule-bound, neoclassical aesthetics, which putatively provided the "know-how" for artistic production, culminated in the Kantian construction of beauty as a moment of receptive judgment. And the rise of biblical, classical, and legal hermeneutics—the necessity of constructing an understanding of texts where once an understanding could, perhaps, simply be assumed—

can be explained by an acute experience of historical alterity. G. E. Lessing learns to ask, how can the "contingent truths of history"—by which he means the scriptural narratives of the life and deeds of Christ —give evidence of the "necessary truths of reason" that form the essential core of Christianity (Lessing 1957)? The answer, according to romantic hermeneutics, is to read, read, and read some more—not extensively but intensively—until one can understand a text even better than its original author. How can one do this? By dissociation. By distinguishing intention from utterance, text from language, author from subject. One understands better by receiving more "information" than was produced, and one does this by constructing infinite texts out of the finite fragments of language that are preserved. The elements of the archive are restricted, but the relations among those elements seemingly endless. And there is no definitive card catalog.

This chapter investigates a paradigmatic feature of romantic hermeneutics: its elevation of misunderstanding (sometimes in the guise of irony) to the status of an indispensable component of all communication. The necessary inclusion of misunderstanding—or noise, as I update the notion here—in all understanding threatens to degenerate into a cute paradox, but what is meant is simply that texts remain readable to the extent that they remain "infinite" and inexhaustible, as both Friedrich Schleiermacher and Friedrich Schlegel maintained. And texts remain infinite to the extent that they remain complex, where complexity registers the "incompleteness" of information. The discussion of noise is framed by the encounter between Hans-Georg Gadamer and Jacques Derrida in Paris in 1981. Like Habermas, Gadamer assumes that communication presupposes common understanding; but unlike Habermas, he believes this understanding to be rooted in a shared, lived experience that is provided by a historically specific yet mutable tradition—a tradition that regards the Enlightenment as a part, rather than as an extrahistorical judge and jury. Derrida resists Gadamer for the same reason he resists Habermas, that is, because the assumption of common understanding brings with it a (premature) foreclosure of difference. Our discussion begins with Gadamer and Derrida, but then moves to information theory, as elaborated by Michel Serres and, for our purposes more interestingly, by N. Katherine Hayles, to examine the role noise plays in the generation of information. Finally, when we move to Schleiermacher's insistence that hermeneutics must presuppose misunderstanding in order to produce (incomplete) understanding—an impulse seconded by Schlegel—we see that the "order from noise" principle articulated in the late twentieth century has its roots in the eighteenth.

## Is Common Understanding Possible?

In his discussion of *Bildung* in the opening section of *Truth and Method*, Gadamer explicitly confirms the Hegelian structure of theoretical knowledge. The basic movement of *Geist*, in his view, consists of two distinct moments, initial self-distancing followed by the eventual return to the Self. He writes: "To recognize one's own in the alien, to become at home in it, is the basic movement of spirit, whose being consists only in returning to itself from what is other" (Gadamer 1988, 14). Such also is the movement of hermeneutics. With the questioning of the self-evidence of classical and Christian traditions, distance is opened up and hermeneutics becomes necessary (174). Understanding, defined as the ongoing process of overcoming distance, is the return to the Self, albeit not the same "self-evident" Self that is presumed to have existed prior to the breach.

Of the two moments, estrangement and return, the return is clearly the center of Gadamer's concern. "Thus what constitutes the essence of *Bildung* is clearly not alienation as such, but the return to oneself—which presupposes alienation, to be sure" (Gadamer 1988, 14). It is assumed possible based on an underlying commonality uniting Self and Other. As Gadamer puts it, "Understanding is, primarily, agreement. Thus people usually understand each other immediately, or they make themselves understood with a view toward reaching agreement." Understanding is natural, it arises spontaneously and "becomes a special task only when natural life, this joint meaning of the meant where both intend a common *subject matter*, is disturbed." Self and Other are not in conflict. Even when misunderstanding occurs, when the Self has to become "aware of the individuality of the 'Thou' and take account of his *uniqueness*," Gadamer assumes in each participant the good will to understand and overcome the distance that has opened up (180).

Needless to say, Gadamer's Hegelian frame and definition of understanding as agreement has not met with universal approval. In the texts that record the now nearly forgotten 1981 encounter between Gadamer and Derrida, Gadamer's assumption of commonality and his invocation of the "good will" required to reach agreement become a pivot around which the elusive dance of the two thinkers turns. Gadamer's notion of understanding, it is claimed by Derrida, replicates the traditional metaphysical gesture of extinguishing difference in its relentless pursuit of the absolute presence of unified knowledge. Rediscovering oneself in the Other, the argument goes, is tantamount to denying the absolute otherness of the Other. It presupposes the "continuity of *rapport*," Derrida contends, where one might do better to presuppose "the interruption of *rapport*, a certain *rapport* of interruption, the suspending of all mediation" (Derrida 1989, 53).

What the Nietzschean "counterposition" of Derrida finds troublesome in the Gadamerian "position," as Josef Simon makes admirably clear in his gloss on their debate, is the subterfuge of a "moral ontology of good will" that is based on the "universal and unshakable presupposition of understandability" (Simon 1989, 169, 164). For Nietzsche and Derrida, interpretation is not mediation, as it is for Gadamer, but appropriation, "the translation of what is alien into one's own self" (162). The "presupposition of a common understanding" is a ruse, a "means of making one's own understanding prevail" (165). Once one acquiesces to the desire to understand, one has already surrendered one's otherness to the Other and become the Same; one has been swallowed up and made to agree in advance to one's own appropriation. This Derridean "counterposition" is articulated from the "standpoint of an other who feels misunderstood even within my best will" (Simon 1989, 169) and who therefore seeks to preserve himself from the menace of a Self who makes of the world of Others a world of Selves.

But of course at this very point, the Derridean "counterposition" takes on the shape of an interested and appropriating "position" of its own. If Gadamer's notion of the good will to understand posits an unquestioned value centered around the notion of agreement, so, it may also be claimed, does Derrida's abhorrence of agreement. The reluctance to involve oneself in the complicity of understanding, the reluctance to surrender one's otherness in the face of the Other, whom one wishes would remain other, creates a world of Others—a world in the image of the Other who wishes to remain other. In this world of Others, disagreement or misunderstanding does not arrive as an aberration against a background of understanding, to be excluded by both participants of a dialogue. Rather, it is thrown up by the Other as a protective screen, a deflection of the gesture of interpretive appropriation. A battle of wills results between a world of harmonious

Selves and a world of absolute Others, a battle that no amount of good will (to power) can resolve.

## The Platonic Dialogue and Information Theory

Michel Serres, in his analysis of the ideal of the Platonic dialogue, relates this battle of Selves and Others to classical information theory. As originally developed and popularized by Claude Shannon and Warren Weaver, information theory set out to solve a limited problem: how to transfer a discrete message from sender to receiver through a channel without having it rendered unintelligible by noise. Serres notes that traditionally in the dialectical game, the relationship of Self to Other (sender to receiver, as interchangeable roles) is too easily seen as antagonistic, as two interlocutors doing battle, each trying to enslave the other. A more plausible scenario is triadic, Serres maintains, and quite explicable in terms of Shannon's model. It, too, sees Self and Other as engaged in a struggle, but not with each other. Rather, they are united against a common enemy, the parasitic third party called "noise," in whose interest it is to interfere and promote confusion. Therefore the two protagonists strive in common, by doing "battle together to produce a truth on which they can agree," to eliminate noise from their discourse. "To *hold a dialogue*," Serres writes, "is *to suppose a third man and to seek to exclude him*; a successful communication is the exclusion of the third man." The problem of understanding, then, "is not the problem of the Other, who is only a variety—or a variation—of the Same, it is the problem of the third man" (Serres 1982a, 67).

Serres sees that the ideal language for this type of specialized discourse, visualized in terms of discretely discriminated components (channel, message, receiver, sender, code), would have to be mathematics, since mathematics is deemed to be the "kingdom of quasi-perfect communication, . . . the kingdom of the excluded third man, in which the demon is most definitively exorcised" (Serres 1982a, 69). Even philology, then, could be understood as essentially a mathematical, or at least a logical, enterprise. No two graphic signs—written letters, words, and so on—are exactly alike. But empirical variation between the way you write the letter "a" and the way I write it does not conceal from either of us or from yet a third or fourth or fifth reader/writer the symbol or ideal type that underlies the empirical manifestation. The concrete graph itself is not the symbol. Rather, the symbol is an "abstract being that the graphs in question only evoke" (68). When one writes legibly, the noise of empirical variation is easily eliminated; when one writes illegibly, one threatens to drown the abstract symbol in a sea of noise that masks the recognition of the Same. Therefore, "the act of eliminating cacography, the attempt to eliminate noise, is at the same time the condition of the apprehension of the abstract form and the condition of the success of communication" (68).

Successful communication, along the lines of this model, entails the desire to "exclude the empirical," the desire "to exclude differentiation, the plurality of others that mask the same" (Serres 1982a, 69). As Serres notes, such a model seems to place us on a familiar continuum, one with Leibniz on one end and Locke on the other. The defender of the universal recognizes the Same in the empirically Other, while the empiricist insists on naming each Other with an other name. We have an untenable opposition, a continuum which, when forced into extremes, cannot communicate with itself. The more the Self recognizes the Same in all Others, the less, it would seem, there is to say. Yet the more consistently empirical one is, the less intelligible one becomes. The more these Others are "right," Serres observes, "the less we can hear them; they end up only making noise" (70). But if the Other ends up only making noise, then the Other has slipped off of the continuum and out of the dialogue. That is, if noise, considered to be the "empirical portion of the message" (70), becomes identified with the Other, then the exclusion of noise no longer is merely the exclusion of an intruding third party, but rather—and this seems to confirm Derridean/Nietzschean fears—becomes the exclusion of the Other. Therefore the Other, who must enhance and include noise as an act of self-preservation, condemns himself or herself to oblivion. No amount of dialogue can eliminate noise and still preserve the Other. We have reached the same impasse.

## Information and Necessary Noise

Missing from the above brief treatment of information theory and from Serres's use of it to ascertain the nature of the Platonic dialogue is what N. Katherine Hayles refers to as "Shannon's choice," that is, Claude Shannon's metaphorical and productive identification of information with entropy (Hayles 1990, 32). This identification has been enticing to some and frustrating to others precisely because of its seemingly counterintuitive nature, for it identifies information not with order, as one might expect, but with maximum disorder. For this identification to work, the notion of information has to be distinguished from the notion of message. Information is seen as the total field of choices from which the choice of the correct message is to be made. Information is proportional to uncertainty: the greater the information, the greater the uncertainty on the part of the auditor regarding precisely which message from the manifold of possible messages is the intended message. So an addition of noise, of perturbations in the system, means an increase in uncertainty and thus an increase in information. "It is therefore possible for the word information to have either good or bad connotations," writes Warren Weaver, the popularizer of Shannon's findings. "Uncertainty which arises by virtue of freedom of choice on the part of the sender is desirable uncertainty. Uncertainty which arises because of errors or because of the influence of noise is undesirable uncertainty" (Shannon and Weaver 1949, 109).

It is interesting to note how traditional—one might even say classically rhetorical—this model of desirable and undesirable uncertainty is, since it hinges on the notion of authorial intention. The intended message is discrete and exists prior to encoding; the code is not constitutive, merely ornamental. The reception of the message, its decoding, is more or less passive, a retracing of the steps taken to encode it. Within this process, noise, too, can be intended; that is, a certain uncertainty, an ambiguity, pun, or irony (in the classical sense of meaning the opposite of what one says) can be introduced, as long as the act is encoded (by tone of voice, use of quotation marks, etc.) as an intended act and then decoded as one. In the end, one must remain certain even about uncertainty. However, the appeal of Shannon's equating of information with disorder lies not in our ability to control the distinction of information from noise by recourse to intentional signals, but rather in the realization that the chaotic noise of the universe can serve, according to the physicist Robert Shaw, as a continuous and spontaneous source of new order and new information that "insures the constant variety and richness of our experience" (quoted in Hayles 1990, 160).

In light of the ambivalent relationship of noise, information, and uncertainty, we must ask whether noise is only an accidental and undesirable component of communication, to be rigorously excluded, or instead an indispensable means by which information is generated and because of which the Same never remains the same? If the latter is true, as Shannon's work has led some to believe, then the fundamental question of how human communication is possible can be broken down into two questions. First, how can the choices that information forces on the auditor be limited or restricted so that information does not defy comprehension? How, in other words, is "too much" noise to be excluded? The answer usually involves the notion of codes as conduits of meaning and, as we saw with Weaver, the notion of intention. But as soon as codes and intentional authority are firmly in place, the complementary question arises: How is the array of choices that information provides to be utilized so as to guarantee that communication is not merely the communication of what is already known? That is, how is the right "mixture of order and surprise, when the message is partly anticipated and partly surprising" (Hayles 1990, 51) to be brought about?[2] This question assumes as its answer the inclusion of noise, or more specifically, assumes a perspective from which noise can be perceived to be something other than interference.

In Weaver's assumption that unintended uncertainty is negative, the perspective taken is that of the original sender. The concern is to eliminate noise (choice) so that a receiver will understand a message in precisely the same way that the sender understood it (as a statement of fact, as irony, etc.). But this concern may not coincide with the concerns of a given receiver or of an observer totally outside of this particular communicative system, and therefore the sender's evaluation of the effects of uncertainty does not necessarily hold for the system at large. In assessing the "apparently paradoxical stimulating effect of low doses of noise-producing factors like ionizing radiation, thermal noise, and time," Henri Atlan concludes that noise may be seen as "destructive" by those interested in the transmission of a discrete message within a particular communicative channel, but when viewed from other perspectives, noise may be seen as "autonomy producing," as transforming a relatively redundant and simple system into a more complex one in which relatively autonomous subsystems emerge (Atlan 1974, 298). Noise can therefore be seen as inherently ambiguous, neither desirable nor undesirable in and of itself.

According to Luhmann, this ambiguity is essential. If understanding is something other than the simple replication of a given message, then what makes communication both possible and necessary is the receiver's ability to differentiate between the selection of information that constitutes a sender's message and the selection of an "attitude" or "interest" that guides the former selection process. "Without the basic distinction of information and utterance[3] as different kinds of selection," Luhmann writes, "the understanding would not be an aspect of communication, it would be a simple perception" (Luhmann 1990b, 12). This distinction between information and utterance generates new information and therefore perpetuates communication by making immediacy, the simple reception of an already constituted message, impossible. The receiver's ability to receive the sender's intention is in fact the ability to receive a multiplicity of intentions, not all of which, or even none of which, were initially intended. Thus the message received is a message constituted as much in the act of reception as in the act of sending. The sender, in turn, perceives the same distinction between the selection of information and the selection of delivery as she receives the reception of her message. The scene of communication, then, is characterized by extreme contingency, since any selection of information or means of delivery is marked by the interplay of ego and alter, who must always take into account the possibility of selections being selected otherwise (Luhmann 1995b, 143). It is only by virtue of uncertainty, the necessity of choice, that communication continues, though the effects of uncertainty can always be variously evaluated.

But if it can be said that communication cannot continue without an element of uncertainty, then the question of how communication is possible can be elucidated as the paradoxical unity of the restriction and the generation of information. Thus the problem of communication can be formulated as the necessity for both a restrictive code and chaotic noise.[4] Again, whereas in the idealized dialogue only the inclusion of the code and the exclusion of noise is permissible, in the more contingent space of social systems communication requires the differentiation of code and noise in order to initiate a reciprocal play of inclusion and exclusion, noise at the expense of code, code at the expense of noise. Which necessity is seen to dominate at any given time may well depend on historical or political conditions, or on individual affiliation. At any rate, Gadamer's good will to understand and the Derridean/Nietzschean will to resist understanding can then be seen as necessarily linked tendencies, not mutually exclusive truths, though as tendencies they can also serve as blinders. In Gadamer's case, blindness comes when his notion of understanding causes him to devalue an important aspect of the romantic hermeneutics of Schleiermacher:

the necessity of including noise, by way of abstract negation, as a means of increasing the ability to deal with communicative complexity.

## The Hermeneutics of Misunderstanding

Gadamer's notion of understanding as agreement is articulated in direct opposition to what he takes to be Schleiermacher's notion of understanding. What Gadamer objects to in Schleiermacher is the assumption "that the experience of the alien and the possibility of misunderstanding is universal" (Gadamer 1988, 179). For Schleiermacher, according to Gadamer, hermeneutics is not grounded in the unity of the subject matter to be investigated or in the unity of the subject matter agreed upon by the participants of a dialogue, but rather is an autonomous process made necessary by the fact that understanding is nowhere thought of as self-evident. "In a new and universal sense," Gadamer writes of Schleiermacher, "alienation is inextricably given with the individuality of the Thou" (179). Gadamer correctly sees in romanticism a "deep conviction of a total strangeness of the tradition (as the reverse side of the totally different character of the present)," and correctly observes that romantic hermeneutics "presupposed the foreignness of the content that is to be understood and thus made its task the overcoming of this foreignness by gaining understanding" (Gadamer 1976, 47). However, in attempting to recover and rehabilitate a preromantic hermeneutic tradition, Gadamer fails to see why the presupposition of foreignness was necessary to guarantee the possibility of understanding.

In his lectures of 1819 on hermeneutics, Schleiermacher notes two basic distinctions: one between spoken words and written texts, and one between contemporary texts and those distanced from us by time and language. However, he explicitly denies that the need for hermeneutics is due to these distinctions. "Were the art of interpretation needed only for foreign and ancient texts," he writes, "then the original readers would not have required it. Were this the case, then in effect the art of interpretation would be based on the differences between the original readers and us." Furthermore, "written texts alone" do not "call for the art of interpretation," otherwise "the art would be necessary only because of the difference between written and spoken words." Yet even the "living voice" and the "supplementary personal impressions" that come with personal interaction must "be interpreted, and that interpretation is never certain" (Schleier-macher 1977, 109).

Schleiermacher rehearses these distinctions to point out that, contrary to what one might expect, they are not the operative ones. Why are they not operative? Quite simply because if they were, understanding would be bound to immediacy. It would be equated strictly with the elimination of distance (noise), linguistic or temporal. If our understanding of a histori-cally and linguistically distanced text were to be measured against the un-derstanding of its "original" audience, who presumably required no media-tion, then we could never know whether our understanding was sufficient, since our understanding of the original audience's understanding of the text is likewise mediated. We would, therefore, be condemned to establishing flawed understandings of historical texts. "We" can never be "they," so we could never have their understanding, and our understanding of "their" text would forever remain subordinate to an unattainable original meaning.

Schleiermacher recognizes the need to universalize distance by posit-ing mediated understanding as the norm. Therefore he replaces these ob-jective distinctions with procedural ones. For Schleiermacher, understand-ing requires the resolution of tensions between the fluidity of meaning inherent in language as a system of infinite potential and the assumed de-terminateness of meaning exhibited in any given historically concrete and psychologically motivated discourse. Interpretation, then, is not a method of set rules but an art of constructing "something finite and definite from something infinite and indefinite" (Schleiermacher 1977, 100); and lan-guage is not an inert body infused with the spirit of meaning at the birth of an utterance, but rather a field of information (selections) that produces meanings only with the help of an auditor, who decides on one of two modes of reception: the artful or the artless. So, for Schleiermacher, the crucial distinction that necessitates hermeneutics lies not in the nature of the text (all texts and utterances, contemporary or historical, potentially re-quire hermeneutic attention) but in the *reception* of the text.[5]

Artless reception assumes that understanding occurs naturally and sees its task as the simple avoidance of careless misunderstanding. This as-sumption of effortless understanding is based on the further assumption that "the speaker and hearer share a common language and a common way of formulating thoughts" (Schleiermacher 1977, 110). On the other hand, the artful appropriation of text or utterance must question identity and assume difference, even where difference does not immediately present itself. Although the goal is still to avoid misunderstanding, misunderstanding is no longer understood as a special case, and understanding is no longer understood to be the self-evident ground of communication. Rather, understanding must be constructed, it "must be willed and sought at every point." This construction, which is grounded in the assumption "that the speaker and hearer differ in their use of language and in their ways of formulating thoughts" no matter what the "underlying unity between them" may be (110), begins with the willful positing of misunderstanding.

One can appreciate Gadamer's uneasiness even if one does not endorse it. To posit the ubiquity of misunderstanding, as Schleiermacher does, is to distance understanding from the object to be understood. Once misunderstanding is injected into the system, understanding, seen from the perspective of the more complex system that emerges, slips the anchorage of immediacy. Neither authorial intention nor representational correspondence can serve as the only, or even the governing, criterion for interpretation. Understanding becomes contingent—all constructions of meaning could be otherwise—when misunderstanding emerges as universalized negation. Consequently, understanding is temporalized, concretized in a present that never remains present. Where once inevitability stood, a space of temporalized possibilities opens up. Time reflexively distances itself from itself. What is the past in the present is not identical with what was present in the past. Indeed, "making society independent from its own memory" is one aspect of the historicist preoccupation with constructing "the past as the present it once was," that is, with constructing "past presents" and not just accepting the self-evident "presence of the past." Historical research "distances the system from its own history. By breaking with all attempts to transfer its subject matter into the present, modern historical research can allow its own interests to select the stance it will adopt toward it" (Luhmann 1982, 306). "Emancipating" itself from a single tradition, modernity can construct a plurality of pasts to allow for a contingent present and therefore an open future. But such a strategy presupposes detaching a text's reception from its production, a process reflected in the hermeneutic trope, cited here in Schleiermacher's formulation, of understanding a text "'at first as well as and then even better than its author.' Since we have no direct knowledge of what was in the author's mind, we must try to become aware of many things of which he himself may have been unconscious, except in-

sofar as he reflects on his own work and becomes his own reader" (Schleiermacher 1977, 112). And since our only evidence of an author's having become his own reader would be the production of another text, we are never
released from this mediated relationship. Yet this uncertain relation between
meaning and reception of meaning proves to be fertile ground. Precisely because we can never achieve immediacy and can never receive a noiseless
message, we must use our mediated relation to the text to generate more information than the author or the author's original audience could ever have
done. "So formulated," Schleiermacher concludes, the potential for misunderstanding "is infinite, because in a statement we want to trace a past and
a future which stretch into infinity" (112).

By virtue of its preoccupation with the reception of texts, hermeneutics (including the deconstructive variety) is continually tempted to construct models of reading, either by way of codified methodologies or, per-
formatively, by means of texts designed to serve as exemplary "readings" of
other texts. One presumably learns to read by reading the way the latter are
"read." The issue at stake is control (in the sense of establishing order out
of chaos), but control becomes tenuous when misunderstanding is seen to
be constitutive of understanding. Schleiermacher's achievement was to de-
temporalize noise, to dissociate it from history and posit its ubiquity. The
goal of understanding, then, becomes not the elimination of noise but the
exploitation of the difference between noise and code, "the construction
and reproduction of order out of order and disorder" (Luhmann 1990b,
85). Yet that element of disorder within all order is never extinguished. It
makes our understanding of order contingent. It forces selection, "whether
intentional or not, whether controlled or not, whether observed or not"
(82). Whatever that selection constitutes can be observed, but since observation itself is "the act of distinguishing for the creation of information,"
whatever "appears can be interpreted as being the exclusion of other possibilities." Meaning, therefore, "involves focusing attention on one possibility among many"; it is "actuality surrounded by possibilities. The structure
of meaning is the structure of this difference between actuality and potentiality" (82, 83).

Not surprisingly, it is precisely in romanticism that one can find this
assumption of the all-pervasive and productive nature of noise as misunderstanding. The placing of misunderstanding on an equal footing with
understanding implies a critique of the Enlightenment contention that to-

tal knowledge from a single, God-like perspective is theoretically possible. Romanticism counters with the assertion that knowledge has its source in darkness, or in an indeterminate mix of light and dark, and that therefore the structure of irony informs the structure of all meaning. Every utterance is infused with the possibility of its own incomprehensibility, and none more so than those utterances that attempt to come to terms with the nature of irony itself. Midway through his famous essay "On Incomprehensibility," Schlegel acknowledges that the supreme irony of irony is reserved for all those who attempt to speak or write of irony. Irony continually deflects the comprehension of irony, Schlegel writes, both "if one speaks of irony without using it, as I have just done," and "if one speaks of irony ironically without in the process being aware of having fallen into a far more noticeable irony," until finally "one can't disentangle oneself from irony anymore, as seems to be happening in this essay on incomprehensibility" (Schlegel 1971, 267).

Perhaps the present endeavor is also becoming entangled in irony. As an ironic confirmation that the structure of meaning is informed by the structure of irony, I offer the above critique of Gadamer's notion of understanding as agreement. In contradicting Gadamer I affirm him by *understanding* Schleiermacher and *agreeing* with Schleiermacher that negation (misunderstanding) and the inextricable foreignness of the Other are essential to understanding. My affirmation of Schleiermacher contradicts the "negativity" of his contentions. I claim understanding of misunderstanding (and appropriate it in terms of a particular interpretation—misunderstanding?—of information theory) and claim that Gadamer misunderstands understanding. And when I now comment on the ironic structure of my argument—ironically? or without irony?—I introduce a further ironic tension that, if allowed to proliferate unchecked, would lead the argument into incomprehensibility, if it has not done so already.

"But," Schlegel counters, "is incomprehensibility really something so unmitigatedly contemptible and evil?" (Schlegel 1971, 268). The answer, as might be expected, is "no." And this "no" is based not on modest claims concerning the lamentable finitude of human understanding but rather on the absolute necessity of incomprehensibility as a constitutive element of understanding. The "unending world," Schlegel maintains, is "constructed by the understanding out of incomprehensibility or chaos," but ultimately the world would be destroyed if it "were ever to become wholly comprehensible in earnest." An element of chaotic incomprehensibility must always be "left in the dark," unanalyzed by understanding, to serve as a foundation for "inner happiness" and social organization (268).

Incomprehensibility, therefore, is not a negative state to be totally overcome, according to Schlegel. When order and meaning arise, incomprehensibility is not used up as if it were a finite substance, nor is the remainder a residue left by the limits and imperfections of the human intellect. Rather, chaos is a self-replenishing and necessary element within all order, including the order of deriving meaning from a text by the act of reading. Referring to the difficulties contemporary readers have had in understanding his *Athenaeum Fragments*, Schlegel wryly notes that the ruminating readers of the nineteenth century will, no doubt, eventually learn to understand what he has written. It will all seem so commonplace. Yet this state of affairs will require adjustments. Citing one of his earliest fragments, he reminds his public that literary texts must never be fully understood since readers must always be able to return to them, must always be able to apply new perspectives and gain new results. Should the nineteenth century bring with it readers who have learned how to read, then outbreaks of currently hidden incomprehensibility would have to occur (Schlegel 1971, 269). Understanding, Schlegel implies, is not commensurate with the image contained in the word "enlightenment." It is not the full and final illumination of a content but an ongoing process that of necessity must bring shadows as well as light with it.[6]

Thus for Schlegel as well as for Schleiermacher, irony and the shadows of misunderstanding and incomprehensibility that accompany every moment of enlightenment ensure the essential freedom and complexity of language. Schlegel maintains that language is ultimately beyond the control of intention and representation, that "words often understand themselves better than do those who use them," and that "the purest and most genuine incomprehension emanates precisely from science and the arts—which by their very nature aim at comprehension and at making comprehensible—and from philosophy and philology" (Schlegel 1971, 260). For this reason, the construction of an ideal reader or reading strategy designed to ensure precise decoding of encoded messages is impossible. Precision is the goal of knowledge, but imprecision is its ever-renewable source. The structure of irony enables the inexhaustibility of texts. Without the autonomy provided by ironic deflection, language could never generate information, only relay messages. If reading strategies were ever developed that could finally and forcefully restrict meaning within the bounds of intention—that could, as Norbert Wiener writes, "create, at the receiving end of a communication system, an enduring state completely characterized in terms of its own past" (quoted in Luhmann 1995b, 530 n. 8)—then new incomprehensibility would have to erupt from within language itself to ensure future communication.

# 3

## Constructivism as a Two-Front War

In the work of Jean-François Lyotard, the information-theory trian-gle—sender ("addressor"), receiver ("addressee"), and message ("referent")—becomes a model for understanding "obligation," or the ethical "call" that comes from an unknown and unknowable source. Like Luhmann, Lyotard rejects the transmission model and focuses on the seminal mo-ment of reception. "It should be said"—and he says it—"that addressor and addressee are instances, either marked or unmarked, presented by a phrase. The latter is not a message passing from an addressor to an ad-dressee both of whom are independent of it" (Lyotard 1988, 11). By identi-fying addressor and addressee as situated effects of phrases, Lyotard wishes to deanthropomorphize language. Language is not a tool used by an indi-vidual to deliver messages; rather, language is a universe in which individ-uals (addressees) emerge when called. The ethical question, Lyotard asserts, "is to know whether, when one hears something that might resemble a call, one is held to be held by it. One can resist it or answer it, but it will first have to be received as a call, rather than, for instance, as a fantasy. One must find oneself placed in the position of addressee for a prescription (the request being a modality of prescription)" (107). A third party, of course, does not hear what you hear, and is thus placed in a different position. A third party could observe Schreber and employ the tag "insanity," could observe Abraham and acknowledge "religion," or observe an SS officer and see effects of "totalitarianism"—these, at any rate, are Lyotard's examples

(108). But the addressee who hears the call cannot translate the moment of obligation—the moment in which he or she has been placed in the irrevocable position of a "you" obligated to an unknown "I"—into a cognitive or descriptive legitimation without losing the ethical calling. To legitimize one's calling descriptively is to render the law "intelligible to cognition," to make it an "object of discussion," and thus to divest it of its "obligatory value." Yet to refuse to discuss one's calling is to see it branded as "irrational" and thus illegitimate (117). Since the "call" is not a discrete message transferred from a legitimate source to an authorized receiver, it remains "unknowable" in an objective sense.

What is true for the communicative reception, that is, generation of obligation is true for other realms of communicative experience as well, and we need not assume the primacy of the ethical. Even the cognitive "tribunal" that attempts to judge the legitimacy of the *communicated* call (communicated, for one interrogates another's sense of obligation only when one has been "irritated" by that other) undergoes a similar "irrational" leap of faith in every bit of cognitive information it generates. As Lyotard states, the addressee who decides she hears a call has already made an "interpretation," has had to "decide" that what she heard was a call and not a fantasy, not a delusion, not a naturalistically explainable fact of nature. In other words, the addressee has already "translated" a difference, a distinction between noise and order, into a particular form of information, which is then left open for others to use in like manner as part of a distinctive, information-processing observation. What the addressee "sees" and "hears" and "feels" are irritations, perturbations seeming to come from the outside, mixtures of noise and pattern that act as excitations. The impulses themselves have no distinct form; they do not "carry" ready-made information; thus any given individual opens her kit of operative distinctions and generates information. One may hear a call and feel obligated; another may simply daydream. All create potentially different "observables" that imply different worlds in which these observables make sense. Some may hear God, others see demons, and still others suffer mental disorders. For some, Schreber and Abraham may be archetypes; for others, they may simply be indistinguishable. For some, God created this world and demands obedience; for others, God is nothing but a Big Bang, and our "obedience" is called evolution. These two groups may, in fact, have a difficult time talking to each other about God and the universe (though not, for instance, about sports, fashion, or money), and if consensus were demanded, "God only knows" which group would have to be condemned to silence (Hell).

But isn't this flat-out idealism?

The question is not only a rationalist one, it is a reasonable one. In highlighting the constitutive nature of "reception" or "observation," in highlighting the inaccessibility of affect (articulated as "obligation"), are we not constructing operationally closed, windowless monads? And, in emphasizing the incommensurability, rather than preestablished harmony, of the worlds that these monads purport to "see," are we not simply flying in the face of common sense—that is, the common understanding that both Gadamer and Habermas, for instance, agree on, even if they do not agree on the methods by which this common understanding is (or should be) achieved? Luhmann has always insisted that his work is not idealist, that his work is empirical, though it is not your garden-variety empiricism. By "empirical" Luhmann simply means not relying on transcendental unities to guarantee the "objectivity" of knowledge. Rather, his stable unities, so to speak, are immanent systems, and his empirical task is to observe how these systems (including the system from within which he observes) construct themselves as internally differentiated unities among a plurality of similar, internally differentiated unities. But in saying that his inquiry focuses on systems, he evidently presupposes the reality of at least one class of objects, namely, systems. The very first sentence of the first chapter of *Social Systems* says—or seems to say—as much: "The following considerations assume that there are systems." Consequently, he continues, "the concept of system refers to something that is in reality a system and thereby incurs the responsibility of testing its statements against reality" (Luhmann 1995b, 12). But in his introduction he had already said something slightly different: "Thus the statement 'there are systems' says only that there are objects of research that exhibit features justifying the use of the concept of system, just as, conversely, this concept serves to abstract facts that from this viewpoint can be compared with each other and with other kinds of facts within the perspective of same/different" (2). Luhmann wishes to have it both ways. The claim that systems exist relates to "objects of research," but these objects, it seems, come into view only when the claim is uttered, because the concept "system" gives one the means to make systems visible. Once we have described systems using the tools the concept provides, we can then test them against reality. But which reality? The reality that preexisted the descriptions of systems, or the reality that emerges with the reality of systems? Both realities exist for Luhmann, but only one of them—the latter—can serve as the reality against which statements can be tested. The former—some sort of physical but indescribable *an sich*—must be assumed in order for a "second-order" reality of observation and description to exist at all, but the "first-order" reality that enables the second-order one remains inaccessible to observation and description. It remains a blind presupposition. Luhmann maintains, therefore, that we must presuppose the (physical) reality of reality even if all we can perceive is perception and all we can know is knowing.

"Having it both ways" seems a necessary consequence of the unsublatability of the constitutive Kantian dichotomies discussed in the introduction to this volume. One cannot just "have it" dogmatically one way nor skeptically the other, nor can one find the perfect third term to cancel and preserve the first two. One oscillates, therefore, between the two positions, neither denying reality nor denying reality's essentially constructed nature. One calls this not idealism or realism but constructivism—in Germany, one now calls it "radical" constructivism.[1] We can call it cognitive constructivism to distinguish it from Anglo-American social constructivism, in which the addressor is unproblematically and unequivocally identified as "capitalism," "the bourgeoisie," "the patriarchy," "the First World," or some other seemingly stable referent. In this chapter I observe Luhmann fight a "two-front war" against idealism and realism. After staking out territory in one passage that most would locate in "idealist" terrain, Luhmann veers dramatically in the opposite direction in another passage, sounding as hard-nosed as any contemporary warrior of the scientific holy grail. I subject Luhmann to a Luhmannian reading, therefore, to isolate the guiding interests of his analyses. Those interests continue to center on a view of modernity that insists that scientific descriptions of physical reality cannot dictate the content of the descriptions emanating from other domains. A realist ontology that might gain support from scientific self-descriptions cannot carry the day without destroying the structure of modernity that, ironically, scientific self-descriptions helped bring about. We cannot reverse the "Copernican turn" in epistemology—even when the subject no longer remains as the site of that turn—without losing the structure of modernity that occasioned that turn in the first place.

⁓

When relativists talk about the social construction of reality, truth, cognition, scientific knowledge, technical capacity, social structure, and so on, their realist opponents sooner or later start hitting the furniture.
—Malcolm Ashmore, Dereck Edwards, and Jonathan Potter, "The Bottom Line"

Those who champion a constructivist epistemology must live in anticipation of a big bang—the bang, that is, of a realist fist crashing down in verification upon a real table. Constructivists, in other words, fear being confused with idealists and are, therefore, perpetually involved in a two-front war. Engaged in hand-to-hand combat with realist common sense on one front, they must also, like Kant before them, mount their own "Refutation of Idealism" on the other front, to maintain their intellectual credibility. The war has its pitfalls, chief among them the tendency to concede too much ground to the realist antagonist when his fist-and-furniture argumentation seems to overwhelm naive idealism. Thus, reality, whose tidily ordered existence prior to representation is customarily denied or at least skeptically suspended by constructivists, often finds itself not only logically but ontologically reconstructed as a precondition of representation. A famous example is Kant's above-noted refutation of idealism, an impossibly intricate balancing act added to the second edition of the *Critique of Pure Reason* as a result of persistent fist-thumping (Beiser 1987, 172–75). Here Kant starts with the logical determination of external reality. "I am conscious of my own existence as determined in time," he writes. "All determination of time presupposes something *permanent* in perception. This permanent cannot, however, be something in me, since it is only through this permanent that my existence in time can itself be determined. Thus perception of this permanent is possible only through a *thing* outside me." So far, so good, if one accepts the initial premise. What Kant sketches is a series of logical presuppositions: "determined in time" presupposes "something permanent," which in turn presupposes "a thing outside me." But what follows seems a wildly "un-Kantian" conclusion: "Consequently the determination of my existence in time is possible only through the existence of actual things which I perceive outside of me" (Kant 1965, 245). Which I perceive outside of me? The logically presupposed object becomes, all of a sudden, the simply perceived object. It appears that in rescuing himself from the charge of idealism, Kant crosses one bridge too many when he moves from logical necessity to a seemingly standard, empiricist, monocausal, physical explanation of self-consciousness.

Poised precariously between two fronts, ever at risk of straying into enemy territory, the constructivist valiantly attempts to claim the middle ground. This middle ground, however, is nothing if not traditional territory. As Luhmann notes: "There was a shift in emphasis in the conflict between realism and idealism, but it is not easy to discover in this a new theory. There is an external world, which results from the fact that cognition, as a self-operated operation, can be carried out at all, but we have no direct contact with it" (Luhmann 1990a, 64). Since access to "external" reality is mediated by representation, the modern starting point, the modern "underlying reality," becomes knowledge itself. "Without knowing, cognition could not reach the external world. In other words, knowing is only a self-referential process" (Luhmann 1990a, 64–65).[2] The act of knowing can know only itself, yet if it is to observe itself as an "act," as an operation, and not as the mythopoetic dream of a deceptive God, then it must presuppose a physical base of operations that can be described, albeit not directly perceived, as reality. "Knowledge can know only itself, although it can—as if out of the corner of its eye—determine that this is possible only if there is more than only cognition. Cognition deals with an external world that remains unknown and must, as a result, come to see that it cannot see what it cannot see" (65, trans. modified). In this particular explanation of knowledge, the logical presupposition of "something permanent" never slides into a direct perception of it.

We seem to be on familiar "Kantian" turf. The inaccessible *Ding an sich*, to be sure, has become an inaccessible but necessarily presupposed *Operation an sich*, a "buzzing booming confusion" of physical operations out of which an observed reality arises, not because reality is inherently observable but because observation happens to be one of the operations that are possible.[3] And the transcendental subject, the unified "I," is no longer the transparent self-reflection of the "mind" but something more like the conceptual unity of the operations of the central nervous system. It is familiar turf, but it has become naturalized. W. V. Quine is perhaps the best witness to this terrain:

Our talk of external things, our very notion of things, is just a conceptual apparatus that helps us to foresee and control the triggering of our sensory receptors in the light of previous triggering of our sensory receptors. The triggering, first and last, is all we have to go on.

In saying this I too am talking of external things, namely people and their nerve endings. Thus what I am saying applies in particular to what I am saying, and is not meant as skeptical. There is nothing we can be more confident of than external things—some of them, anyway—other people, sticks, stones. But there remains the fact—a fact of science itself—that science is a conceptual bridge of our own making, linking sensory stimulation to sensory stimulation; there is no extrasensory perception. (Quine 1981, 1–2)

So, where does this leave us? Our denial of skepticism (our fear of the fist—after all, realist impatience will eventually ignore the table and seek more direct means of convincing us) has led us to proclaim our unqualified confidence in the reality of external objects; while our equally empirically minded (positivistic?) caution has us also claiming that our "talk" or notion of things is "just" a "conceptual apparatus." That apparatus, it seems, must presuppose as real that which it conceives in order to conceive it. But it cannot assume that its conception of reality is a necessary and accurate *reflection* of reality. It must, on the contrary, construct the reality it presupposes in the very act of presupposing it. So, where does this leave us? It leaves us talking. It leaves us in the circle of communication about communication that Luhmann is at times so good at evoking. It leaves us operating "autologically and thus circularly, as we derive the demands made on a theory that describes a world and the society in that world from the structures of that very society itself. The describing system and the system that is described in its system/environment world-form are the same system" (Luhmann 1970–95, 5: 25–26). The Kantian problem finds a Fichtean solution—which is to say, a "practical" solution. The self-positing *Ich* (system) emerges simultaneously with its necessary other, its *Nicht-Ich* (environment); and communication enacts the circular emergence of this bifurcated world-form, since the world is presupposed by every description but must also be seen as the effect of these same descriptions.

   Luhmann, however, is not always this good at enacting or evoking the autological qualities of observation. In this regard, his occasional references to the concept of causation in *Die Gesellschaft der Gesellschaft* (The society of society, 1997) can be puzzling. The following brief treatment of the causal principle, therefore, will take as its starting point two passages from this work.

   The first passage is a radically constructivist description of causation as attribution:

Furthermore it is clear today that causality requires decisions regarding attributions [*Zurechnungsentscheidungen*], since one can never relate all causes to all effects (or vice versa). The decision about which causal factors are to be taken under consideration and which ones are not rests with the observers who use the causal principle. Consequently, one must observe the observers if one wants to determine which causes bring about which effects, and there is no "nature" today that will guarantee consensus on the matter. Causal judgments are "political" judgments. (Luhmann 1997, 1011)

Here we have, *in nuce*, a number of tropes immediately recognizable to readers of Luhmann. The principle of causality is the result of attributions, and attributions are a result of selective (contingent) observations; hence, to understand causality we do not directly observe the world but observe the observer who, by way of interested selections, attributes causal connections to a chain of events. Finally, we are reminded that no ontological unity (e.g., nature) exists to guarantee consensus regarding the composition or operation of the world. In a somewhat uncharacteristic flourish, Luhmann adds an intriguing exclamation point to the passage: All causal judgments are *political* judgments. One can only surmise that the lack of ontologically grounded consensus produces an agonistic ("political") clash of perspectives with no standard that might adjudicate among attributions, no single perspective of a totality that could distinguish *correct* attributions from incorrect ones. Different observers make their attributions differently, depending on . . . well, depending on what yet another observer decides is the "cause" of the first observer's choices.

But if we consider the second passage, an earlier reference to causality (Luhmann 1997, 129–30), we run into some trouble. The constructivist's two-front war against realism and idealism appears to have taken its toll. At first, all the familiar tropes make their appearance: the necessity of drawing distinctions (here, between operation and causality), the notion of contingency, and the importance of observing the observer. Thus, here too we have the makings of a theory of causality as attribution. "Causal statements" (*Kausalfeststellungen*), Luhmann explains, are the results of attributions, and attributions work by way of selection. From an unlimited number of possible causes, effects are attributed to a select few, depending upon "attribution-interests" (*Attributionsinteresse*). Attribution of causality is, therefore, both contingent and "political," since it depends on a selection of factors, a selection that, of course, could always be otherwise, depending on the observing system's "interests." One need not even argue for this point any-more, Luhmann interjects, because it has become so obvious (since Marx, one might add, or Nietzsche, or Freud). Accordingly, if one wishes to know which set of causal connections are assumed at any particular time, one must observe the observer who is responsible for the selection. Luhmann raises two cautious qualifications, though, in this initial run-through: con-tingency is not to be confused with either arbitrariness or mere fiction, and effects are generated not just by systemic operations but also by the envi-ronment. Both qualifications can be seen as gestures toward the necessary physical reality that must be presupposed by operations of a system—the reality that can be glimpsed, as it were, "out of the corner of one's eye." It must be presupposed, in other words, that physical constraints, not just cul-tural or historical ones, channel and limit the selective process.

This initial caution about contingency and environmental effects in-cautiously becomes a full-fledged counterattack that threatens to domesti-cate, if not make irrelevant, Luhmann's entire theory of observation of ob-servation. For convenience, I quote the paragraph in full:

> Therefore, it is entirely incontrovertible [*nicht zu bestreiten*] that systems-opera-tions depend causally on environmental conditions, which either are mediated by structural coupling or are simply destructive. It is equally incontrovertible that systems-operations causally change environmental conditions. To put it another way, system boundaries block causalities in neither direction. A communication sets air in motion or colors paper, changes the electromagnetic conditions of a par-ticular apparatus and the conditions of the participating conscious systems. . . . There is no doubt about that, and it cannot be thought away without having com-munication disappear altogether. The question is only, what social meaning does such an environmental cause have? Does it somehow change—and within which time horizon—the condition of the selection of further operations in the system? (Luhmann 1997, 130)

The first thing to note is the heavy rhetorical artillery brought to bear: "It is entirely incontrovertible," "It is equally incontrovertible," "There is no doubt," "it cannot be thought away." The negation of doubt seems to ape the Cartesian method, but instead of clear and distinct ideas, instead of ar-gumentation, evidence, or any kind of theoretical chain of reasoning, we get an insistence on incontrovertibility. These phrases emulate the fist that pounds upon a table, hoping thereby to demonstrate its existence. Are we to assume that we have arrived at the bedrock of certainty? More interesting than the brute force of the assertions, however, is the example given, the physical description of communication in terms of sound waves, light, and so on. A nonemphasized distinction between the physical and the social universes emerges in full force. The physical universe not only operates as a necessary presupposition, it presents itself as immediately perceivable (or, at least, describable) as a set of substances with definite properties. This apparent slide from logical to perceptual (or intuitional) necessity resembles the surprising shift we witnessed in Kant's "Refutation." In equating the description of sound waves, light, and electromagnetic fields with their incontrovertible reality, Luhmann sidesteps or at least diminishes the issue of attribution and, thus, of observation. Here, it seems, a simple subject/object dualism reemerges, and the issue raised is merely one of deriving social significance from the noncontroversial preexistence of the material universe. Over here, we have physical reality; over there, social interpretation —the result, social hermeneutics and an old-fashioned perspectivism that presumes the existence, if not the accessibility, of a unifying God's-eye view. In this passage, is Luhmann inadvertently retreating, not just to a methodological dualism between the natural and the human sciences but also to an underlying ontological distinction between nature and Geist?

We can respond to the above by thinking with Luhmann against Luhmann and asking the very question he habitually demands that we ask, namely: Who is the observer that so describes the causal chain of physical attributes allowing for spoken, written, and electronic communication? In answering this question, would we not—more to the point, would *he* not —want to say that such a description issues from the social system called science, more precisely, from some sort of subsystem like physics? Is not this physical description concerning sound waves and the nature of light and sight, not to mention the nature of linguistic or other sign-systems, a "cultural" or social achievement? Is it not system-specific, even temporally specific? Remember, had such a physical description been uttered a mere hundred years ago, the phrase "world ether" most surely would have come up, a phrase now meaningless and not at all obvious. Is this incontrovertible description not a product of contemporary science, and can we not, then, observe the observer who produces such a description? In so doing, can we not ask about the "attribution interests" of such an observing system, as well as the interests of the one who demands we observe the observer? Is this not the "deconstructive" mechanism by means of which constructivism constructs (Luhmann 1993)? And are not the fist-thumping rhetorical gestures of "incontrovertibility" designed precisely to beg this observation-question?

In raising these issues, we do not deny reality but rather ask whether what we should regard as real are descriptions or the things described. We need, therefore, to face the equivocation inherent in the notion of observation. Does observation of an operation in some way constitute that operation, or is it merely a reflection, one that can be judged according to its representational adequacy? We can get at this question, briefly, via the famous battle between Einstein and Bohr (as explicated by Hübner 1983) over the nature of quantum mechanics. The differences between the so-called Copenhagen interpretation of quantum physics and the view positing "hidden parameters" or "hidden variables" are based not on differences in empirical or mathematical evidence but on differing philosophical presuppositions.

For Einstein, David Bohm, and other adherents of hidden-variable theories, the universe is still basically Cartesian (Hübner 1983, 82–84, 138–54), and "reality consists of substances that have properties which remain unaffected by the relations between substances." Bohr, however, views reality precisely in terms of these relations. Thus, "for Bohr a measurement constitutes a reality" (75). If one translates these contentions into observational terms, we can state that Einstein's universe is still Cartesian, consisting in an "implicate order" (Bohm 1981), hence observable and subject to a unified description that is "neutral for all systems of reference" (Hübner 1983, 83). If, however, for the Copenhagen interpretation, relations, not preexistent substances, are the basic component or operation of reality, then the world consists of observables that are brought forth by means of observation (i.e., measurement and experimentation). "Being," in Hübner's summary of the Copenhagen position, "is only the possible, which, with the aid of a measurement procedure, is produced or brought forward as the real" (19).

These philosophical skirmishes occasioned by twentieth-century physics have naturally affected the principles of classical physics, among them causality. Whereas one party wishes to preserve an unlimited principle of causality by postulating the incompleteness of quantum theory (an incompleteness that needs to be compensated for by the presupposition of "hidden variables"), the other party is willing to question the universality of causality, is willing, in other words, to entertain a limited principle of causality. Hübner views the issue as undecidable by either empirical or philosophical means. Indeed, the causal principle, on his view, cannot be grounded in an ontology of any sort, but must be viewed simply as an imperative. It "lays claim to expressing neither an empirical fact nor an a priori necessary constitutive structure, whether of nature or of a cognizant being." Neither the Cartesian solution nor the Kantian transcendental solution suffices. Rather, the principle of causality "implies only the *demand* to *presuppose* and to *seek after* the existent Y for every X. Thereby the causal principle becomes a *practical postulate*" (Hübner 1983, 22).

Hübner's "demand to presuppose," it seems to me, is Luhmann's "demand to attribute." Further, the way Luhmann frames his demand, his stress on the incompatibility of observational perspectives, on their "complementarity," if you will, aligns him rather with Bohr in Copenhagen than with Einstein and a God who refuses to play with dice—at least Luhmann in general, if not the Luhmann of the paragraph cited above. Now, one can sympathize with his insistence on the reality of physical reality (to put it redundantly), and one can also agree that the attribution of causality is essential for communication (as attested by the many times I have, in this short chapter, rhetorically urged cause-and-effect reasoning on my readers by means of simple terms like "thus," "if . . . then," "therefore," "accordingly," "consequently," and the like). Yet when Luhmann moves from attribution, from presupposition, to what can only sound like the positing of metaphysically established substances with inherent causal properties that can somehow be directly "known" (i.e., cannot be doubted), he cedes too much ground to a world picture against which, elsewhere, he explicitly argues. This sudden lurch toward realism has its consequences. If there is a radical disparity between physical reality and social interpretation (implied by the closing lines of the cited paragraph), then not only does one maintain that "science" is the system that uses the generalized symbolic medium "truth" to reduce complexity and channel communication, but one also arms those who would claim that science is the only means by which (metaphysical) Truth is discovered. The old Platonic distinction between truth and opinion reemerges, only now, not philosophy but the natural sciences become the repository of the only kind of truth there is, namely, mathematical truth. All else is relegated to opinion and, as such, is seen as entertainment.

What seems key in Hübner's description of how we ought to view causality is a certain pragmatic turn. The causal principle is to be judged not by its adequacy of representation but by the adequacy of its effect. As he puts it, "how the causal principle is expressed is no longer determined according to what is, but rather according to what one wills (the end that is sought)," since "there is no empirical or metaphysical high court which is able to pass any judgment here" (Hübner 1983, 22). Causality, like so much else in modern scientific rationalism, is evaluated not against a metaphysical standard of reality but according to its performance. The question asked of it, then, is the following: Is causality an effective means when it comes to manipulating the world via experiment, measurement, and observation? The answer clearly is yes.

But the question we must ask ourselves is somewhat different: What purpose does it serve to assert the pragmatic rather than the referential truth of causality? Obviously, we cannot assert that the pragmatic interpretation *corresponds* to reality without getting ensnared in the rationalist's favorite trap—the self-referential paradox. The pragmatic definition of causality must also serve an interest. If, as many have noted, the natural sciences have become the modern substitute for the medieval church (e.g., Hübner 1983, 105), then our ability to keep alternate, "heretical" visions of the world visible depends on our ability to relativize the self-understanding of science. More precisely, if modernity is characterized by the differentiation of autonomous systems, as Luhmann contends, then we have to envision this ordering of perspectives much the way we might wish to view a cubist painting. No single perspective can be adopted as the one that gives us a neutral reference system, not even the one that purports to describe the bedrock of physical operations that serve as our logically derived, necessary presuppositions, the physical "conditions of possibility" for observing physical conditions. Thus, unless one wishes to see in the natural sciences the system that can dictate to all other systems, unless one wishes to see the horizontal ordering of systems give way to a new hierarchy in which science usurps the position once enjoyed by theology, then Luhmann's rather Cartesian outburst must be seen as an aberration "caused" by fear of the realist fist. Consequently(!), one is tempted to say that Luhmann's "Refutation of Idealism" overshoots its mark, much as Kant's seems to. But perhaps there is no mark to overshoot, no perfect middle ground that could be hit like the bull's-eye of a target. Perhaps the constructivist position is really no position at all but rather a continual oscillation between positions, now defending the presupposition of reality with a rhetorical flair that evokes Cartesian certainty in the sea of modern doubt, now defending, with an ironic gesture or two, the "political" nature of the whole enterprise of describing the nature of reality, both physical and social. Perhaps the constructivist is condemned to this perpetual two-front war, a constant battle of assertion and revision. If so, then the "critical" rejection of both dogmatic realism and skeptical idealism can never definitively secure the conditions of its own possibility, but must parasitically forage on the fringes of both its enemies. That it can occasionally stray too far is the risk it inevitably takes.

# 4

## In Search of the Lyotard Archipelago

The dichotomy between idealism and realism is based on the quintessential dichotomy of the Cartesian worldview, that between mind (*res cogitans*) and body (*res extensa*). When we follow the basic Luhmannian injunction to observe the observer, we ask: Who makes this distinction, the mind or the body? If *mind* distinguishes between mind and body, then any reference to mind is self-reference, and any reference to body is external reference. The traditional problem has been to understand how mental reference to a physical body is possible. Since the distinction is made within the mind, and since mind has only mind to operate with, it is difficult to see how reference can be made to a "real" body, as opposed to a fictionally postulated one, for the mind's "body," its external reference, must be simply a logical necessity for enabling self-reference. The mind's evocation of body is the *Nicht-Ich* that makes the identity of the *Ich* (mind) possible. The external world thereby threatens to disappear, threatens to have existence only in and as the mind's fantasy—preferably the fantasy of God's mind, and not some demon's. If, on the other hand, the *body* distinguishes between body and mind, then the physical universe presupposes itself as basal reality, and the mind emerges as a concatenation of epiphenomena of the brain and nervous system. We could call this the revenge of the *Nicht-Ich*, if you like, for now the mind loses not only its claim to primacy but also its claim to autonomous reality. Its functions can be reduced to the functions of the fully deterministic natural world. Hence, in the world as seen by the body (as seen, in other words, by modern science), we talk no longer of mind but of synapses and nerve endings. But if, on this view, the mind is just the body writ ephemeral, what is the status of the theory that says this of the mind? Must not that theory also be part of the epiphenomenon called mind? Would not "theory" be simply the self-reflection of the firing of nerve endings, a narrative "caused" by the firing of nerve endings in order to "explain" the firing of nerve endings (whatever the firing of nerve endings might "really" be)? One of the fascinating aspects of this question is the realization that the very theory that declares mind to be an unintended by-product of deterministic physical operations would itself have to be such a by-product of those same operations. And then we can ask whether the body's self-description still wishes to deny to the realm in which it finds itself the status of autonomous reality. If it does, then in both instances—the mind's observation of the mind/body distinction and the body's observation of the body/mind distinction—we are faced with the problem of self-reference, either the mind's or the body's.

There is a third choice: to locate oneself directly on the (invisible) line that must be drawn for there to be a distinction (mind/body) in the first place. Yet when one attempts to land on that perfect center, one finds oneself, as we saw in the last chapter, oscillating wildly from side to side, perhaps preferring the mind side, but (over)compensating to the body side —or vice versa. The history of post-Kantian German idealism is a history of the failed search for this perfect middle, this origin or neutral ground outside both mind and body that would nevertheless actualize itself as a perfectly transparent mind/body within history. Thus, much of contemporary philosophy that both follows and rejects that tradition has become fascinated by, even as it is trapped in, the mind/body oscillation. What do we call this oscillation? We call it paradox.

Self-reference and paradox—sort of like love and marriage, horse and carriage.

Let us briefly return to twentieth-century physics and its discontents. In the clear and elegant words of N. Katherine Hayles, Einstein's theory of relativity "contains two fundamental and related implications . . . : first, that the world is an interconnected whole . . . ; and second, that there is no such thing as observing this interactive whole from a frame of reference removed from it. Relativity implies that we cannot observe the universe from an Olympian perspective" (Hayles 1984, 49). For Einstein, then, there is a totality, though there is no perspective from which this totality can be totally seen. Since we can never extricate ourselves from the totality of which we are a part, we can never see but a portion of it. Our instruments, so to speak, are imperfect, finite. Quantum mechanics radicalizes this finitude of perspective into something qualitatively other. Heisenberg's uncertainty principle, which is "concerned with how precisely the position and momentum of a particle can be known simultaneously," stipulates that "the more sharply the one value is determined, the more diffuse the other becomes." This "indeterminacy . . . is not just a result of limitations in the measuring instruments, but fundamental to the process of measurement itself. It implies that there is no way to measure a system without interacting with it, and no way to interact with it without disturbing it" (Hayles 1984, 50, 51). Observing the universe, then, is limited not because the observer is situated but because the observer is in fact engaged in a form of self-observation that partially transforms what it observes, which is to say, partially transforms itself, for it cannot cleanly separate itself from what it observes. Whereas Einstein and those who follow him with the thesis of "hidden variables" attempt to make the metaphysics of quantum physics conform to the meta-physics of both relativity and classical physics, Heisenberg and Bohr are driven to other conclusions. Heisenberg sees measurement as constitutive. In ways not clearly explicable, it transforms potentialities into actualities (Hayles 1984, 51–52). Bohr, on the other hand, rejects an ontological explanation in favor of an epistemological one. That is, he seeks an answer not on the level of emergence but on the level of description. Language presupposes a subject/object split, and thus a specific viewpoint from which a subject speaks. Accordingly, every utterance "will always result in an incomplete and partial description," and these incomplete and partial descriptions, which are uttered from different viewpoints (for the subject/object split is spatially and temporally local), will be "mutually exclusive." To move from one viewpoint to another "will render indistinct and hence indeterminate aspects that may have been clear in the former viewpoint" (Hayles 1984, 53). Unlike believers in the theory of hidden variables, which serves as a sort of *Prinzip Hoffnung* that the truth of totality is out there (even if fallible humans are too weak to locate it), Bohr and Heisenberg believe that the inability to integrate the observations made from the various perspectives into a comprehensible whole is constitutive and unsurpassable. Different observations are not observations of the same "thing" from different places but observations of different "things."

Now, it is easy to see how Bohr's statement, if one accepts it, dashes Einstein's hope, for his hope is the hope that there is, "out there," one comprehensible object, no matter how fragmented this object may appear when filtered through its own observation devices (i.e., us). It is also possible to see how Bohr's statement relativizes Heisenberg's ontology, for after all, Heisenberg's view that observation actualizes potentialities is also just that—an actualization of a single potentiality. But when applied to itself, Bohr's statement clearly relativizes Bohr's own statement as well, for his description of the perspectival descriptions that language executes is also just a linguistic description made from a particular perspective, a particular subject/object split in space and time. Bohr's statement purports to account for the constitutive partiality of all other statements, but can do so only by subjecting itself to the same criteria of partiality. Thus "absolute knowledge," to reprise a phrase that we have already had occasion to use, is not knowledge of the absolute, thought of as a totality, but knowledge of the limits of knowledge. Not surprisingly, Bohr's statement gives an example of what Luhmann looks for in a universal theory. In his words: "Theories that make a claim to universality are self-referential. . . . They always learn something about themselves from their objects. Therefore they are forced, as if by their own logic, to accept a limitation of their meaning" (Luhmann 1995b, xlvii). Bohr's truth is a relativized truth, but a compelling one, because it does not, not even in the service of hope, exempt itself from itself.

Luhmann's theory of modern differentiation, it seems, is equally "quantum" (if I may be permitted the layman's sin of misusing that word), not only because "as a theory of differentiation, [it] can understand itself as the result of differentiation" (Luhmann 1995b, xlviii), but because it rejects the part/whole way of dealing with the modern puzzle of perspective. Systems define themselves in distinction from their environments. Environments do not preexist systems but are called into being, through exclusion, by the systems they thereby help define. There is no system from which one can observe all others, tally their features, fit their "edges" back together, and come up with the "whole" from which these "parts" were originally cut. Rather, systems, when they define themselves in distinction from everything else (their environments, which may include other systems), "actualize" a world. Thus "world," for Luhmann, designates the unity of system and environment, but there is no way to "see" this world, not even imaginatively, as a whole constructed of parts, because to see it would require making another "cut," another system/environment distinction, thus another incompatible world. Each system is universal in the same way that theories are. And each system is partial in the same way that Bohr's viewpoints are partial. Systems articulate a world judged in terms of truth, beauty, profitability, or any of a number of other properties; aspects of these worlds fade from view when other systems apply their distinctions and make their judgments. Systems remain "mutually exclusive"—or, as Lyotard would say, incommensurable. The paradox of observation is far from paralyzing; it is productive.

The field in which self-referential paradox has been most popularly explored in recent decades has been the field of language. Because Nietzsche, Heidegger, and Derrida "take the destructive aspects of reflexivity to their limit," Hilary Lawson explains, "they can be seen to open up the post-modern world—a world without certainties, a world without absolutes. This new impact of reflexivity is in part due to a critical shift of focus, from the individual subject to the text" (Lawson 1985, 10). The problem of the self-reflection of the subject, which sought to stabilize itself in its transcendental form in order to serve as a source and foundation, is translated into a problem of the self-referentiality of language. The initial formalist "turn" to language during the first half of the twentieth century was also intended to stabilize, not undermine, external reference, even if it did so exclusively by examining the structure of language as if it were examining the features of a closed system. Derrida's famous critique of structuralism, however, demonstrated (or sought to demonstrate, depending on your viewpoint) not only the inescapably self-referential nature of linguistic "pointing" but the inherently immanent ordering of linguistic self-reference. Signs do not refer to "things," but things emerge—"objects of experiential research" emerge, you might say—when signs refer to themselves and each other. Inherent within every linguistic construction is the threat of its deconstruction, by virtue of a series of further possibilities that serves as a reservoir of complexity. The point is to show not that meaning is impossible but that meanings arise as a result of a contingent relationship among elements. "Metalevel" reflection forces one to realize that examining the operations of language can take place only within the domain of the object examined—that is, language. Talk of language is language talking. Thus one confronts such simple and obvious paradoxes—paradoxes that have delighted and exasperated audiences from coast to coast over the past few decades—such as: "There is no truth."

Lyotard, too, is part of this general linguistic turn of philosophy. Where Luhmann investigates the emergence of systems and environments, Lyotard studies phrases, phrase regimes, genres, and language games. Both face the inevitability of self-referential paradox, for both reject the construction of some permanently transcendent or transcendental level from which the conflicts of systems and languages can be absolutely resolved. The task of dealing with paradox, Luhmann therefore feels, entails neither hunting them down with rationalist SWAT teams nor worshipping them in stunned and paralyzed awe, but rather recognizing their inevitability in order to investigate their productive "unfoldings" (Luhmann 1990b, 123–43; see also 1991b; 1995a). The difference between Luhmann and Lyotard might lie in their differing Kantian commitments. Whereas they both respect the distinction between theoretical and practical reason, Lyotard, like Kant, looks to aesthetic judgment (without criteria) to ameliorate the effects of the chasm. To be sure, Lyotard constructs no bridge and conducts no search for hidden variables, but he does shy away from the consequences of his own thinking by exempting judgment from the rules of the language game that he sets up. Luhmann remains unmoved by this particular pathos.

Luhmann and Lyotard's commonalities and differences are the subject of this chapter and the next.

## The Dance

Postmodernist critics and critics of postmodernism are like a bickering couple in a dance contest. They mechanically circle, locked in a dance they no longer enjoy, but also no longer know how to stop. The postmodernist keeps accusing her partner of stepping on her feet; the critic of postmodernism rejoins that his partner unknowingly steps on her own feet. And so they go on, each confident of the other's ineptitude. The judges, if there ever were any, left the hall long ago, and now the spectators are filing out.

In the eyes of the rationalist critic of postmodernism, postmodernists cannot help but trip over their own feet in maintaining their radically ungrounded and therefore paradoxical positions. The classical version of this critique is articulated in the Habermasian contention that it is impossible to use critical reflection to critique reflection without falling into contradiction. Once the rationalist critic makes the central contradiction visible for all to see, the postmodern utterance is said to collapse under its own weight. Yet this critique has been remarkably ineffectual. Postmodernist critics continue to perform paradoxically; they continue to imply, through their persistence, that self-referential paradoxes are not careless oversights and not merely banal "You Are Here" signposts. Rather, they say, the presence of paradox makes a claim about the inescapably self-referential nature of language and therefore of efforts to understand the world.

## Paradox and Differend

In his critique of judgment in *Just Gaming*, Lyotard claims to locate a paradox, based on logical contradiction, in the traditional Western notion of justice. At the same time, he seems to enact the very paradox he locates in his analysis. According to Lyotard, a traditional "scientific" notion of justice (which could be characterized as Platonic, as Marxist, or in a variety of other ways) conceives itself as an essence of justice that can ground a just society. Such grounding proceeds in two steps: First, the essence must be described; this is "a theoretical operation that seeks to define scientifically . . . the object the society is lacking in order to be a good or a just society." Second, the object or essence thus defined serves as a model to guide improvements in society: "plugged into this theoretical ordering, there are some implied discursive orderings that determine the measures to be taken in social reality to bring it into conformity with the representation of justice that was worked out in the theoretical discourse." In Lyotard's view, traditional notions of justice thereby conflate and confuse the workings of two radically incommensurate language games—the theoretical or descriptive game and the practical or prescriptive one. It is in this confusion of games that Lyotard finds a paradox. "The paradox is as follows: what is implied in the ordering in question is that the prescriptive can be derived from the descriptive." Using Aristotle's notion of classes of statements and "a very schematic logical analysis" that could, he assures us, "easily be refined," Lyotard claims that commands cannot be derived from propositional statements. "This passage from one [class of statements] to the other is, properly speaking, unintelligible. There is a resistance, an incommensurability, I would say an irrelevancy, of the prescriptive with respect to the functions of propositional logic." In short, "all this thought is actually futile, inasmuch as a command cannot find its justification in a denotative statement" (Lyotard and Thébaud 1985, 21, 22).

Rejecting this "Platonic" notion of justice, Lyotard proposes a "pagan" one, in which judgments are not made in conformity with a concept of justice, that is, "not regulated by categories," but are rather made "without criteria" (Lyotard and Thébaud 1985, 14). But in enjoining us to adopt this model—in urging, "Let us be pagan"—Lyotard violates the proposition he is at pains to demonstrate: "To be Platonic is to commit a logical fallacy." In offering judgments without criteria as a model of justice, Lyotard performs the very paradox he claims to diagnose. He utters a simple descriptive statement—namely, that a prescriptive statement cannot be logically derived from a descriptive one—and then uses this descriptive statement to justify the prescriptive statement that one ought not derive or claim to derive prescriptions from descriptions. That is, because there is a radical discontinuity or incommensurability between language games, one cannot logically derive a statement in one game from a statement in another; therefore prescriptions that in some way claim as their ground a descriptive statement are illegitimate and should not be uttered. So stated, Lyotard's prescription violates its own principle, for it uses the theoretical (descriptive) assertion—that theoretical assertions cannot logically justify moral (prescriptive) ones—to justify itself.[1]

The situation is rich in irony. In *The Postmodern Condition*, Lyotard invokes Gödel's incompleteness theorem to stress that all formal systems, including logic, have "internal limitations" and therefore allow for "the formation of paradoxes" (Lyotard 1984, 43). Thus, older forms of legitimation based on truth as internal consistency have given way to legitimation through performativity or paralogy, that is, the quest for new moves "played in the pragmatics of knowledge" and the assumption of "a power that destabilizes the capacity for explanation" (61). In *Just Gaming*, he defends his notorious *The Libidinal Economy* by stating that its rhetorical violence is nothing more than a strategy for producing effects. Far from attempting to control opinion, prevent dialogue, or obstruct negotiation, he meant only to send this book off, as he has all his others, like a "bottle tossed into the ocean" (Lyotard and Thébaud 1985, 6). He conceives the reader of these messages in a bottle not as an arbiter of intentions or logical consistencies but as an "addressee." Yet, with regard to systems of justice, Lyotard forsakes the uncontrollable waves whipped up on the sea of performance for the solid ground of logical analysis, and his strategy for delegitimation reverts to a quintessentially rationalist tactic: the hunting down and elimination of contradiction and paradox, coupled with the denial that his hunt engenders its own paradoxes.

As Samuel Weber has noted, the web of paradox ensnaring Lyotard results from his insistence on the strict autonomy of language games. It is a manifestation of the antifoundationalist's unstated, contradictory desire for a perspective from which the particularity of all perspectives can be guaranteed. Consequently, the discourse that claims that no discourse enjoys a special status enjoys a special status. Weber writes: "The concern with 'preserving the purity' and singularity 'of each game' by reinforcing its isolation from the others gives rise to exactly what was intended to be avoided: 'the domination of one game by another,' namely, the domination of the prescriptive" (S. Weber 1985, 104). The "great prescriber"—the title that Thébaud bestows on Lyotard at the end of their seven-day discussion (Lyotard and Thébaud 1985, 100)—in fact proscribes, "while at the same time obscuring the necessity for proscription. . . . He guards over the multiplicity of the games as if that multiplicity could be delimited without exclusion—while at the same time excluding himself from the field he thus claims to dominate" (S. Weber 1985, 104–5). The paradox Weber locates is generated by self-reference. In what way can a discourse, which claims that no hierarchy of discourses exists, give a description of the field of discourses without implying that it exists on a "higher" level of explanatory power than the discourses it describes?

In *The Differend*, Lyotard discusses self-referential paradox in connection with his first example of a "differend," the dilemma or "double bind" that victimizes one party in a legal dispute. Protagoras demands that a fee be paid by one of his students, Euathlus, who refuses, stating that he does not owe his teacher any money because he has never won a case that he has argued. In reply, Protagoras confronts his former student with the following dilemma. Protagoras will take Euathlus to court, and if he, Protagoras, wins, then Euathlus will of course owe him the money; but if Euathlus wins, then the latter will still owe Protagoras the money, because by winning, Euathlus can no longer say that he has never won a case. Euathlus, in other words, faces a double bind: if he loses, he loses, yet if he wins, he also loses. "The paradox," Lyotard writes, "rests on the faculty a phrase has to take itself as its referent. I did not win, I say it, and in saying it I win." A logician, Lyotard notes, would reject Protagoras's argument and solve the problem serially. Protagoras's pupil has unsuccessfully argued $n$ litigations; the "litigation between master and pupil is added to the preceding ones, $n + 1$. When Protagoras takes it into account, he makes $n = n + 1$" (Lyotard 1988, 6, 7). Thus the logic turns the paradox into a simple contradiction.

The logician's solution works, but only by compounding the original injustice. In the first instance, Protagoras's aggressive use of paradox effectively silences Euathlus, and in the second, the logician's use of the "Russellian axiom of types" (7) juridically silences Protagoras by disallowing self-reference. "The phrase whose referent is *all phrases* must not be part of its referent. Otherwise it is 'poorly formed,' and it is rejected by the logician" (6). Logic thereby presents itself as the arbiter of difference, but can do so only by setting itself up as the sole admissible standard. It insists that all phrases, if they are to be ordered in a meaningful universe, must be translatable into propositions, so that all discourse may be regulated by a single metadiscourse: logic (Lyotard 1988, 65). But this regulation is not mediation. What Lyotard diagnoses as the differend does not disappear; it is merely rendered imperceptible. If in the first instance, one partner of the litigation is silenced, in the second, not only is the second partner silenced but, since the outcome is labeled a "solution," the very act of being made to fall silent is silenced. One discourse cannot be translated into another without loss. The space where that loss occurred is called the differend. If, then, a third discourse claims to be able to adjudicate between the first two discourses, the differend—that original sense of loss—is itself lost. Paradox is not eliminated by logic. Paradox and its effects are rendered invisible although they still exist. Euathlus still says, "I've never won," in the very moment that he wins.

Self-referential paradox is not the major focus of *The Differend*; the differend is. They are related, however, and given the nature of Lyotard's philosophical project, self-referential paradox is every bit as inevitable as the differend. In his preface he argues that with the "'linguistic turn' in Western philosophy" and with the "decline of universalist discourses," the "time has come to philosophize" (Lyotard 1988, xiii). With the linguistic turn, traditional problems of philosophy, specifically problems of thought, reflection, and consciousness, are rewritten as problems of language. Therefore, since philosophy is a particular discourse, or genre, or "use" of language, philosophy becomes the linguistic observation of linguistic phenomena, that is, a field of linguistic self-observation. How is this self-observation organized? One can conceive of a universalist, metalinguistic discourse—such as the one that ruled against paradox above—that can analyze other discourses without including itself in what is analyzed. As is well known, however, Lyotard has steadfastly questioned the validity of such a discourse on two grounds. Descriptively, he has questioned the possibility of fashioning a metadiscourse that can extricate itself from the field of its observations—as if a discourse could somehow rise above and remain untouched by the language it uses. Prescriptively, he has questioned the use of metalanguages since it results in the formation of differends and the victimization of those trapped by them. By consistently raising both objections, Lyotard indicates that self-reference and self-referential paradoxes cannot be avoided as easily as the metadiscursive Russellian sleight of hand would have us believe. Lyotard acknowledges that his are metalinguistic moves—he makes them continually just as I have been making them here—but he gives them "no logical status" (69). He sees them as "part of ordinary language" (76). Therefore, any metalinguistic reference to ordinary language is also a self-reference. If any utterance purports to speak of language as a whole, then it necessarily speaks of itself as well. They may be metalinguistic utterances by virtue of their claim to speak of the entire entity called language, but they are not metalinguistic in the sense that they can claim to be above or beyond the consequences of their phrasing. They cannot assert that they are exempt from the rules they utter about language, and they cannot dictate to others without dictating to themselves.

This problem of self-reference is not merely a logical problem, nor is it new. It continually presents itself as the defining problem of modernity. Once the apparently solid, external ground of tradition, God, and the monarchy was replaced by rational self-grounding, self-reference became unavoidable, whatever its guise: that of historicism (all statements, including this one, are historically conditioned), psychoanalysis (all intellectual achievements, including this one, are the result of sublimation), political philosophy (all philosophies, including this one, are ideological), or rhetorical analysis (all statements, including this one, are rhetorical). Of course, the "including this one" phrase has generally been excluded: all *other* philosophies are ideological, and so on. But if postmodernity can be distinguished from modernity, it is in the various ways that the self-inclusive phrase has entered discourses purporting to describe the universe of which they are incontestably a part.

But if discourses are horizontally ordered, not vertically or hierarchically, and if each discourse "phrases" a distinct universe, independent of and on an equal footing with all others, and if conflicting discourses create differends whenever they attempt to resolve disputes in which they are both involved, then what role is left for the discourse of philosophy? By definition, it has no metanarrative role. It cannot use the traditional rationalist tools of logic, argument, and the assumption of metadiscursive norms to establish the relative validity of other discourses, because in so doing it suppresses—according to Lyotard—what it should not be allowed to suppress. Yet despite philosophy's past claims to preeminence and its affiliations with the politically hegemonic discourse of intellectuals, Lyotard does not shy away from assigning philosophy a specific role. It is no longer the science of all sciences, as speculative idealism would have it, nor the theoretically guided determinant of political action, but rather the guarantor of the inviolability of discursive boundaries. It is designed to protect discourses from being encroached upon by other, self-aggrandizing discourses, and to preserve the evidence of differends—exclusions, silences, victimizations, incomprehensibilities—from obliteration. "One's responsibility before thought," he concludes in *The Differend*, "consists . . . in detecting differends and in finding the (impossible) idiom for phrasing them. This is what a philosopher does. An intellectual is someone who helps forget differends . . . for the sake of political hegemony" (Lyotard 1988, 142). At this point the self-referential paradox Weber located in *Just Gaming* comes back around to bite Lyotard in his rhetorical tail. At the very moment he maintains the radical incommensurability and radical, horizontally structured autonomy of discourses, he seems to remove one such discourse from the field of play. One does not need to make the deductive, logical move Weber makes to arrive at this conclusion. It is suggested by Lyotard's famous image of the archipelago in his third "Kant Notice" (130–35). In this archipelago, Lyotard reports:

Each genre of discourse would be like an island; the faculty of judgment would be, at least in part, like an admiral or like a provisioner of ships who would launch expeditions from one island to the next, intended to present to one island what was found (or invented, in the archaic sense of the word) in the other, and which might serve the former as an "as-if intuition" with which to validate it. Whether war or commerce, this interventionist force has no object, and does not have its own island, but it requires a milieu—this would be the sea—the Archepelagos or primary sea as the Aegean was once called. (Lyotard 1988, 130–31)

Why does the faculty of judgment not have an island of its own? Is this because, as Lyotard emphasizes elsewhere, judgment in its "most humble form" is "feeling" (Lyotard 1992, 7)? But is not feeling, when articulated as a judgment, an exercise of language (after the "linguistic turn"), and therefore is it not a genre, or at least a "concatenation" of genres, that is, an island, or at least a cluster of islets? Why is this particular exercise of language—judgment—not subject to the same limitation—immobility—as the others?

Lyotard's apparent privileging of the genre of philosophy and the faculty of judgment (over speculative and intellectual modes of discourse) points to a weakness that has often been noticed and variously commented on, either as a hidden nostalgia for unity or as a self-condemning performative contradiction.[2] The antipostmodernist critic asks: from what place is this denial of metalinguistic capabilities uttered if not from a place endowed with metalinguistic capabilities? Lyotard astonishingly (inadvertently?) answers: from a ship that navigates (impossible?) passages between the islands of discourse. The critic responds: by postulating a discourse that navigates passages between other discourses, you privilege what you say cannot be privileged. Furthermore, you commit a performative contradiction. You can maintain the inevitability of differends only by counterfactually presupposing unity. By defining the stakes of your philosophical project with verbs like "convince," "refute," "defend and illustrate," "show," and the theologically tinged "bear witness" (Lyotard 1988, xii, xiii), you reaffirm the validity of rational argumentation, moral persuasion, and consensus, or at least a consensus about dissonance, difference, and the inevitability of differends. With this disclosure of a performative paradox, the critic closes his or her case. Lyotard's project is exposed as internally incoherent, and no further discussion is deemed necessary. Indeed, his use of the archipelago metaphor can be taken as evidence that he recognizes the inevitable contradictions of a consistently self-referential position. He confronts self-reference—and flinches. He does not seek refuge in a universalist discourse, but he also fails to maintain a "consistently" self-referential position; as a result, wearing his admiral's cap, he flounders in mid-ocean, fending off the sharks of modernism.

Such, at any rate, is the picture painted of all conventionalist and postmodernist thought by many a rationalist critic.[3] In light of the unavoidability of self-contradiction, James L. Marsh, for instance, writes: "The post-modernist . . . has the option of either remaining silent or joining fully in the philosophical community. If he opts for the former and moves into a post-rational, post-metaphysical solitude, then there is nothing we can do for him. If he opts for the latter, then we can welcome him back as a Prodigal returned. In making such a return, however, he has to cease being a post-modernist" (Marsh 1989, 349). On this view, postmodernist discourse is a truly impossible (not just parenthetically impossible) discourse; so impossible, in fact, that it is commanded to disappear. Either speak our language, Marsh declares, or sit down and shut up.[4] But what Marsh intends as a devastating indictment of postmodernism can of course easily be deflected and turned back on itself, for do we not find in his own words a telling enactment of what Lyotard defines as a differend? Does not Marsh want to silence his opponent, or at least force "him" to renounce "his" heresy and speak the correct idiom? And if Marsh, in the name of Reason, thereby enacts what Lyotard describes, does he not verify the chief postmodernist suspicion about the terrorism of rationalism in the very act of refuting postmodernism? If so, does he not come perilously close to performing a contradiction that, by his own criteria, could be construed to condemn him and, by extension, the entire "philosophical community" to silence? With such an outcome, would not Marsh's postmodernist critic be justified in dusting "himself" off and smugly observing, "It takes one to know one"? But where does that leave us? At the grave site of philosophy? The junkyard of used contradictions?

Lyotard describing his archipelago exemplifies the postmodernist committing his paradoxical act. In making a global claim denying the possibility of global claims, he seizes for his own words the special status enjoyed by the one discourse that claims that no discourse has a special status. Instructed by this example, we can see that the task at hand is to go beyond mere denial on the one hand and mere accusatory pointing out of paradox on the other. Any denial of universality falls prey to self-referential paradox and thus, given the current climate, to paralysis. To get a glimpse of a universe that thrives on self-reference, one can develop Luhmann's observa tions on observation in order to formulate a contingent universality, which, as the oxymoronic phrase indicates, does not try to avoid paradox but rather tries to avoid the avoidance of paradox.

## Observing Paradox

The modern European claim (made since about 1600) to a universal perspective is predicated on distinguishing between thought and thing, mind and matter, spirit and body, the realm of freedom and the realm of necessity. Classical notions of observation assume a clear separation of the human observer from observed nature, and this separation implies that the observer observes from a level distinct from and higher than what is observed. The human observer is part of nature only in body, not in mind, and mind is the agent of observation. The early-twentieth-century logical resolution of paradox is one form of this observational hierarchy. The logician wishing to extricate Euathlus from his dilemma institutes a hierarchical relation between the series of litigations to be observed ($n$) and the litigation ($n + 1$) that will observe (and judge) that series. Without this distinction, a clear judgment, valid for all observers, cannot be made. The hierarchical distinction defines a (meta)language into which all other languages can be translated, a perspective from which all observers may see the same thing. Thus, the logical solution to the problem of self-referential paradox formalizes the model of early modern science, in which the physicist/astronomer is able to determine with God-like precision a discrete and closed system (the solar system, say) with the aid of a few basic mathematical operations, operations that are not applied to the thoughts performing them. The observing mind remains apart from the matter observed. This distinction allows the observer to be thought of as standing quasi-divinely outside nature and as attaining, in theory, absolute knowledge of it. That the light of the mind may never be able to illuminate every nook and cranny of the universe is blamed on human fallibility, not on the constitutive limits of observation.

Following Luhmann, one might use the term "first-order observation" for this level of empirical observation of an external universe. Kant would argue that it is dogmatic to assert or to reject assumptions based strictly on direct observation. His task, then, is to subject such assumptions to a transcendental critique by introducing a second level of observation, an observation of the constitutive nature of observation. He accomplishes this by reproducing the basic observer/observed distinction within the realm of the observer, thereby making self-observation a component of all observation. Kant's analysis of the conditions for the possibility of knowledge is not a simple regress of reflection. In his discussion of the formative media of space and time and the category of causation, he notes how our observation of sense perceptions constitutes the world that these sense perceptions are said to reflect. Observation (mind) does not create nature (matter) *ex nihilo*, but what we know of nature is the observational grid we place on it. Nature is intelligible not because mind and nature are congruent but because mind imposes intelligibility on nature by way of fundamental categories. The intelligibility of nature arises because mind (by way of rational reflection and not immediate intellectual intuition) has privileged access to itself, not privileged access to nature. Thus nature, in and of itself, thought of as something essentially separate from us, is in a profound sense unintelligible. We impose intelligibility, but we do this by watching ourselves watch our sense perceptions, without knowing precisely whence these sense perceptions come.

By displacing our knowledge of how we know the world, however, Kant did not alter the accepted scientific knowledge of his day. He speaks in the assured tones of Newtonian mechanics and Euclidean geometry. More to the point, he continues to use the observer/observed distinction to fix the ontological realms of freedom and necessity. It is only in the realm of freedom that self-observation is introduced. The observing mind is not part of the realm of necessity—nature—and nature cannot observe itself—it remains inert. Consciousness can no longer view nature as a simple object standing over against itself, for it knows its own complicity in the construction of this object. Still it struggles to free itself from its entanglement with materiality, that is, from the consequences of this complicity, and this struggle is victoriously marked by the construction of a "transcendental" metaperspective. In the immediately post-Kantian writings of Schiller, Fichte, and Humboldt, this struggle is not construed as a total denial of the body—though monastic imagery sometimes prevails—but as a triumphant taming of it. The mind/body distinction is reproduced in the realm of mind, where mind overcomes the "body" of nature by overcoming its own "body," by purging itself of the influence of materiality, of what can only be observed. Thus, necessity is brought into conformity with freedom, and the observed universe is stripped of its mute recalcitrance.

If pre-twentieth-century science was, as Warren Weaver notes, "largely concerned with two-variable problems of simplicity," in which observation was defined as the mathematical determination of the velocity and position of individual bodies, then early-twentieth-century science's "disorganized complexity" (Weaver 1948, 537), in which observation consists in statistical averaging of large bodies of randomly moving (subatomic) particles, plays havoc with the all-controlling observer. Perhaps more than anything else, Heisenberg's uncertainty principle has come to symbolize this change in the nature of observation. Briefly, Heisenberg demonstrated that the precise velocity and position of a subatomic particle cannot be measured simultaneously since the measurement of its position affects its velocity and vice versa, and that in both cases these changes are unpredictable. This impossibility is not the result of the imperfection of our measuring instruments. It is, as Stephen Hawking puts it, "a fundamental, inescapable property of the world." Therefore,

the uncertainty principle signaled an end to Laplace's dream of a theory of science, a model of the universe that would be completely deterministic: one certainly cannot predict future events exactly if one cannot even measure the present state of the universe precisely! We could still imagine that there is a set of laws that determines events completely for some supernatural being, who could observe the present state of the universe without disturbing it. However, such models of the universe are not of much interest to us ordinary mortals. (Hawking 1990, 55)

Relinquishing the belief in classical determinism does not, of course, mean relinquishing faith in discoverable laws governing the universe. Quantum physics has impressed on us, however, that observation is a physical process using physical tools (such as light waves and neurons) to observe physical processes, and that natural laws govern their mortal, physical discoverers in the same way that they govern the observed universe. If physical processes are said to be physically determined but unpredictable, then the physical processes involved in observation are just as determined but unpredictable as those involved in what is observed. A complete theory of the universe would then have to account not only for the workings of the universe but also for the conditions of the theory's own possibility (Hawking 1990, 12). The picture of observation here becomes undeniably circular. Observers lose their quasi-divine status since the distinction between mind and nature no longer holds in an unqualified manner. Therefore, the aspect of self-observation introduced by Kant cannot be limited to the self-reflection of a consciousness safely embedded in its material base, but must rather encompass a universe no longer neatly divided into distinct domains. As the following passage by the mathematician George Spencer Brown indicates, the universe can thus be envisioned as an amorphous entity straining to see itself from as many angles as possible:

Let us then consider, for a moment, the world as described by the physicist. It consists of a number of fundamental particles which, if shot through their own space, appear as waves and are thus . . . of the same laminated structure as pearls or onions, and other wave forms called electromagnetic which it is convenient, by Occam's razor, to consider as traveling through space with a standard velocity. All these appear bound by certain natural laws which indicate the form of their relationship.

Now the physicist himself, who describes all this, is, in his own account, himself constructed of it. He is, in short, made of a conglomeration of the very particulars he describes, no more, no less, bound together by and obeying such general laws as he himself has managed to find and to record.

Thus we cannot escape the fact that the world we know is constructed in order (and thus in such a way as to be able) to see itself.

This is indeed amazing. (Spencer Brown 1979, 104–5)

Thought of in this way, the observer/observed distinction no longer delineates ontological realms of freedom and necessity, or of thought and physical reality. Rather, it becomes a formal tool the universe uses to observe itself. As Spencer Brown notes, in order to see itself the universe "must first cut itself up into at least one state which sees, and at least one other state which is seen." But such self-deformation for the sake of self-observation is of necessity accompanied by blind spots and is therefore incomplete: "In this severed and mutilated condition, whatever it sees is only partially itself. We may take it that the world undoubtedly is itself (i.e. is indistinct from itself), but, in any attempt to see itself as an object, it must, equally undoubtedly, act so as to make itself distinct from, and therefore false to, itself. In this condition it will always partially elude itself" (105). It is as if contemporary science has taken the step from Kant to Hegel by incorporating the latter's "originary paradox" of a consciousness that has to objectify itself—refer to itself as other—in order to become aware of itself.[5]

No matter how aesthetically pleasing and Escher-esque this collapsing of levels may be, however, it can be epistemologically unnerving. If one accepts the incompleteness and circularity of observation, how can one frame a theory that can account for its own ability to formulate observations on the incomplete and circular nature of observation? Any observation about observation is self-referential and yet, in the form that it takes, implicitly universal. If the claim made by Spencer Brown and others is true —that is, that all observation contains at least implied or collateral aspects of self-observation and is thereby "false" to itself and will "always partially elude itself"—how can this claim be made, based as it is on observation? What claim to authority can observation make when observation does not (or does not just) find observables, but creates them, by way of the formal observer/observed distinction. Under these circumstances, is anything that could be called universality still possible?

Although the sciences have come to thematize self-reference only in the twentieth century (Hayles 1984, 15–59), the problem of circularity is the basic problem of the self-grounding of modernity. What Lyotard sees, linguistically, as the demise of the grand narratives and the proliferation of incommensurable language games or genres of discourse, Luhmann describes as the shift from a hierarchically structured, stratified society to a horizontally structured, functionally differentiated one. Whereas formerly one part of society—the "top" part, the aristocracy or the court—assumed the privilege and responsibility of representing the whole, since the eighteenth century this claim has lost its force. In Luhmann's view, as in Lyotard's, the social world has been "flattened," not in the sense that a general egalitarianism has been achieved but in the sense that no single social entity or system enjoys a fixed relationship of hierarchical dominance over all the others, as in premodern, "feudal" societies. That is to say, each system is irreducible. No system can take over the functions of any other system, nor can a system subordinate the functioning of any other system to its own. "We live," Luhmann writes, "in a society which cannot represent its unity within itself because this would contradict the logic of functional differentiation. We live in a society without a top and without a center. The unity of society no longer appears within this society" (Luhmann 1990c, 16). Luhmann would, then, agree with Critical Theory (and, for that matter, all of modern sociology) that we live in an "administered" society, if we can read "administered" to mean functionally differentiated. He is not, however, tempted by "sympathy" or "hope" to look for pockets of redemption, whether figured as outside or inside the system. Since the basic element of society is communication, all modes of communication are social; thus no social system—not the religious system, not the aesthetic system, not even the new social movements—can provide an outside, that is, a nonadministered, non–functionally differentiated perspective from which to critique society. "Even the criticisms of society," Luhmann tirelessly repeats, "must be carried out within society. Even the planning of society must be carried out within society. Even the description of society must be carried out within society. And all this occurs as the criticism of a society which criticizes itself, as the planning of society which plans itself and always reacts to what happens, and as the description of a society which describes itself" (Luhmann 1990c, 17).[6]

This loss of a hierarchical top or perspective from which to write a universal narrative, as found in contemporary philosophy, serves as a springboard for Lyotard's war on totalizing theory. Luhmann nevertheless agrees that the only way to come to terms with the paradox of observing and describing the system from within the system is to pursue the project of universal theory, all the while accepting self-reference as an unavoidable conceptual cornerstone and methodological procedure. For Luhmann, the explicit acknowledgment of self-reference distinguishes theories that can make claims to universality from those that cannot. Universal theories do not claim absolute vision, as if a totality of systems could be seen from somewhere outside that totality, but rather include themselves in the domain they observe. For example, a sociological theory of social systems must acknowledge and examine the social subsystem of sociology in its investigations, just as a physical theory of the universe must acknowledge the physical basis of the system (brain/mind) that derived the physical laws governing the universe. In other words, universal theories subject themselves to their own laws.[7]

The discipline of sociology has had to grapple with the problem of self-reference almost from its inception. It surfaced as the problem of historicism and is usually found under the heading of the sociology of knowledge. Even so, theories of the social construction of knowledge have, in the past, evaded exploring their own social constructedness. Notions of the free-floating intelligentsia, the historical subject, the critique of ideology, communicative action, and even, to a certain extent, the Foucauldian power/resistance distinction have provided an explicit or implicit promise of an unblemished perspective from which to perceive the blemishes of others

(Luhmann 1990d, 68–72). As a social philosopher unabashedly interested in the possibility of a general theory of social systems, Luhmann has been inexorably pushed to consider the recurrent epistemological problem of paradox.[8] Therefore, he is concerned to devise a sufficiently abstract, universal theory that is capable of acknowledging, on a formal level, the constructed —that is, "blemished" or limited—nature of radically constructivist theories. Since self-reference, or self-observation, is what both limits and universalizes theoretical considerations, Luhmann has increasingly focused on the nature of observation in his most recent writings. His discussions can be read both as an elaboration of Spencer Brown's contention that the universe "cuts itself up" in order to observe itself and as a more detailed account of Lyotard's notion that a phrase "presents" a universe, a universe that includes the enunciator of that phrase as a construction of the phrase.

Following Spencer Brown's operational logic, Luhmann defines observation as the ability to mark and label unmarked space, to make left/right, inside/outside, foreground/background, system/environment, self-reference/hetero-reference distinctions and label them in such a way as to construct an observable universe. These distinctions enable observables to materialize, but they cannot be perceived by the observers who use them —except by way of further distinctions that remain invisible in the moment of their operation. They are blind spots, the unseen and temporary "ground" from which a world can be seen. Observers can be aware of the contingency of their activity. They can know that there is something they cannot know, but, as Luhmann is fond of saying, they cannot know *what* they cannot know—again, except by a process of self-enlightenment that has its "source" in another recess of darkness.[9]

With this relatively simple and not unfamiliar model,[10] Luhmann hopes to show that organized complexity can evolve and be observed without an appeal to logically or metaphysically determined hierarchies of perspective. There are "levels" of observation, but these levels are not distinguished qualitatively. Second-order observers can observe the blind spots of other observers by utilizing their own enabling distinctions, with the result that a social network of observers of observers evolves, observing what other observers cannot observe, and having what they cannot observe be observed. But no matter whether we are dealing with first-order, "naive" observation (of "objects") or the observations of observations, the mechanism of observation remains the same (Luhmann 1998, 49). Observation

—the construction of a visible universe—proceeds by way of enabling distinctions and exclusions, that is, by way of what constitutively remains invisible. The "angle" or "perspective" achieved, the particular universe that is thus "presented," is determined by what remains latent.

The problem of observing latencies, Luhmann maintains, has been *the*—at times unrecognized, at times disowned—epistemological problem of the past two hundred years. It has manifested itself as the Marxist critique of ideology, as Freudian psychoanalysis, and as the sociology of knowledge, but in such manifestations latencies have not been seen as the necessary, enabling blind spot for the production of knowledge. Rather, they have traditionally been interpreted in Enlightenment fashion as error, as a deformation of knowledge that can be cleared up, brought to the light of day, and cured (Luhmann 1990d, 90–91). Once one understands the nature of observation, however, one is forced to recognize, formally, the contingent nature of such universal models. The original procedure— Spencer Brown's command "Draw a distinction. . . . Call it the first distinction" (Spencer Brown 1979, 3)—is itself made within a space marked by the unseen and unseeable distinction that allows for the conceptualization of observation to begin with. The phrase that calls forth the observable world is already made within that world. Observation, from its very "beginning," can only be carried on within the field of observation. It can never observe the unmarked space that is constructed as its origin. Once one accepts that the injunction to observe from its very inception is enmeshed in a paradox that unfolds over time but never resolves or becomes transparent to itself, then one is forced to acknowledge that the Enlightenment ideal of observation gives way to more complex, statistical, and "uncertain" models in which the illumination of shadows casts its own shadow and every gain in information, every gain in order, is accompanied by loss and increased disorder.[11]

## The Stakes

All of which causes Luhmann to wonder why Lyotard, who appeals to the same critique of Enlightenment science and of Enlightenment presumption to an Archimedean perspective, is still tempted to think the "unity of the difference" and phrase his version of the inevitability of latency in terms of a "victimology." From Marx to Lyotard, Luhmann writes, "the excluded is determined as a class or in some other way observed as human, mourned, and reclaimed for society. Were society to respond as demanded to this complaint, it would still not become a society that excluded nothing" (Luhmann 1994c, 36). Such a response would always produce further "silences" and further exclusions, for exclusions cannot be thought except by way of exclusion. Any attempt to think the unity produces an excess that cannot be contained in the unity thought. "If one wants to observe unity," Luhmann writes, "difference appears. Whoever pursues goals produces side effects" (Luhmann 1990d, 194). In a word, bearing witness to the differend produces its own differend. In response, Lyotard would bemoan the lack of a sensitivity to the singularity of loss, the lack of feeling for the sublime. "The sublime," Lyotard notes, "does not exist for Luhmann. And if it did exist, it would in any case be destined to become incorporated" (Lyotard and Pries 1989, 338).[12] For Luhmann, paradoxical circularity cannot be avoided by appeals to the outside; what escapes the system can be observed, and therefore communicated, only from within the system, and what can be communicated is, by definition, part of the system. The "sublime," once it is distinguished and designated, becomes an element of the space from which it is observed. For the systematizer, no matter how the system may be conceived, there is no "call," no prescription, no obligation that is not marked by the immanent distinctions that confine us. But Lyotard fears that without such an unmediated reminder coming from the unknown and unmarked space beyond the realm of communication, a morally and politically worthwhile sense of justice is impossible.

So, what distinguishes Lyotard and Luhmann can be best described by what is at stake—to frame it in Lyotard's terms—in their arguments. Given the collapse of the grand narrative of knowledge, originally built on an ontology that claimed to provide a solid ground for physical reality, Luhmann is in search of an epistemologically consistent—and that means unavoidably paradoxical—theory of the evolution and function of social systems. Lyotard, on the other hand, celebrates and mourns the collapse of the grand narrative of emancipation by searching for a nonfoundational foundation for political action. It is this search for a viable politics in a "postpolitical" world that has led him to stray into yet shy away from the minefield of self-referential paradox. These stakes make for a certain incommensurability between their two discourses, but for those observing the contemporary quarrels between the "project of modernity" and the "postmodern condition," perhaps any future Franco-German debate worth having will not be the one between hermeneutics and deconstruction, or the one between rational consensus and anarchical resistance, but the one between an epistemologically correct, self-referential, constitutively incomplete systematicity and a politically committed, negatively theological, fragmented asystematicity—in sum, the one between a contingent universality and an impossible particularity.

# 5

# The Limit of Modernity and the Logic of Exclusion

The unity of a distinction is paradoxical because a distinction is made from within the space that the distinction demarcates. A distinction can only follow, so to speak, what it distinguishes. The paramount distinction of much of Western modernity, for example, the one between rationality and irrationality, is made not by God but by rationality itself. This paradoxical relationship between a distinction and its resultant, yet presupposed, space is what allows distinctions to be so easily deconstructed. Despite the efforts of Kant, who drew limits around reason, Hegel, who historicized it, Marx, who materialized it, and Popper, who made it criticizable, we still can see—as Jacobi, Kierkegaard, Nietzsche, and others saw—that the belief in reason is just as much an irrational leap of faith as the belief in God. We do not, however, therefore give reason up. We use reason where we think reason ought to be used; we argue reasonably, we operate rationally; and the lack of assurance that by so doing we are on holier ground than thou does not bother us. Distinctions are contingent—could be made otherwise—but inevitable—cannot not be made.

Some distinctions seem almost doubly paradoxical, in that their "unfoldings" produce primarily what they are designed to preclude. Take, for instance, the distinction between transcendence and immanence, which Peter Fuchs, following Luhmann, identifies as the religious (at least Christian) code par excellence. Codes, he states, usually demarcate desirable entities from undesirable ones—justice, say, from injustice, or truth from falsehood. In the case of religion, transcendence—as God, heaven, or simply the realm of pure spirit—is the wished-for goal, while immanence, or the carnal world to which our bodies chain us, is what is to be escaped. Yet since we, in body and mind, inhabit the carnal world, the distinction transcendence/ immanence can be made only from within immanence. "The effect," Fuchs writes, "is the negative occupation of the immanent world" (Fuchs 1989, 24). Every attempt to escape the world, or rather, every communication of one's attempts to escape the world by employing the transcendence/imma- nence distinction, leads to the production of more world. Hermits remove themselves to the desert and leave behind literary artifacts that become part of the (worldly) Christian tradition; monks move to monasteries that be- come essential institutional components of the (very worldly) Catholic Church. Thus, the attempt to escape the world serves as "catalyst" for the world's replication and complexification, because the very act of denying the world inescapably produces more of what is denied.

The distinction between inclusion and exclusion operates in a similar way. Indeed, since all distinctions work by way of inclusion and exclusion, preferring the desirable at the expense of the undesirable, the distinction in- clusion/exclusion is quintessentially self-referential. It desires inclusion but can achieve it only by excluding exclusion. At first this seems to be a trivial, even contrived problem. If you have 100 nails on your desk and you wish to "include" all of them in a glass jar, and if after you have done so all you have "excluded" is the "exclusion" of any nails, then you have succeeded in your goal. In the political arena, however, this does not seem to work quite as well. Let us take the traditional liberal problem of tolerance as an example. If we tolerate difference of opinion and "exclude" only intolerance, do we not thereby "exclude" different opinions, at least certain different opinions that legitimate intolerance? How do we deal with intolerance toward gays based on religions conviction? Do we tolerate it? But how can we tolerate something that does not tolerate us? So, do we not tolerate it? But does that not violate our own principle of toleration? There are, of course, all sorts of traditional, political solutions to these problems, usually involving the ap- plication of yet another distinction: public/private. We tolerate the private intolerance of gays, but not the public intolerance of them. Such a solution deftly "unfolds" the paradox of the original problem, making it at least tem- porarily invisible. But it never *permanently* solves the original paradox, es- pecially for those unsatisfied with the public/private sleight of hand. The point to be made is that these provisional solutions, these solutions that switch attention from one set of distinctions to another, are the only solutions we have. There is no solution to the "founding" paradoxes that give us the problems with which we build our world.

"The supreme paradox of all thought," Kierkegaard writes, "is the attempt to discover something that thought cannot think." What should we call this something that we cannot think? "Let us call this unknown something: *the God*," he responds (Kierkegaard 1962, 46, 49). Let *us*, however, be a bit more modest. Let us simply call it: the limit. The limit of what? The limit, among other things, of the differential structure of modernity. The question this chapter poses is whether we can think this limit politically, or only logically. Or whether thinking the limit logically is not itself a political act.

Lyotard's *The Postmodern Condition* is a deeply divided work. On the one hand, it ceremoniously rejects the so-called Enlightenment projects of modernity, the metanarratives, as the famous phrase has it, of emancipation and knowledge. Thus, the condition labeled "postmodern" paradoxically recognizes that no great alternative, no absolute knowledge or historical subject is waiting in the eschatological wings to transform modernity into its utopic other. On the other hand, this recognition does not transform Lyotard into a champion of the modernization process or an apologist for the "system." Like Max Horkheimer and Theodor Adorno, whose analyses of the horrors of immanence echo throughout *The Postmodern Condition*, Lyotard retains a profound distaste for what remains after the great alternative projects have failed. Accordingly, modernity as the "administered society" (Horkheimer and Adorno) or as the "performativity of the system" (Lyotard) can be seen only as a hell on earth that is exacerbated by the absence of any messianic promise of salvation. The solution to this problem—the problem being the need for an outside—is to posit the hope for an immanent (albeit not imminent) self-transformation of modernity. If Horkheimer and Adorno endeavored to move beyond the concept by way of the immanent critique and micro-deconstructions, Lyotard attempts to move beyond the performativity of science by way of its paralogy, or "search for instabilities" (Lyotard 1984, 53). The other of the present, therefore, is said to arrive not from the outside, as revelation or apocalypse, but parasitically from within, as an ethical imperative housed in what the system excludes or marginalizes. This ethical redemption of the system, then, is said to compensate for the collapse of the political projects of the utopic alternative. What remains problematic about this solution, however, is not the notion that a body—a "system"—can carry a "subversive" parasite but the idea that this parasite can be considered a moral agent or can otherwise be ethically steered.

Lyotard's relationship to Luhmann, as fleeting and oblique as it has been, registers Lyotard's ambivalence about the "unsurpassable horizon" of the ever-expanding "interior space of modernity" (Wellmer 1991, vii), as well as about the possibility of an ethic of the excluded other. If, in *The Postmodern Condition*, Lyotard linked Luhmann, via Parsons, to Comte, and made him stand for totality, efficiency, and terror (Lyotard 1984, 12, 61–64), by the late 1980s Lyotard came to see Luhmann more as an ally than an enemy. In response to a meeting with Luhmann in 1988 at a conference in Siegen, Germany, Lyotard wrote:

N.L., hardly loquacious, calculating his words with his Baudelairian elegance (which is much more than a systematic strategy), knows this kind of complexity. He wants to simplify a different kind of complexity. And he can only do it at the cost of a supplement of differentiation. It is this apparent "aporia," assumed with calm and tact, that I like most in his thought, from which I am in a sense so distant. It was possible for us to form a small common front against the waves of ecologist eloquence. A two-sided front. There is no nature, no *Umwelt*, external to the system, he explained. And I added: of course, but there remains an *oikos*, the secret sharer [*hôte*] to which each singularity is hostage. (Lyotard 1993, 81)[1]

Lyotard now stresses a common rejection of an accessible outside. The affirmation of immanence is no longer recorded by Lyotard as an indicator of efficiency, but rather appreciated for its paradox, the "aporia" of a necessary "supplement of differentiation," or, as Luhmann would say, the reentry of the system/environment distinction within the system. However, that the system itself can produce effects that appear only as disturbances, as if they had come from without, is for Lyotard not only a logical imperative but also, as his emotive language suggests ("secret sharer," "hostage"), a last residue or possibility of ethical action. The system produces noise; Lyotard wants to hear that noise as a "call." It is on this issue that a profitable *Auseinandersetzung* (debate) between the two can continue. The point of contention is whether that which presents itself as the other of a system—and ultimately that which presents itself as the other of modernity—is to be thought of as modernity's logical limit or as its moral conscience.

## The Logic of Exclusion

In a succinct if indirect manner, Lyotard expresses the dilemma felt by many who are no longer tempted by the call for a radical transformation of society. "All politics," he writes, "is only (I say 'only' because I have a revolutionary past and hence a certain nostalgia) a program of administrative decision making, of managing the system" (Lyotard 1993, 101). With a touch of self-deprecatory irony, he acknowledges the collapse of a 200-year-old Enlightenment/Marxist tradition of oppositional politics, yet distances himself from what remains in its place in the aftermath. This dual gesture is key to understanding his attempt to think both the inevitability and the possible instability of modernity. In *The Postmodern Condition*, the famous demise of the metanarratives of emancipation and *Bildung* already signals the rejection of this political tradition. Even the opposition between "traditional" and "critical" theory no longer holds, Lyotard realizes, because the Archimedean efforts of critical theory have disintegrated into postulates of "utopia" and "hope." In essence, critical theory, which has variously grounded itself in some historical subject (first the proletariat, then "the Third World or the students"—and one can easily add to Lyotard's list) or in categories such as "man or reason or creativity" (Lyotard 1984, 13), has lost its ability to occupy an outside or oppositional position and has therefore become just one more regulator of the system. In "countries with liberal or advanced liberal management," critical theory has, in so many words, become co-opted, while in communist countries (to the extent that they still exist) it has become the system itself. Thus, "everywhere, the Critique of political economy (the subtitle of Marx's *Capital*) and its correlate, the critique of alienated society, are used in one way or another as aids in programming the system" (Lyotard 1984, 13).

Dismantling the eschatology of emancipation remains a theme throughout Lyotard's writings of the 1980s and early 1990s. In "Rewriting Modernity," Lyotard attacks the hermeneutics of remembering, which has proceeded "as though the point were to identify crimes, sins, calamities engendered by the modern set-up—and in the end to reveal the destiny that an oracle at the beginning of modernity would have prepared and fulfilled in our history" (Lyotard 1991, 27). In "The Wall, the Gulf, and the Sun: A Fable," oppositional criticism and the interest in emancipation, far from opposing the system from the outside, are seen as necessary means by which the system improves its efficiency (Lyotard 1993, 113–14). But perhaps most telling, and most poignant, is his 1989 introduction to a republication of his essays on the Algerian war for independence, essays originally written during his association with the group "Socialism or Barbarism" in the 1950s and 1960s. Here, the demise of the Enlightenment/Marxist political project is delineated with great clarity:

The presumption of the moderns, of Christianity, Enlightenment, Marxism, has always been that another voice is stifled in the discourse of "reality" and that it is a question of putting a true hero (the creature of God, the reasonable citizen, or the enfranchised proletarian) back in his position as subject, wrongfully usurped by the imposter. What we called "depoliticization" twenty-five years ago was in fact the announcement of the erasure of the great figure of the alternative, and at the same time, that of the great founding legitimacies. This is more or less what I have tried to designate, clumsily, by the term "postmodern." (Lyotard 1993, 169)

Yet, with this acknowledgment of the total collapse of the project of emancipation, Lyotard is faced with a dilemma: If one rejects the traditional/ critical opposition as outdated, and if one rejects the historical narratives of emancipation and knowledge from which this opposition could gain nourishment, where does one turn to escape the deadening embrace of what Lyotard variously calls the system, the monad, and the ethos of development? If one can no longer think the disenfranchised other as the site for oppositional political activity, is the attempt to think the other bereft of all significance? Lyotard is certainly not claiming that the problem of exclusion in the form of political oppression has disappeared, or that exclusion is now somehow to be preferred. Rather, he simply observes that the inclusion of the excluded (the proletariat, the Third World, women, etc.) as the subject of history can no longer be proposed as the basis of an emancipatory political program. The challenge then becomes one of thinking exclusion in ways not compromised by utopian projections of the great alternative.

The dynamic logic of exclusion is an inherent feature of Luhmann's systems theory, a feature that has become increasingly highlighted with reference to George Spencer Brown. Spencer Brown's "laws of form" serve as a refinement, a logical shorthand, for the enforced selectivity that is the hallmark of Luhmann's notion of complexity and thus of his notion of system formation. All choice, all observation—as the act of making distinctions, of making "cuts" in the world—is a process of inclusion by way of exclusion. As Luhmann explicitly points out:

The concept of form refers to the postulate that operations, insofar as they are observations, always designate one side of a distinction, actualize it, mark it as the starting point for further operations—and not the other side, which is, as it were, simultaneously carried along empty [*die im Moment gleichsam leer mitgeführt wird*]. . . . The theoretical provocation of the concept . . . rests on the fact that it postulates that something is excluded with every execution of an operation—at first purely as a matter of fact, then, however, as a matter of logical necessity for an observer who has the ability to distinguish. (Luhmann 1970–95, 6: 240)

What is interesting here is the distinction between matters of fact and logical necessity. On the level of operations, exclusions are by-products of an enforced selection, a reduction of complexity, an identity formation. A system—living, social, or other—defines itself against a background, which, as the system's environment, remains inaccessible. We start off, as it were, in a room with two doors. When we walk through one (marked, for instance, "male"), the other door ("female") disappears from view. The door not chosen, however, remains with us (*wird leer mitgeführt*) precisely *as* the door not chosen, as an included exclusion, a potentiality that can be activated, but never as if from ground zero. We can never walk back out the door we chose, only through additional doors, which may now be marked differently, just as we, by now, are marked differently too. One can walk through the "male" door (or, more precisely, be walked through it at birth), and then, if one happens to be of a romantic habit of mind, attempt to think androgyny, but it will always be a male-centered androgyny, an androgyny "seen" from the perspective of one who initially entered the "male" door and who therefore "carries with him" the rejected "female" door as a permanent blind spot.[2]

As an operation, all this remains rather unproblematic. It is the way of the world. Controversy—that is, choice of perspective—arises on the level of observation, indeed, the level from which the above description was made. Exclusion was presented as a logical necessity, not just a factual occurrence. Of necessity, choice precludes other possibilities. By way of the inclusion/exclusion distinction, observation sees that the operation of observation includes what it chooses and excludes what it does not. Seen from this "logical" point of view, exclusion is presented as unavoidable.

Just because one can observe the excluded as excluded does not mean that the excluded can now be painlessly included, for this logical observation also operates by way of exclusion and can see a former exclusion, a "latency," only by way of a new exclusion. Try as we might, we have not developed alternative logics, ones that could promise exclusion-free inclusion. Thus, *remediating* the effects of the process of exclusion can only happen by *replicating* the effects of the process of exclusion.

## The Differend of Logic and Politics

Such a depiction of logical inescapability, however, raises more than a few hackles and takes on a different shading when a moral or political distinction is substituted for, or superimposed upon, the logical one. From a political perspective, the excluded becomes the other (of the system, of the dominant discourse, etc.). If we stick with the example used above, we can see that in a patriarchal society, the male "self" awards himself the attributes of an assumed universality (i.e., desired traits such as strength, rationality, educability, seriousness), while the female "other" becomes the source of unwanted (or, more rarely, idealized) deviance (with traits such as weakness, irrationality, "natural" immutability, frivolousness). More than a logical necessity, exclusion is thus read as a series of existential consequences of ideological choice. From such a political perspective, to maintain a logical or scientific (*wissenschaftlich*) observation of the logical necessity of exclusion is deemed an evasion or denial of the victimized other, if not, in fact, a further masculinist strategy of domination. Indeed, according to this view, logic itself, by hiding (excluding) the political analysis, becomes ideological. If a whole culture, in the name of humanism, is walked through the door called "Man," and if "Man," not so coincidentally, bears a striking resemblance to "man," then the logical exclusion is no longer merely the way things are but rather the way things have deliberately been made to be and, therefore, the way things ought not to be. Thus, to remain "neutral" about the excluded other is tantamount to a moral affirmation of what is included, the privileged self; and this affirmation, it is felt, must be met with critique in the name of the excluded.

With impeccable severity, Luhmann opposes the political reading of exclusion, referring to it, as noted in the previous chapter, as a "victimology." Within this "victimological" tradition, the excluded (*das Ausgesch-*

*lossene*) is personified as a class, or as some other form of human collectivity, and mourned. To repeat: "Were society to respond as demanded to this complaint, it would still not become a society that excluded nothing. It would communicate out of other considerations, with other distinctions, and perhaps resolve the paradoxes of its communication differently, shift sorrow and pain and, by doing so, create a different silence" (Luhmann 1994c, 36). The pathos of personification is simply no match for the inexorable grinding of the logic of exclusion. Inclusion, even the inclusion of the oppressed other, is predicated on exclusion. Such an observation need not be construed as irrevocably hostile to particular political activity. Oppressed minorities and exclusionary ideologies undeniably exist, as well as laws and legal systems that are inherently and systemically prejudicial with regard to the rights of select groups. And political activity that attempts to rectify perceived injustices and inadequacies is part of our daily lives. But all this does not erase the logical fact, Luhmann argues, that a politics claiming to give voice to the excluded other for the sake of egalitarian inclusivity is a constitutive impossibility.

Therefore, if we attempt to think both the logic and the politics of exclusion, we find ourselves in the presence of what Lyotard calls a differend. "A case of differend between two parties takes place," he explains, "when the 'regulation' of the conflict that opposes them is done in the idiom of one of the parties while the wrong suffered by the other is not signified in that idiom" (Lyotard 1988, 9). In our case, however, even identifying the differend seems to be inextricably entwined with the differend we try to describe. If we say that the wrong suffered by women is not signified in the neutrally logical idiom of inclusion/exclusion, we would, of course, already assume the position of the political. And if we say that the differend registers the indeterminate conflict between incommensurable language games, between the logical or descriptive and the political or prescriptive, then the very attempt to *describe* the nature of the conflict would be a descriptive gesture, hence a gesture that participates in the dispute it seeks to explain. Thus, we find ourselves here at an impasse. More precisely, we find ourselves replicating the Kantian antinomy between theoretical (descriptive) and practical (prescriptive) reason; and in the modern world of unresolved antinomies, there is no *Aufhebung*.

Perhaps because of his "revolutionary past," Lyotard feels the need to deal with the necessity of the differend by way of a kind of "anamnesis," a mournful nonforgetting of the mechanism by which forgetting happens, because to forget that forgetting happens is to fall victim to the beautiful illusion of reconciliation, to a type of Hegelian sublation that claims that nothing is left behind, that all is remembered in a transformed, higher stage of knowledge. This rejection of *Aufhebung* brings Lyotard back to the Kantian starting point of the antinomy between theoretical and practical reason, that is, the impossibility of deducing a prescription from a description, which leads to the impossibility of cognitively justifying an ethical "call" or obligation received from an unknown source (Lyotard 1988, 107–27). For Lyotard, as for Kant, an ethical observation is autonomous, not derived from, and therefore not subordinated to, knowledge. Autonomy, however, does not mean isolation; it means perpetual conflict, a battle in which each side—theory and practice—attempts to assert the hegemony of its own observer-position. This continuous struggle, however, must remain a stalemate if we are to be true to the differend. We can represent the situation as follows: We start with an event (or, if we wish to speak with Luhmann, an operation) by generating both a theoretical and a practical observation of the event, and these two observations stand in an incommensurable relationship to each other. We mark this relationship as a first-order differend—$differend_1$—and then proceed to observe this first-order differend from both theoretical and practical observer-positions. These observations of observations likewise stand in an incommensurable relationship to each other, and therefore we can mark this relationship with the term $differend_2$, and say that this second-order differend replicates the structure of its first-order cousin and in no way resolves the dispute.[3] If we have lost faith in logical resolutions by way of neutral third terms, then we see that syntheses of these observations are, in fact, translations of differends into completed litigations, that is, successful adjudications of disputes, achieved by phrasing one idiom in terms of the other. A synthesis would in fact be an ethical domination of the theoretical, or a logical domination of the practical; it would not resolve the original incommensurability but only render it invisible. Syntheses are decisions that mask themselves as the *avoidance* of decisions. They thus compound the "violence" (the exclusion) that all decisions perpetrate under the pretense of excluding violence.

Does this mean that the structure of the differend leads to paralysis? No, for choice is necessary. If the above sketch of the import of the differ-

end has any meaning, then Lyotard's injunction to "bear witness to the differend" (Lyotard 1988, xiii) can be read as an attempt to make the ineluctable violence of enforced selectivity visible.[4] The question to be asked,
then, is the following: Is the imperative to bear witness to the differend a
practical observation of the differend, or a theoretical one? In other words,
is the imperative to acknowledge the necessity and the necessary violence
of choice an ethical or a logical imperative?

We can find evidence for both options in Lyotard. Certainly there is
a strong moral, even religious, flavor to much of his writings, especially
with regard to the Holocaust. Indeed, Lyotard attempts to use the figure of
"the jews" as an abstract marker not only for real Jews—who have, quite
literally and in a variety of quite violent ways, been excluded from European civilization over the centuries—but also for "all those who, wherever
they are, seek to remember and to bear witness to something that is constitutively *forgotten*, not only in each individual mind, but in the very
thought of the West. And it [the expression 'the jews'] refers to all those
who assume this anamnesis and this witnessing as an obligation, a responsibility, or a debt, not only toward thought, but toward justice" (Lyotard
1993, 141).[5] In a more Freudian register, "the jews" stands for the unrepre-
sentable originary shock of the West, its constitutive exclusion, and the "Final Solution was the project of exterminating the (involuntary) witnesses
to this forgotten event and of having done with the unpresentable affect
once and for all, having done with the anguish that it is their task to represent" (Lyotard 1993, 143). Given this evocation, the demand to "witness"
rereads the logical necessity of exclusion as The Fall. Anamnesis serves,
then, as a ritualized nonforgetting of primordial forgetting, of Original Sin.
It is not that lost innocence could be thereby regained—that would be the
eschatological project of emancipation—but that it would be remembered
and mourned with every choice, every exclusion, every reenactment of the
original fall from grace. But can this act of memory escape the forgetting it
mourns? Does it not already also replicate the exclusion that would be the
object of the justice it demands? One could ask whether the figure "the
jews" does not attempt the type of reconciled neutrality Lyotard knows is
not possible. Does not "the jews" evoke real Jews, and thus exclude other
potential markers for the other of the West—"the native americans," say, or
"the africans," or "the homosexuals"?[6] To raise these questions, of course,
implies observations just as morally and politically charged as the observa-

tions they question. That, in fact, would be the logical point of asking them in the first place.[7]

## The Spasm of Limits

There is, however, a way of reading Lyotard that is stripped, or nearly so, of the theological pathos. It relies on a distinction different from the one between the theoretical and the practical, and it brings Lyotard back into closer association with Luhmann. Lyotard is of course famous for his resurrection of a particular kind of Kantian aesthetic, especially for his championing of the notion of the sublime. The distinction of importance in this regard is the one between determinative judgment, which is constitutive of conceptual knowledge, and reflective judgment, constitutive of the nonconceptual aesthetic response to particularity. Even though the sublime can be linked, in both Kant and Lyotard, with ethical thinking, I would like to elucidate the determinative/reflective distinction in terms of function and nonfunction. The attempt here is to think the limit of function (or *Zweckmäßigkeit*) and thus to think the limit of modernity itself.

"The differend cannot be resolved," Lyotard writes. "But it can be felt as such, as differend. This is the sublime feeling" (Lyotard 1994, 234). One hesitates to conceptualize the sublime, because here the sublime—a "feeling"—marks the limit of conceptualization. It does not describe the differend, because as we have seen, any such description already phrases the dispute in one of the contentious idioms, or masks itself with some supposedly neutral third term. Instead, the sublime marks the limit, the incommunicable other of communication, the event that announces nothing, causes nothing. The sublime represents no lost or transcendent *Ding an sich*, but rather presents itself as the realization of the either/or of limits, the distinction that irrevocably cuts the world, making it visible in the very same moment it makes it invisible. Simply and most directly put, the sublime presents the impossibility of thinking the sublation of antinomies. Thus, it would not be overly dramatic to say that Lyotard's notion of the sublime registers the pain of the "severed and mutilated condition" of Spencer Brown's universe, a universe that cuts itself in two to observe itself (Spencer Brown 1979, 105). "Reflection thus touches on the absolute of its conditions," Lyotard observes, "which is none other than the impossibility for it to pursue them 'further': the absolute of presentation, the absolute of speculation, the absolute of morality. . . . The consequence for thought is a kind of spasm. And [Kant's] Analytic of the Sublime is a hint of this spasm. . . . It exposes the 'state' of critical thought when it readies its extreme limit—a spasmodic state" (Lyotard 1994, 56). Lyotard, then, certainly does not appropriate Kant's *Third Critique* for the sake of building a bridge between theoretical and practical reason, nor simply as a way to return to the ethical as something like the gravitational pull of the Law (though this is always present in Lyotard, too). Rather, the sublime provides an emphatic demonstration of the radical impossibility of such a bridge and the constitutive impossibility of any straightforward reclamation of victims for the sake of politics or morality. With the sublime, we have not an observation of the excluded but a "feeling" of, and for, the mechanism of exclusion. What this "feeling" consists in might best be put as the attempt *not* to think either side of the differend, neither to conceptualize nor to mourn it. Thus, the import of the sublime resides in drawing the line, not in overstepping it.

We cannot communicate this "feeling," for then it would cease to be a "feeling." But we do communicate this feeling, conceptualize it, and thereby we retreat from the limit and confront the dilemma of the differend once again. If the sublime marks the cut that both enables observation and guarantees that observation will always be partial, casting shadows along with its light, then we find ourselves returning to the logic of exclusion with which we began. Our reflections on the necessity of exclusion have all taken place within the immanent space of a modernity that is marked by untranscendable differends, that is, exclusions. By definition, there can be no point of indifference from which this space can be thought of as an undifferentiated unity. It is this lack of indifference, this impossibility of indifference, that sets limits to the projects of emancipation envisioned in the name of the excluded other. However, by the very same logic of exclusion that has got us here, must not this immanent space that we call modernity also be a limited space? Must not there be an other to modernity that is contained, as an exclusion, within modernity itself? How are we to think this other of modernity as modernity's limit?

Lyotard offers the following fable. "In the incommensurable vastness of the cosmos," he writes, there are "closed, isolated systems" called galaxies and stars. These systems are marked by entropy, the gradual decrease in "internal differentiation." However, within the vastness of the universe, there are also pockets of negentropy, pockets of unexpected and improbable increases of complexity. "With the advent of the cell, the evidence was given that systems with some differentiation were capable of producing systems with increased differentiation according to a process that was the complete opposite of that of entropy." In time, that recursive and self-referential mode of communication called "language" developed, allowing for "improbable forms of human aggregation . . . according to their ability to discover, capture, and save sources of energy." Finally, the inner differentiation of these social aggregations into "social, economic, political, cognitive, and representational (cultural) fields" led to "systems called liberal democracies," whose task was to control "events in whatever field they might occur. By leaving the programs of control open to debate and by providing free access to the decision-making roles, they maximized the amount of human energy available to the system" (Lyotard 1993, 120–23).

This more recent fable "updates" the one offered in *The Postmodern Condition* and gives evidence of a more sympathetic reading of Luhmann. The "performativity of the system," once decried as "terrorist," turns out to have been the only viable model available, with no "paralogy" left to oppose it, for instabilities and the unexpected maximize a system's energy. Yet the system still has its other. The distinction entropy/negentropy is reentered into the negentropic space, to the effect that within the sea of entropy (the cosmos) we find an island of negentropy (the earth), on which pockets of entropy can be found. Perhaps these pockets can be labeled the "Third World" (Lyotard 1993, 99), or perhaps they can be found in the form of the unconscious (100). But no matter what form it takes, entropy "is an otherness that is not an *Umwelt* at all, but this otherness in the core of the apparatus. We have to imagine an apparatus inhabited by a sort of guest, not a ghost, but an ignored guest who produces some trouble, and people look to the outside in order to find out the external cause of the trouble" (100).[8] So entropy comes to stand for the limit of development, an internally generated "spasm," with no other function than to be the other of function itself.

Surprisingly, Luhmann has also recently found a hidden guest lodged within the heart of modernity. More surprisingly still, he locates this guest in the Third World and in the ghettos or *favelas* of the large cities in industrialized nations like Brazil and the United States. Unlike the new social movements—which, according to Luhmann, have the specific function of pointing out the failings of functional differentiation (Luhmann 1996)—these pockets of exclusion are neither utopic nor dystopic alternatives to functional differentiation, but areas of "negative integration," so to speak, "because the exclusion from one function-system brings with it quasi-automatically the exclusion from others" (Luhmann 1970–95, 6: 259).[9] What emerges from this exponential process of exclusion is a form of "supercoding," a superimposition of the inclusion/exclusion distinction over modernity that contradicts the logic of functional differentiation (6: 260). Exclusion, of course, is no less a feature of functional differentiation than it is of anything else, but since differentiation manages exclusion by way of system reference and not globally, the type of negatively integrated, total exclusion represented by the *favelas* contradicts modernity's own self-understanding, making the "improbability" and "artificiality" of functional differentiation visible (6: 260). Thus, even for Luhmann, the existential reality of exclusion—that is, the excluded observed as *Personen*—is registered and correlated with the logical necessity of distinction. Like all designations of a distinction, functional differentiation must have its opposite term. Luhmann has traditionally displaced the other of functional differentiation in history as segmentation and/or stratification. But now, from within modernity itself, modernity's other emerges as a logical necessity and a limit function of function itself. What modernity cannot "modernize" returns as a violent spasm, indicating that even functional differentiation, the great ethos of development, has its other and its limit. Even it excludes as it includes, and even evolution can make no sense of this process. Modernity's other, it turns out, is neither "pre-" nor "post-."

One is reminded, here, of Carl Schmitt's indictment of liberal universalism. "As long as a state exists," he writes, "there will thus always be in the world more than just one state. A world state which embraces the entire globe and all of humanity cannot exist" (Schmitt 1976, 53). Perhaps the same can be said of the "state" (status) of modernity as well. It too needs its "adversary." But now that the Western eschatological imagination has run its course—for the time being, at any rate—attempts to invest modernity's self-generated other with political or moral authority (as subject of history, as epistemologically privileged "slave" or margin) appear quixotic at best. If we do without these political readings of the limit of modernity, then we reconfigure that limit simply as a logical space. As such, it becomes the latency that houses the excluded as potentiality. Perhaps, when actualized, these potentialities can be felt as disturbances coming as if from the outside, but since we have walked through the door marked "modernity," and since we carry that marking with us, the disturbances that actualized potentialities may cause can be disturbances that are felt only within modernity, within the supplement of differentiation that both creates the space beyond its limit and is created by that space. Modernity cannot be transformed into its other by such spasms; it can only be extended. Given the spread of fundamentalist revivals of antimodern sentiment around the world, it is fittingly ironic to realize that this logical observation of modernity and its limit cannot help but be a political one as well.

# Immanent Systems, Transcendental Temptations, and the Limits of Ethics

The Hegelian-Marxist tradition has a very powerful way of thinking inclusion and exclusion, a way that is, at least metaphorically, based on Hegel's master/slave dialectic. Within this tradition, the figure of the excluded is epistemologically privileged, for the excluded serves as the source of a comprehensive vision of society and of the dialectical self-actualization of humanity. Historically, the place of the excluded other has been occupied by a number of collective subjects: the proletariat, the colonized Third World, and women, among others. In her attempt to adapt this tradition for a feminist project, Nancy Hartsock articulates well what she calls Marx's "metatheoretical" claims. The main points of this metatheory, as Hartsock enumerates them, include the fact that "material life" both "structures" and "sets limits on the understanding of social relations," such that not only will the vision of dominant and oppressed groups "represent an inversion" of one another, but the vision of the ruling class will be "both partial and perverse." The vision of the oppressed, however, when properly (scientifically and politically) educated, will "expose the real relations among human beings as inhuman" and thus serve a "historically liberatory role." Against the "dualism" that she would no doubt see in our ongoing discussion of distinctions and observations, she pits a "duality of levels of reality, of which the deeper level or essence both includes and explains the 'surface' or appearance, and indicates the logic by means of which the appearance inverts and distorts the deeper reality" (Hartsock 1987, 159–60). Though the oppressed group is very much caught in the web of material social relations (included in them by way of exclusion, we might say), its collective vision, when trained, has the potential to transcend the partiality of its involvement and, by being the repressed object of history, eventually becomes its emancipatory subject. In the end, "generalizing the activity of women to the social system as a whole would raise, for the first time in human history, the possibility of a fully human community, a community structured by connection rather than separation and opposition" (175). For the first time, exclusion would be truly, nonparadoxically, excluded.

Hartsock solves the paradox of exclusion by locating an essence ("a fully human community") on the far side of modernity, an essence that, by abolishing distinctions ("separation and opposition"), eliminates all limits as well. Modernity lost, paradise regained. But what sort of paradise is this? A collective subset of the world's population (who indeed may be empirical subjects suffering the most horrid conditions imaginable) is determined to have privileged (if theoretically mediated) access to a vision of the whole (or at least to the means—science and praxis—for obtaining that vision) and is thus endowed with a privileged political position. In fact, these oppressed members of the collective now possess the *only* legitimate political position, for their interests coincide with the interests of the whole, while the interests of those who oppose them are inherently partial and perverted. Politics is therefore "overdetermined," one might say; it acts in a correct manner not just politically but also epistemologically, ontologically, and perhaps most importantly of all, morally. Once the true world is actualized, particularized viewpoints disappear, for without distinctions, all will have the same vision. And with the disappearance of difference comes the disappearance of the necessity of politics. A fully realized humanity need no longer oppose itself. Indeed, any opposition would be a "betrayal" and a fall from grace. Accordingly, politics exists only in the postlapsarian world, for it was never needed "originally," and its ultimate aim is to consume itself fully in its dialectic journey back to the garden.

Currently, however, we still live in the lapsed world, and we have learned to have our doubts about paradise. If what has gone by the names "poststructuralism" and "postmodernism" have taught us anything, it is to beware of the paradoxical and "insidious ruse of power" of any position, to use Judith Butler's words, "that places itself beyond the play of power, and which seeks to establish the metapolitical basis for a negotiation of power

relations," as well as the "insidious cultural imperialism" that "legislates itself under the sign of the universal." It has taught us that any "comprehensive universality" that sets out to eliminate exclusions "could only be
achieved at the cost of producing new and further exclusions." It has also
taught us that we *cannot do without* foundations and universalities, because
"theory posits foundations incessantly" that "function as the unquestioned
and the unquestionable within any theory" and that are "constituted through
exclusions which, taken into account, expose the foundational premise as a
contingent and contestable presumption" (Butler 1995, 39–40). We have
learned that exclusions proliferate far more rapidly than Marx's metatheory
allows, that even *his* metatheory, which aims at recuperating the excluded,
produces new exclusions that, because of their perversions, would seem to
be constitutively denied the right to participate in political activity. We have
learned, in short, that there are other others than the ones we name and el-
evate as the Other, and that there are other *we's* who wish to do the naming.
Butler's aim in "Contingent Foundations" (which, by the way, is a response
to Seyla Benhabib's more modest but still "foundational" Habermasian
feminism) is neither to endorse nor to condemn exclusion, but to acknowledge that exclusion remains an irrefragable part of the field of possible political negotiations, a field she demarcates with the terms "contingency" and
"contestation." If, for Hartsock and the tradition she comes from, politics
cannot begin until it has found sure epistemological and ontological footing, for Butler and the tradition she represents, politics begins and continues with the undermining of that footing. "The term 'universal' would have
to be left permanently open, permanently contested, permanently contingent," Butler writes, because "a social theory committed to democratic contestation within a postcolonial horizon needs to find a way to bring into
question the foundations it is compelled to lay down. It is this movement of
interrogating that ruse of authority that seeks to close itself off from contest
that is, in my view, at the heart of any radical political project" (Butler 1995,
40–41). With this inward turn, politics becomes self-reflexive, questioning
itself as it questions others.

　　Butler's musings seem to me to provide the appropriate image of a
"universal" politics, provided one now uses the term in the way that Luhmann does—a politics, namely, that applies itself to itself and thus includes
itself in its own field of operations. Politics, on this view, is not strictly the
realm that locates empirical others for the purpose of transforming them

into transcendental ones, but also the realm in which these transcendental constructions are deconstructed. It is a field of selves and others who continually exchange roles, for one cannot help but don the dominant mantle in the very moment that one sovereignly names the other for the purposes of emancipation. In this chapter, therefore, we look at how the logic of inclusion and exclusion works its way through various "temptations" to occupy both the transcendent and the "quasi-transcendental" other. It is Luhmann's contention that morality represents the foremost impediment to the continued working of the political, both on the "macro" level (in terms of "the good life") and the "micro" (e.g., "family values" or "empathy"), because it acts as a virus, destroying the codes of the function systems to which it attaches itself. How to isolate this virus becomes the task of ethics, a task very different from the one usually associated with that word on the American scene.

### Anxieties of Immanence

Perhaps modernity—as an obsessive process of self-description—should describe itself yet again as a force field of competing anxieties. We have become distinctly suspicious of transcendental attempts to construct inviolate and panoramic levels of vision labeled God, Reason, or Truth. Yet, because of political or moral commitments, we are equally disinclined to relinquish "critical" perspectives from which we presume not only to see the world as it is but also to utter judgments about its inadequacy. From their midcentury vantage point, Max Horkheimer and Theodor Adorno found themselves uneasily negotiating this terrain. According to them, the "pure immanence of positivism," which they described as the "ultimate product" of Enlightenment, was driven by a fear of the outside. "Nothing at all may remain outside" for the positivist, "because the mere idea of outsideness is the very source of fear" (Horkheimer and Adorno 1972, 16). In the years immediately surrounding the 1969 republication of their *Dialectic of Enlightenment*, Critical Theory waged war against positivism in the name of an outside that was seen as the (at least utopic) other of the all-pervasive administered society, an other that may inhere in the cracks and fissures of immanence, but an other that nevertheless remains outside of the Same. The fear that motivated Adorno and his compatriots was not the fear of the outside they had attributed to positivism but rather a fear of the loss of the outside, a fear that lingers in much of what calls itself postmodern. Yet Enlightenment, once loosed on the world, can apparently never be denied, for in the decades since then, a new "ultimate product" has appeared on the scene—a revised and revitalized systems theory in the life and social sciences, whose immanence and whose evacuation of the outside promises to be even more radical and complete.

According to Luhmann, the traditional question of access to or knowledge of the outside has forced itself upon us again in the twentieth century, paradoxically as the result of empirical research in the various sciences. As examples he cites the inevitable self-referential aspects of quantum physics ("the best-known example"), linguistics ("the fact that research into language has to make use of language"), the sociology of knowledge ("which had demonstrated at least the influence of social factors on all knowledge," including, of necessity, "this statement itself"), and, perhaps most significantly, cognitive science: "Brain research has shown that the brain is not able to maintain any contact with the outer world on the level of its own operations, but—from the perspective *of* information—operates closed in upon itself. This is obviously also true for the brains of those engaged in brain research" (Luhmann 1990a, 64). It would seem, then, that what the disciplines claim to have discovered about the world has made it exceedingly difficult—indeed, has made it impossible—for them to say that they can in fact discover anything about the world. Luhmann concludes: "Knowing is only a self-referential process. Knowledge can know only itself, although it can—as if out of the corner of its eye—determine that this is possible only if there is more than only cognition. Cognition deals with an external world that remains unknown and must, as a result, come to see that it cannot see what it cannot see" (Luhmann 1990a, 65, trans. modified).

That Luhmann emphasizes "brain research" is no accident. He refers here to the work of the biologist Humberto Maturana, who developed the notion of autopoiesis—the self-reproduction of a system's network of elements from that very same network of elements—to describe the essential feature of living systems. According to Maturana's own accounts, the need to define living systems as operationally closed arose from efforts to describe the activities of the nervous system in light of empirical experiments on visual perception, especially the perception of color.[1] The experimental and experiential evidence of frogs, pigeons, and humans led Maturana (first alone, then with his colleague Francisco Varela) to conclude that the nervous system as such cannot distinguish between illusion, hallucination, and perception. Such a distinction can be made only retrospectively, "through the use of a different experience as a meta-experiential authoritative criterion of distinction" (Maturana 1990, 55). In other words, one can affirm an optical illusion only by reference to some other standard (touch, say), which is then constructed as authoritative. Therefore, bucking the orthodoxies of the 1950s and 1960s, which viewed perception in terms of representations of the outside world or as informational "inputs" into a system open to its environment, Maturana defined the nervous system as operationally closed, autonomous, and self-referential: "All that is accessible to the nervous system at any point are states of relative activity holding between nerve cells, and all that to which any given state of relative activity can give rise are further states of relative activity in other nerve cells by *forming* those states of relative activity to which they respond." Thus, "the relations with which the nervous system interacts are relations given by the physical interactions of the organism," and what the nervous system can be said to "represent" are "the relations given at the sensory surfaces by the interaction of the organism, and not an independent medium, least of all a description of an environment" (Maturana and Varela 1980, 22, 23).

As a result, all "communication" between system and environment is blocked. On the one hand, the environment can have no direct causal relationship with a system. All changes in a system are internally determined; the environment merely serves as a "triggering" device, a "perturbation" that is the catalyst for internal activity, but not the determining factor of how that activity takes shape. In like manner, a living system has no access to its environment. What it presents to itself as the outside world are representations of its own internal states. Though Maturana's model of living systems shares much with early cybernetics and systems theory (especially the notion of circular or recursive organization), it differs radically in this claim to operational closure. There simply are no informational exchanges, no informational input-output relations between autopoietic living systems and their environments.

Luhmann has appropriated and generalized Maturana's concepts of autopoiesis and operational closure in his effort to formulate a general theory of modern society as the functional differentiation of autonomous social systems.[2] There is, according to Luhmann, no causal relationship between environment and autopoietic social system, just as there is none between environment and living system. Social systems receive no informational inputs, no directives, no instructions, and no programs from their environments. They can be "perturbed"; they can react to these "perturbations"; but these "perturbations" do *not* enter the system as "units of information" that can dictate the way a system organizes its own reactions. Therefore, systems have no direct access to their environments, cannot "refer" to their environments, and can make no representation of what is external to them. The problem systems are faced with, then, is not one of adaptation and adequacy but rather one of how the tautology of self-reference can be interrupted and unfolded in a productive manner. Systems are faced with the interesting and circular problem of generating "meaningful" external references where none exist.

Luhmann considers this "loss" of reference, or "loss" of the outside, to be a defining feature of the modernity we find ourselves in, and as such it makes no sense to condemn it. The task of social theory, he maintains, is not to wish for an alternative universe but to account for the social aspects of the one we inhabit. In Adorno's nightmare vision, on the other hand, this seemingly complacent and aggressively *descriptive* articulation of modernity as the proliferation of operationally closed and functionally differentiated social systems can be seen only as the crushing victory of administered society from which there is no escape, not even an aesthetically pleasing, utopic peephole through the cell walls. Of course, framed in this way, the issue moves beyond considerations of epistemology. When access to the outside is "lost," it is generally mourned, and mourning attempts to invest this lost outside, this all-but-present absence, with a moral force that wants to make us "feel" environmental perturbations in the same way we once "heard" the voice of God, the traditional source of moral and political authority. If, however, moral codes (commandments), Holy Scripture, papal and royal edicts, and the voice of the prophets and visionaries no longer deliver direct evidence of the transcendent realm, but rather become historicized and seen as socially constructed artifacts, the task of reclaiming authority must be negotiated within the domain of an immanence that has been loosed from its transcendent anchorage. The world is as it is, but could be otherwise. How that "otherwise" is to be thought becomes the "quasi-transcendental" task of an immanence trying to think itself.

## The World Is As It Is

"Ethics is transcendental." This, at any rate, according to Wittgenstein.[3] His is the most straightforward articulation of the absolute inarticulateness of ethics. In the *Tractatus*, the world is a closed system. It is as it is. Because "all propositions are of equal value" (Wittgenstein 1961, 6.4), the world, in itself, has neither sense nor value. To put it another way, because everything in the world is contingent, nothing in the world can express lack of contingency. Whatever guarantees the noncontingency of the world, as opposed to the contingency of the "facts" within the world, must be outside the world, or else it, too, would be contingent and incapable of guaranteeing noncontingency. Absolute value is absolutely different and distant from the world. What can be articulated in the world can make no sense of what eludes the world, but what eludes the world makes for the possibility of sense. There can be no communication between the mundane system of sense making and its extramundane, "senseless" environment. For these reasons, then, there can be no ethical propositions. Ethics cannot be articulated, cannot deal with the world, and cannot leave describable evidence of itself in the world; it serves as the unspeakable limit or condition of the world. "Ethics is transcendental."

In "A Lecture on Ethics," Wittgenstein expresses the relationship of contingency to determinateness in terms of relative versus absolute value. A judgment of relative value is not really a judgment of value at all, but a mere statement of fact (i.e., a "good runner" is simply a person who "runs a certain number of miles in a certain number of minutes"), and "no statement of fact can ever be, or imply, a judgment of absolute value" (Wittgenstein 1965, 5–6). Wittgenstein explains: Suppose it were possible to include a description of the entire world—"all the movements of all the bodies in the world dead or alive" and "all the states of mind of all human beings that ever lived"—in a "world-book." Such a book might contain all the facts of the world, but it would contain no ethical propositions. Remember the *Tractatus*: "All propositions are of equal value." That means that even the description of a "murder with all its details physical and psychological" would be on "exactly the same level as any other event, for instance the falling of a stone" (Wittgenstein 1965, 6). "The world is as it is" means that the world is this way, not that way. It also means that at any given instant, the world *could* be *that* way, and not this way. Within the world, within the book that is the description of the world, preference for these statements of facts over those statements of facts can be expressed only with statements that themselves are chosen from a set of equal possibilities. There is no absolute preference, no necessity for choosing this set over that, and because necessity is the mother of ethics, there is no ethics uttered in the world-book.

Could there, however, be a book on ethics separate from and other than the hypothetical world-book? Wittgenstein answers: "I can only describe my feeling by the metaphor, that, if a man could write a book on Ethics which really was a book on Ethics, this book would, with an explosion, destroy all the other books in the world" (Wittgenstein 1965, 7). A book on ethics could not be just one of many books in the world that could have been written otherwise. It could not sit on a shelf of books that, in fact, *have* been written otherwise. Neither could such a book sit on a shelf by itself as something unique, as a one-of-a-kind event. It would have to sit outside of the world of books that sit on shelves, outside of the world represented by the representations found on the pages of the books in the world, all of which could have been written otherwise. Therefore, a book on ethics would have to obliterate the books of the contingent world, including the book in which a book on ethics could be described. It would have to exist outside of the world that desired a book on ethics for it to be a book on ethics and not a book that desired a book on ethics. A book on ethics would have to be a book outside of the world of language, because there is no language in which a book that could not be written otherwise could be written.

But of course no book, in any meaningful sense of the word, could be written outside of the world of language. The paradoxical twistings and turnings of such statements are meant not to posit propositional truths but rather to reveal the basic experience one has when confronted with the impossible task of ethics. At best, one can attempt to describe this experience. "I believe the best way of describing it is to say that when I have it I *wonder at the existence of the world*" (Wittgenstein 1965, 8). I do not wonder that the world is as it is, for that would ensnare me in the web of contingency. Rather, I ask the quintessential metaphysical question: Why is there something rather than nothing? I could also be "tempted to say that the right expression in language for the miracle of the existence of the world, though it is not any proposition *in* language, is the existence of language itself." I have thereby shifted the "expression of the miraculous from an expression *by means of* language to the expression *by the* existence of language" (Wittgenstein 1965, 11). But of course, in so expressing it, I have recaptured the miraculous in language, and in language, the miraculous ceases to be miraculous. The entire project is fraught with paradox. If ethics can exist only in the transcendental realm of necessity, then ethics can never be glimpsed from within the immanent world of contingency. To marvel at the existence of the world or at the existence of language is to imply the possibility of the nonexistence of the world or of language. To wonder at the existence of the world is to place the "fact" of the existence of the world alongside all the other contingent "facts" of the world. To wonder at the existence of the world is to attempt to place oneself outside of the world, but this attempt can occur only as a conceptualization within the world and therefore becomes part of it. And even if the expression of the impossibility of ethics is said to point beyond the realm of possibility to the realm of necessity, both the expression itself and the sense that it shows something beyond itself are simply two of the many facts of the inescapable world.

Attempting to imagine ethics as absolute value is as noble and as futile as attempting to escape language by means of language. It cannot be done, but one can show that it cannot be done, and the pattern of its impossibility is said to give a glimpse of a world outside of language. Expressions of absolute values, absolute good, and the ultimate meaning of life are nonsense, but, for Wittgenstein, the *function of* nonsense is to point away from the relative world in which sense is made.

I see now that these nonsensical expressions were not nonsensical because I had not yet found the correct expressions, but that their nonsensicality was their very essence. For all I wanted to do with them was just *to go beyond* the world and that is to say beyond significant language. My whole tendency and I believe the tendency of all men who ever tried to write or talk Ethics or Religion was to run against the boundaries of language. (Wittgenstein 1965, 11–12)

Yet, no matter how successfully nonsensical language may show the possibility of a realm beyond sense, it can never cross over into that realm. Even nonsense in language is forever doomed to make sense of itself. Therefore, the attempt to escape the boundaries of our language, which are the boundaries of our world, is—ironically—"perfectly, absolutely hopeless" (Wittgenstein 1965, 12).

Does this mean, then, that ethics is its own impossibility? The transcendental realm of ethics is defined by terms like "perfect" and "absolute," terms that have no meaning in the contingent world of "relative" values; therefore, the transcendental project of ethics is marked by a "perfect" and "absolute" hopelessness. If it is to remain true to its own transcendence, ethics, it seems, must maintain the necessity of its own impossibility. In fact, ethics is identified *as* the necessity of its own impossibility. The figure traced is quite paradoxical. Wittgenstein starts with a basic distinction— call it immanence/transcendence, inside/outside, relative/absolute, contingency/necessity, or sense/nonsense—and attempts to think the possibility of crossing over from the left side of this distinction to the right. The world of language in which this attempt is made is radically immanent. It is a world in which sense is made, in which every proposition implies its own negation, that is, the possibility of its own nonexistence. The attempt to think ethics (defined as absolute value) is an attempt, made from within the contingent world of sense-making, to transcend the contingent world of sense-making. The inside stretches to become its own outside in order to see itself and know itself as absolute necessity. But the task is "hopeless," necessarily doomed to failure. The act of making sense is the act of making distinctions. The attempt to overcome the making of distinctions by making a distinction between making distinctions and not making distinctions is quite obviously impossible. In fact, it has the unintended consequence of expanding the boundaries and increasing the territory of the world of distinctions. For every inside that succeeds in seeing itself from its own outside, there is a further outside that can be discerned, distinguished, and designated. The inside turned outside is recaptured as an inside.

The immanence/transcendence distinction, coupled with the impossibility of escaping the domain from which this distinction is made, results in a vast and oppressive immanence, the inescapability of which is guaranteed by the attributes given to that side of the distinction that cannot be reached. The world thus becomes absolutely contingent. It cannot be otherwise than the fact that the world can be otherwise. The impossibility of necessity is necessarily the case. Transcendence guarantees the conditions for the possibility of immanence by removing itself from the field of observation, for if observed, it would disappear into the vast immanence it calls forth. And so immanence becomes the closed system of the world whose contingency is not contingent. We are left with a systemic solipsism. The outside is acknowledged as the absolute condition for the existence of the inside, but it remains supremely unknowable. It is the silence that delimits the world. Wittgenstein writes of the *Tractatus*:

My work consists of two parts: the one presented here plus all that I have not written. And it is precisely this second part that is the important one. My book draws limits to the sphere of the ethical from the inside as it were, and I am convinced that this is the ONLY *rigorous* way of drawing those limits. In short, I believe that where *many* others today are just *gassing*, I have managed in my book to put everything firmly into place by being silent about it. (Letter to Ludwig von Ficker, quoted in McGuinness 1988, 288)

This, then, is the final paradox. Because the search for ethics is the quixotic attempt to run up against the limits of language (Waismann 1965, 13) with no hope of occupying the position of the extralinguistic, transcendental observer, there is nothing to be done but resign oneself to the position one does occupy. The supreme power of transcendence, then, is its undoing. One cannot evoke the outside and demand a radical change of the world, because the only change that could satisfy the claims of absolute ethics would be the absolute destruction of the contingency that is the world. The result, in the words of Wittgenstein's friend Paul Engelmann, is "an ethical totalitarianism in all questions, a single-minded and painful preservation of the purity of the uncompromising demands of ethics" (Engelmann 1968, 109). But these demands, Wittgenstein makes clear, can neither be taught (Waismann 1965, 16) nor articulated in such a way as to have "the coercive power of an absolute judge" (Wittgenstein 1965, 7). They are felt as the pressure simultaneously to accept and to distance oneself from the world as it is. To experience "the discrepancy between the world as it is and as it ought to be" (Engelmann 1968, 74) is not a mandate to rail against the world but a mandate to realize "that that discrepancy is not the fault of life as it is, but of myself as I am" (Engelmann 1968, 76). For Wittgenstein, the ethical call is transcendental and absolute, but, ironically, its absoluteness is also its impotence. It does not result in moral precepts or political programs; it merely demands recognition of a simple fact: The world is as it is.

## The Other, and Other Others

The world is as it is. If the givenness and valuelessness of the world lead to acceptance of the world as it is, then, as Wittgenstein recognizes, not only does the discrepancy between "I" and world disappear, but so does the opposition between solipsism and realism (Wittgenstein 1961, 5.64). "The world is as it is" becomes identical with "the world is as I see it." The subject is not a part of the world, nor does it stand opposed to the world, but rather is its horizon, beyond which the world ceases. "The world is my world," as Wittgenstein says (Wittgenstein 1961, 5.641). For most, the simple equation "I = World" is an intolerable tautology, an eternal reproduction of the same and exclusion of the other. The "Not-I," the other as excluded middle, is squeezed out of the system and condemned to the unknowable realm that surrounds the world and allows for the definition of the limits of the world. If, however, ethics is proclaimed to be transcendental, then the domain of the ethical is simultaneously the domain of the other, and the question of the relationship of this ethical outside to the immanent inside becomes a meditation on the relationship of self to other. If the excluded other becomes invested in this way with ethical force, does it then take on messianic qualities and arrive as a thunderclap, as the static and noise come from the outside to disrupt the smooth functioning of the self-reproducing system? If so, how is one to heed this ethical call from the infinitely other? Can the Messiah be perceived as the Messiah, or is thunder just thunder? That is, how can one accommodate disruption and hear noise as something other than noise, without denying the alterity of the other? How can the transcendental call of the other be heard without reproducing the dialectic of inclusion and exclusion that forever pushes the other back outside the system and domesticates transcendent ethics in terms of moral codes or political prescriptions?

One could construe this situation, with Jacques Derrida, as the "original tragedy." "*My world*," he writes, "is the opening in which all experience occurs, including, as the experience par excellence, that which is transcendence toward the Other as such. Nothing can appear outside the appurtenance to 'my world' for an 'I am'" (Derrida 1978, 131). Or, one could pose it as the essential philosophical question: "*Why* is the essential, irreducible, absolutely general and unconditioned form of experience as a venturing forth toward the other still egoity? *Why* is an experience which would not be lived as *my own* (for an ego in general, in the eidetic-transcendental sense of these words) impossible and unthinkable?" (131). But one "cannot answer such a question by essence, for every answer can be made only in language, and language is opened by the question" (131). The condition—the tragedy, if you will—of language is the originary violence that both allows us to distinguish ourselves from others and condemns us never to cross the limits of that distinction. "Space" is the "wound and finitude of birth . . . without which one could not even open language" (112). Language can never be "weaned" from "exteriority and interiority," one could "never come across a language without the rupture of space," because "the meanings which radiate from Inside-Outside, from Light-Night, etc., do not only inhabit the proscribed words; they are embedded, in person or vicariously, at the very heart of conceptuality itself" (113). Therefore, any attempts to overcome language and violence lead only to their replication. "Discourse . . . can only *do itself violence*, can only negate itself in order to affirm itself, make war upon the war which institutes it without ever *being able* to reappropriate this negativity, to the extent that it is discourse" (130). The first word is the first wound in a chain of wounds that never heal. "Violence appears with *articulation*" (147–48).

Nevertheless, precisely because of the inescapability of violence and of language, Derrida resists in Levinas what we have seen in Wittgenstein, the absolute transcendence of the other. As we saw in Wittgenstein's acceptance of the world, far from guaranteeing the otherness of the other, positing absolute transcendence only collapses it into the world of absolute immanence. For Derrida, what *does* guarantee the otherness of the other is its ability to reappear in the world distinct from the world. The inside/outside distinction that arises with language and constitutes the system and its other cannot be obliterated in or by language, but it can be replicated and can reenter the system, the inside, as "trace" of the outside in the form of an ego / alter ego distinction. Because "I" can perceive only "my" world, the other has to be presented in it for me to be exposed to it, and only by perceiving the other, analogically, as an other ego, can "I" perceive it *in* "my" world as something *other* than my world. "If the other were not recognized as a transcendental alter *ego*, it would be entirely in the world and not, as ego, the origin of the world. . . . If the other was not recognized as ego, its entire alterity would collapse" (Derrida 1978, 125).

At this point in Derrida's reading of Husserl, Levinas, and Heidegger a tension occurs that might tempt one to think of redemption. On the one hand, with the original tragedy (or should we say *sin*) of language comes "irreducible violence" (Derrida 1978, 128) and universal "war" (129), which, as we have seen, only reproduces itself, even when it attempts the opposite.

"The very elocution of nonviolent metaphysics is its first disavowal" (148). Yet "this necessity of speaking of the other as other, or to the other as other," is not only "the transcendental origin of an irreducible violence" but also "at the same time nonviolence, since it opens the relation to the other" (128–29). The initial word inevitably institutes violent separation, but that originary alienation is required if a nonviolent relation between ego and other as alter ego is to be possible.

One can catch a glimpse here of a familiar teleology. History may be the "infinite passage through violence" (Derrida 1978, 130), but "between original tragedy and messianic triumph [i.e., within history] there is *philosophy*, in which violence is returned against violence within knowledge, in which original finitude appears, and in which the other is respected within, and by, the same" (131). We need to ask, however: Is this respect that is due the other nonviolent, and if so, how are we to think nonviolence within a history defined as violence? Surely philosophy does not transcend history and language. Within history, the messianic triumph can never occur, not even as philosophy. But is Derrida saying that, even if the Messiah never arrives, even if we are to believe in the impossibility of his arrival, we are to figure the ego and the alter ego as the lion and the lamb in order to hold the image of reconciliation as pledge and hope? Is this pledge capable of being redeemed? As respect? If so, is this respect, then, to be read as a prayer to the unattainable but eternally longed-for Unity that lies beyond the distinction between distinction and unity?

These are temptations that Derrida is normally said to resist. More to the point, these are temptations that Derrida normally observes and condemns in others (alter egos?). But redemption does have its allure, and it is out of this glimmer of a utopian moment in Derrida that Drucilla Cornell attempts to construct a "quasi-transcendental" ethics in her study *The Philosophy of the Limit*:

For my purposes, "morality" designates any attempt to spell out how one *determines* a "right way to behave," behavioral norms which, once determined, can be translated into a system of rules. The ethical relation, a term which I contrast with morality, focuses instead on the kind of person one must become in order to develop a nonviolative relationship to the Other. The concern of the ethical relation, in other words, is a way of being in the world that spans divergent value systems and allows us to criticize the repressive aspects of competing moral systems. (Cornell 1992, 13)

Here it is clear that Cornell wants to establish a hierarchical relationship between ethics and morality. Morality, which is to be subordinated to ethics, is equated with the enunciation of behavioral norms and the generation of a system of rules. The ethical relation, on the other hand, does not manifest itself as discourse. Rather, it is embodied by a carefully semi-specified way of being that allows it to sit in judgment on moral systems. Over against morality—which, as the enunciation of rules and norms, inextricably forms part of any system—the ethical relation would seem to occupy a transcendental position, the simple "outside" of any articulated moral code. However, the rudimentary specification of this ethical relation as "nonviolative," contrasting with the specification of morality as "repressive," reveals that what surveys "divergent value systems"—ethics—is itself rooted in a value system. The ethical relation dictates that we have a "nonviolative" relationship to the other, and the way of being that results from this relationship specifies that we are to criticize "repressive" aspects of the moral systems we observe. Both adjectives suggest a moral code: "Thou shalt not violate or repress the Other." The "outside" of morality now finds itself "inside" a specific, if only partially specified, moral system. This passage, then, traces the figure of a dual transcendence. The ethical relation "bootstraps" its way out of its underlying code to serve as the quasi-transcendental perspective from which moral systems can be judged. The ethical relation cannot, however, judge the code with which it is implicitly linked—that is, it cannot criticize nonviolence—without ceasing to exist as the quasi-transcendental self-reflection of morality. The ethical relation, then, displays itself as both the master and slave of morality.

One is tempted to ask why the relation to the other has to be nonviolative. Why does nonviolence (a term Cornell uses interchangeably with "nonviolative") serve as the unquestioned ground for an ethics, which, in turn, is to serve as the ground for political (or, at least, juridical) action? The answer lies in Cornell's fear for the fate of the other in the inexorable and impersonal grindings of legal machinery. As a legal theorist, she is concerned to establish a distinction between justice and existing law, since in her view, social criticism hinges on the deconstructibility of extant law, and the deconstructibility of law depends on the undeconstructibility of justice. Cornell argues that for the legal positivism of a Stanley Fish, no such distinction, no "true *difference* from the system," exists. "Because for Fish there is no divide between justice and law, the deconstruction of law is not possible," making, therefore, "social criticism and radical transformation" also impossible (Cornell 1992, 145). The tautology that results from the equation "justice = law" needs, according to Cornell, to be disrupted so that justice may be dislodged from its all-too-close proximity to the law. But precisely because absolute transcendence, absolute distance between the system and its outside, collapses into effective immanence (as we saw happen with Wittgenstein), Cornell's transcendental other must have a way of entering into the system while still retaining its status as outsider.

The dilemma Wittgenstein faced was the impossibility of occupying the transcendent position dictated by ethics while still remaining in the world that is to be judged by this position. That is to say, he was confronted with the logical paradox of attempting to be simultaneously outside and inside the system, a paradox he could resolve only by embracing immanence in the name of transcendence. Cornell feels that for a transcendental perspective to be ethically and politically effective, it cannot simply remain as a Godlike position supremely distant from and outside of the system. The solution to the paradox can be neither apocalypse nor resignation. She therefore reproduces the system/environment (inside/outside) distinction *within* the system itself (the very definition of "transcendental") and anthropomorphizes it as an ego/other relationship, in which it can be said that the *absence* of the other within the system occupies a form of transcendence. For a system to define itself, it must distinguish itself from what it is not. What is thereby excluded from the system is defined as the system's other. But, says Cornell, this act of self-definition by way of exclusion involves a "responsibility to memory." The "system, through the critical observer, is called to remember its own exclusions" (Cornell 1992, 149). The "trace" of the other is the history of the other's exclusion. The act of remembrance— or mourning, if you will—becomes, then, the quasi-transcendental position that is accessible and capable of being occupied within the system, and from which the system can be seen as the other of its other.

The argument is compelling when anthropomorphized as ego/alter in this way. The other as transcendental perspective lingers like a bad conscience in the shadows of the world from which it has been banned. Thus victimized by the machinery of exclusion, it is thought of no longer as the silence that surrounds the world but as the *silenced* one *in* the world. And as the silenced, oppressed, and marginalized, not only can the other serve as the extramundane critique of the world as it is, but, by way of empathy and

affiliation, the quasi-transcendental position of the other can be imaginatively occupied by those *not* excluded from the system, allowing the system
to critique itself in the name of justice. In this way, the aporia of a Wittgensteinian (or Levinasian), transcendent notion of ethics is overcome.

But the question remains, who or what is the other? More to the
point, if the other is defined as the silenced and the excluded, who or what
*names* the other if not the very system that silences and excludes? Cornell is
of course aware of the inherently paradoxical nature of attempting to name
the other, or attempting to hear the other name itself, and she realizes that
Derrida, whom she takes as her guide in this matter, "leaves us with the
paradox that the Saying can never be said"; yet she still believes that her attempt to "nam[e] the ethical force of the philosophy of the limit" remains
"true to the paradox" (Cornell 1992, 89, 90). But can it remain true to the
paradox? If violence is original sin, if the world of selves and others, systems
and environments, arises out of the violence of distinguishing and naming,
then the attempt to base an ethics on a nonviolent relationship of self and
other represents a desire for the healing of the wounds of existence—in
short, for redemption. Now, Cornell realizes that redemption does not remain true to the paradox; it obliterates it. It can be present only as the
promise of an indefinitely postponed (first or second) coming, for if the
Messiah, wearing the robes of justice, were actually to arrive, the world of
desire would be destroyed. Justice can only be Justice Deferred. There can
be no paradise on earth, because paradise annihilates the earth that desires
paradise as surely as a book on ethics would annihilate all the books that desired ethics. And yet—Cornell's desire to name the ethical force is founded
on the desire for what she calls a "radical transformation" of the system
(142, 145). What needs to be questioned, then, is whether this desire for
radical transformation is simply the wish to give direction to necessary
change, or whether it does not harbor a certain longing for that final un-
changing change, that prescription against change, that comes with any
and all Messiahs.

The problems with Cornell's raising of the other to quasi-transcendental heights become apparent in her discussion of *Roe v. Wade*. Here, the
position of the other is said to be occupied by woman, and the "critical observer" is called upon "to remember the history in which women did not
have the right to an abortion" (Cornell 1992, 149). Justice Blackmun (as author of *Roe v. Wade*) is praised for "imaginatively recollect[ing] a legal norm

from within our heritage that would allow us to make crucial distinctions about the status of the fetus for the purposes of law," and Justice Rehnquist (*Webster v. Reproductive Health Services*) is chastised for "substitut[ing] his own standards in lieu of those which already existed" (150). In particular, Rehnquist, in his advocacy of the rights of the fetus over the rights of women, is accused by Cornell of deliberately disregarding "the genealogical considerations demanded by integrity. These considerations are demanded by the call of the Other for Justice" (152). As a defense of abortion rights, this seems to be a dangerous tactic. Could it not be claimed by anti-abortion activists that Rehnquist did in fact heed the "call of the Other for Justice," that at least at the time of *Webster v. Reproductive Health Services*, the "Other" *was* the fetus? Once the other is identified as woman and the observer in the quasi-transcendental position is called upon to acknowledge "women's demand for the right to abortion," has not the other—Woman— become the quasi-transcendental subject, if not the plain old transcendental subject of history (since, as empirical subjects, women are quite divided on the issue), and could it not be argued, using Cornell's own reasoning, that the responsibility to memory now urges us to recognize the (literally) excluded fetus as the new other, the new quasi-transcendental position from which the critical observer is to utter judgments? Is there not a dialectic of self and other that prohibits ultimate calls to justice based on the other, as if the other were always the same?

The issue ultimately rests on what we think the nature of change is. Does the call to change a particular system presuppose ultimate and inevitable contingency (i.e., things can always be other, even after they have been changed), or is change, when intensified into radical transformation, conceived of as arriving at a final destination? Is the imperative for change, in other words, another term for contingency, or is it contingency's termination? With regard to abortion, what would a radical transformation be? What resolution to the conflict between those who claim priority for the rights of women and those who claim priority for the rights of the fetus can there be that is not a violent repression of a perceived right? We have here a paradigmatic instance of what Lyotard calls a "differend," and no adjudication of the matter can avoid violence. What purpose does it serve, then, to camouflage this fact with a quasi-transcendental construction of justice? Cornell invokes justice as the absent judge. By being invoked, justice is inhabited, and the voice of the other is incarnated in memory and ventriloquized, but is such a ventriloquy ever the voice of the other, and is the invocation of justice (or Justice) ever anything more than the enunciation of the law? Once a law is enunciated, another other has been prepared for future ventriloquy, and the cycle of violence that is history—no, that is politics—continues. If guaranteeing abortion rights is a necessarily violent, political act, why "dress it up" in ethical discourse? Is not this desire for an ethics that invokes the absolute authority of the outside in its attempt to banish violence really a type of violence that longs for the end of the "unclean" world of disputation and politics? And if so, is this not ultimately a paradoxical position—one is tempted to say, a conservative position—for Cornell to espouse, a position that harbors a traditional fear of the loss of transcendental authority even as it attempts to critique traditional transcendental arguments?

In this attempt to figure the outside as the returning other, we can see a concern with opening an otherwise closed system to the possibility of change. The assumptions that seem to guide Cornell's ethical imperative are that (1) closure precludes change because (2) change must be morally guided. On this view, closed systems naturally tend toward equilibrium, and in order for change to occur, the environment (that is, the other, correctly imagined as environment) must instruct the system, must determine change, not simply act as its occasion. The other—at least as ventriloquized by Cornell—authorizes Blackmun, not Rehnquist, to be its spokesperson. But such an authorization would seem to subject the legal system to moral oversight, a position the system has fought long and hard to escape. The "ethical moment" threatens to become, then, the moment that jeopardizes the autonomous self-reproduction of the system by dissolving the clear distinction between system and environment. The law ceases to be the law when the ethically occupied other lays it down. It becomes a commandment.

## The World Can Be Otherwise, Because It Is As It Is

As is well known, in his "Politics as a Vocation," Max Weber distinguishes between an ethics of responsibility and one of ultimate convictions, adding that political action can never be successfully linked to the latter. "He who seeks the salvation of the soul, of his own and of others," he writes, "should not seek it along the avenue of politics, for the quite different tasks of politics can only be solved by violence" (M. Weber 1946, 126). This disjuncture between the spiritual and the material, the religious and the secular, is a result of the rationalization and functional differentiation of modernity. A "specialization of ethics" follows from the fact that "we are placed into various life-spheres, each of which is governed by different laws" (123). In such a modern world, the dreamed-of universal ethics or moral integration of society (Habermas) seems to be gone forever. Whereas most, including Weber himself, have seen this compartmentalization of morality as a cause for anxiety, Luhmann unabashedly endorses it. For him, it is the only way to preserve what he considers to be the hard-won and improbable victory of systemic autonomy that marks differentiated modernity. Unlike the traditions of early German sociology and Western Marxism, which describe modernity (with varying degrees of nostalgia) in terms of reification, rationalization, and colonization of prerational lifeworlds, Luhmann assesses modern differentiation positively, without indulging in 1950s fantasies about the benefits of modernization in individual function systems. In his view, modern society is a horizontally (not hierarchically) ordered plurality of autonomous social systems, with no one system able to control or dictate to any other system how it is to discharge its function. Through this functional differentiation—that is, the self-division of society into the specialized systems of politics, economics, art, science, law, religion, pedagogy, and so on—modernity develops the "resiliency"[4] to withstand environmental assaults and deal with increased environmental complexity (which it also helps create). Recall that Luhmann, adapting Maturana's notion of autopoietic closure, thinks of social systems as operationally closed with respect to information. A system runs blind, so to speak. It does not receive informational inputs from its environment; rather, environmental "perturbations" simply catalyze the operations of a system's internal organization. The outside "impinges" on a system, but remains unknown, unoccupied, unthought. The only position the system can occupy is the position of the system. Luhmann, therefore, is not interested in investing this outside with moral agency, nor is he concerned with constructions of high culture (Adorno) or lifeworlds (Habermas) that could somehow serve within society as society's other. His concern, on the contrary, is with the continued self-reproduction of modernity's differentiated function systems.

Since Luhmann considers communication—not individuals, not subjects, not humans—to be the basic element of social systems, the notion of systemic closure and functional differentiation can be conveyed by saying that the "language" of one system cannot be adequately translated into the "language" of another system. Much like Wittgenstein's language games or Lyotard's genres, Luhmann's system languages are incommensurable, a fact that guarantees their autonomy (or, as Lyotard would say, a fact that guarantees the lack of a grand, totalizing narrative). A system's communication is channeled and directed (i.e., complexity is reduced and managed) by its unique, binary code.[5] Each system uses environmental perturbations as the "excuse" to generate information by way of its own code, and these codes, as Luhmann puts it, stand in an "orthogonal" relation to one another. Simply put, they do not overlap. Science may process information according to a true/false schema, art according to a beautiful/ugly or interesting/uninteresting one, and economics according to a profitable/unprofitable one, but this does not make what is true automatically both beautiful and profitable or what is profitable both beautiful and true. We are not dealing with homologies.

The insistence on the incommensurability, autonomy, and autopoietic closure of social systems like science, economics, and politics—which should imply not a lack of interaction or interpenetration but rather a means of establishing identities—is of crucial importance for Luhmann's handling of the problem of morality in modern society. In fact, in his various treatments of the topic,[6] Luhmann's political commitments clearly emerge, though, characteristically for him, they emerge in the form of a circle. What presents itself as a description of modernity also takes on the force of a prescription. The description of modernity as differentiated needs to be read both as an empirical fact—"differentiation exists"—and as an imperative—"differentiation ought to (continue to) exist." That differentiation exists and ought to exist translates, then, into a political injunction: "Thou shalt not dedifferentiate!" This perceived imperative dictates Luhmann's concern with ascribing limits to the applicability of the moral code.

This problematic relationship between descriptions and prescriptions is reflected in the way binary distinctions both create and "unfold" paradoxes. In Luhmann's view, morality also operates in society as a communication steered by a binary code—good/bad, articulated in terms of approval or disapproval. But whereas the other codes that Luhmann analyzes (government/opposition, profitable/unprofitable, true/false) are housed, so to speak, in the institutional structures of social systems (the state, the capitalist marketplace, the university and academic publishing industry), and whereas the legal system has taken over the function of determining social norms (along the axis legal/illegal), the moral code has detached itself from its premodern locus in religion and has become a self-replicating, parasitic invader of the various modern, functionally differentiated social systems (Luhmann 1989b, 421, 434–35). Luhmann actually writes of morality as a bacterial infection, and concedes that "like bacteria in bodies, morality can also play a role in function systems." But if morality is not to destroy the system it inhabits, it must orient itself toward "the structural conditions of the respective function systems" and not according to some "metacode" that aims at totalization (431). The danger comes, according to Luhmann, when the moral code—good/bad—attaches itself "isomorphically," one might say, to the prevailing codes of the respective function systems, when it seeks, that is, to impose a binding translation of "true" or "government" or "profitable" into "good" (or "bad"). Such a debilitating moral "infection," or parasitic overlay of the good/bad grid, would paralyze the autonomous functioning of the system, eventually causing it to lose its identity and disappear.

The ever-present temptation to moralize politics is an example of the danger of such an infection. If, as Luhmann contends, the political system in modern parliamentary democracies orients itself toward the distinction government/opposition, then it cannot allow the value "good" to attach itself only to the governing party (or opposition party) and still exist as an autonomous social system. "Neither the government nor the opposition," he writes, "should entangle the model of government/opposition in a moral scheme in the sense that one side (ours) is the only good and respectable one, while the other side acts immorally and reprehensibly. For this would inhibit the very idea of a change from government to opposition as such and the idea that democratic rules work" (Luhmann 1990c, 237–38). Thus, the incongruence of codes formally guarantees the circulation of power and thereby the legitimacy of political decision making in the political system. In a similar manner, the value "good" cannot be allowed to be coterminous with "legal," for otherwise how could one challenge existing law without exposing oneself to moral condemnation, or, what amounts to the same thing, how could one continue the replication of the legal system through legal (not moral) communication? If one does not preserve the "orthogonal" relation between the moral and legal codes, how else—to return to the abortion debate—could one distinguish between the morality and legality of abortion, a distinction Bill Clinton made in his acceptance speech at the 1992 Democratic National Convention when he affirmed his opposition to abortion while still defending the right of a woman to choose. Given the climate that surrounds this debate, such a statement by a politician strikes most as hypocritical, dishonest, and opportunistic—and maybe from the perspective of "sincerity" or "authenticity," whatever those qualities may be, it was. But from the perspective of the political system in which it was uttered, it could also be construed as distinctly "modern" in the sense of a radical—and radically desired—disjuncture between legal and moral codes.

If, as I have claimed, there is a prescriptive element in Luhmann's treatment of morality, and if, as Luhmann claims, the moral bacterium can have positive effects, then the question arises: To what *should* the moral value "good" attach itself, if not exclusively to one side or the other of a given code? It is clear that the value "good," in Luhmann's own description of modernity, should attach itself to the very *distinction* each code embodies, that is, to the *difference* "government/opposition" (or "legal/illegal," etc.), which defines the political system and by which the system communicates and reproduces itself. Preserving the autopoiesis of the system (not its historically contingent structure) by preserving the independent functioning of its code becomes Luhmann's moral imperative, an imperative he expresses with yet another distinction, the one between morality and an ethics that is set up to serve as morality's self-reflective conscience.

This distinction between morality and ethics is historically conditioned. Ethics as the reflection theory of morality becomes necessary when caste-based moral codes of conduct—defined by Luhmann as the unity of morality and manners—along with the stratified ("feudal") societies in which it flourished, give way to increasingly complex, differentiated modernity (Luhmann 1989b, 416). In both its utilitarian (Benthamian) and Kantian varieties, this new emphasis on ethical reflection is registered as the need to establish criteria for choice (413). In other words, ethics becomes formalized, moved from a consideration of the moral "fiber" or substance of an individual to a consideration of action in the face of competing alternatives. The Kantian solution, as is well known, relies on the validity of the transcendental/empirical distinction and therefore, in Luhmann's view, is no longer tenable. Historically speaking, the circle that this distinction interrupted is back in operation because of the demise of the transcendental subject. Any renewed efforts to determine the function of morality by utilizing the morality/ethics distinction must locate ethics—that is, ethically determined choice—inside the system called society. Ethics, then, as a decision-making process, is anchored not in free-floating, morally educated subjectivity but in the need of social systems to protect themselves from the effects of morality (371).

The effects Luhmann fears can be elucidated historically by listing the countless crusades, wars, inquisitions, and persecutions that moral discourse has fueled. In mediating between morality and society, ethics is charged with minimizing the devastation morality can unleash. This attempt to shield society from the consequences of moral communication explains, in part, the limited and formal definition of freedom and democracy with which Luhmann operates. As has been noted, social systems exist and reproduce themselves by virtue of communication. Communication is defined not as the transfer of information from active producer to passive receiver but as the production of information through choice on the part of the recipient. Communication could be said to be the result of continuously constructing the distinction between information and noise. Communication offers itself, then, as connectivity (*Anschlußfähigkeit*), as the opportunity to continue or discontinue communication. Freedom arises in systems as the ability to affirm or reject communication, and democracy is thus defined as the precariously evolved formal structure of differentiation that holds open the possibilities for affirmation and rejection, assent or dissent, in the political system. The resulting democratic principle par excellence is defined as maximization of choice. Modernity, as the functional differentiation of social systems that reproduce themselves through communication, is a highly evolved structure that continuously enforces the necessity for selection, and therefore continuously reproduces freedom in this highly abstract and formal sense.

Now, morality, too, is a form of communication, and therefore morality helps produce the choice between affirmation and rejection as well. But the moral code, Luhmann contends, has the additional function of inhibiting or "suggesting away" (*wegzusuggerieren*) the freedom it produces by coding approval and disapproval of the consequences of communication. Its aim, in short, is to eliminate choice (even as it produces it) by preselecting affirmation and rejection (Luhmann 1989b, 439–40; 1991a, 91). That is, morality, with its code of approval/disapproval, attempts to limit the choice it cannot help but engender. It attempts to impose its means of reducing complexity on the systems it inhabits by attempting to replace a "legitimate," system-specific means of generating and processing information with an "illegitimate," totalizing and parasitic one. This description of morality, of course, is not a self-description of morality but rather comes from the perspective of a social system's general theory of social systems. Its interest is the preservation of the autopoiesis of the system it describes (including, it must be added again, the autopoiesis of modernity as functional differentiation).[7] Ethics, therefore, described from this systemic perspective, is a kind of *immune system* or *on/off switch*, and we are advised that "perhaps the most pressing task of ethics is to warn against morality" (Luhmann 1991a, 90). But, as a version of the traditional intolerance of intolerance, it can do so only as paradox. As a reflection of and on morality, ethics operates with morality's code, only what it subjects to this code is morality itself. Because of morality's limitation of others' freedom, its own freedom must be limited, or, as Luhmann puts it, because of its negative, violent effects, morality undergoes a (violent) civilizing process (Luhmann 1989b, 435, 436). Thus, by way of ethics, morality is called upon to discipline itself for the sake of the system. "No progress without paradox" (Luhmann 1991a, 91).

If we remain within the immanence of systems that Luhmann not only advocates but sees as inescapable, we are left with this paradox. Ethics emerges as the by-product of a system's attempt to preserve its own reproduction from the ravages of moral infection. The only moral preselection said to be ethically permissible is the preselection that guarantees the freedom of selection. Thus ethics, though it can make moral judgments regarding morality, reaches its limit when it attempts to judge itself, and it must resign itself to this inherent limitation. As a reflection theory of morality, not of society, ethics must use (a particular description of ) society as its ground, shielding that ground from internal and external threats. In this way, Luhmann resists transcendental temptations—or at least attempts to. His minimalist liberalism—intent on preserving operations, not contents —and his formal definitions of freedom and democracy leave no room for talk of emancipation as an achieved or even as a utopically desired state. Democracy, according to Luhmann, is not "about emancipation from societally conditioned tutelage, about hunger and need, about political, racist, sexist and religious suppression, about peace and about worldly happiness

of any kind" (Luhmann 1990c, 231); it is simply the prerequisite for the political, economic, and legal observation and discussion of such problems.
Democratic discussion cannot successfully mandate outcomes, nor does it
proceed along the lines of consensus or predictated rules, other than the
"rules" of the various observing systems that are and that will remain at
odds with each other. Democratic discussion simply reproduces the conditions for its own possibility, and the rights we fight for, it would seem, arise,
when they arise, as the by-products of this continuous activity. It is not a
utopic vista that Luhmann paints, but simply an improbable and, he seems
to think, highly fragile condition. And it is *this* condition—not project—
of modernity that he invests with an ethical imperative.

7

# Locating the Political

If we abolish all salvation religions in the field of politics, the "backward-looking" fundamentalist varieties as well as the "forward-looking" secular and dialectical ones, what sort of politics do we have left? It seems that we would be stuck with some sort of liberalism, but a liberalism of a peculiar kind, a contentious and antagonistic pluralism that proposes to overcome the shortcomings of classic liberal foundationalism. One can account for the increased interest in a newer, more radical liberalism in a number of ways. From within the liberal tradition itself, a reclamation of what is valuable is coupled with a critique of the rationalist universalism that continually threatens to make liberalism a fundamentalist dogma of the kind it purports to combat. John Gray's reading of Isaiah Berlin, for example, stresses the latter's "insistence that fundamental human values are many, that they are often in conflict and rarely, if ever, *necessarily* harmonious, and that some at least of these conflicts are among incommensurables—conflicts among values for which there is no single, common standard of measurement or arbitration," neither reason nor tradition (Gray 1996, 6). Added to this internal revaluation of liberal values are streams from "post-Soviet" Marxism, which wishes to retain the primacy of "social conflict" and reject the burden of a redemptive eschatology, and streams from poststructuralism, with its emphasis on the unresolvable paradoxes of political life.[1]

Ironically, Carl Schmitt has also been incorporated into this neo-pluralist project. While more traditional liberals like Stephen Holmes and Charles Larmore dismiss this preeminent critic of liberal modernism (Holmes 1993, 37–60; Larmore 1996, 175–88), and while liberal warriors like John McCormick and William Scheuerman condemn his thought as fascist (McCormick 1997, Scheuerman 1999), Chantal Mouffe finds it helpful "to think, with Schmitt, against Schmitt, and to use his insights in order to strengthen liberal democracy against his critiques" (Mouffe 1993, 2). As Mouffe intimates in the title of a collection of her essays, *The Return of the Political*, her chief grievance echoes Schmitt's own. They both set out to combat liberalism's alleged neutralization of politics, the traditional complaint that, within liberal modernity, questions of politics are shunted off into the spheres of economics or culture and handled as matters requiring specialized or technological expertise. By using Schmitt's famous friend/enemy distinction, refigured as a fundamental "we/they" relationship, she sets out to combat the old primacy of the economic with a new primacy of the political. "As a consequence," she concludes, "the political cannot be restricted to a certain type of institution, or envisioned as constituting a specific sphere or level of society. It must be conceived as a dimension that is inherent to every human society and that determines our very ontological condition" (Mouffe 1993, 3).

As the previous chapters should have made clear, if by "the political" Mouffe means a realm of conflict in which decisions are made and unmade, I welcome the return of the political—which is to say, I endorse the antagonistic pluralism advocated by Mouffe and others—by asking where the political is to be housed. In spite of the wailing and gnashing of teeth by antimodern critics of liberalism such as Leo Strauss and his followers, one of the achievements of liberal modernity has been to translate moral questions into political ones. In reconstructing liberalism as contentious pluralism, then, we must ensure that the political is not thought in so amorphous, "ontological" a manner as to be consumed once again by an ever-opportunistic and predatory moralism. Such a reconflation of the two domains would result not merely in a renewed neutralization of the political but in its very extinction. I argue in this concluding chapter, therefore, that the political can remain the political only if it retains its autonomy, and it can do so only in a society where autonomy of spheres is the rule, not the exception.

### The Friend/Enemy Distinction

In his 1932 review of *The Concept of the Political*, Leo Strauss perceptively locates an ambivalence or tension in Schmitt's essay and attributes it to
the impossible undertaking of an immanent critique of liberalism. Schmitt,
he argues, attempts "the critique of liberalism in a liberal world," which
means that "his critique of liberalism takes place within the horizon of liberalism; his illiberal tendencies are arrested by the as yet undefeated 'systematics of liberal thinking'" (Strauss 1976, 104–5). This seemingly inextricable
complicity with the liberal structure of modernity is perhaps nowhere more
evident than in Schmitt's critique of pluralism, a critique that very much
seems to take place within a field staked out by liberal assumptions. Indeed,
one can read the brief second section of Schmitt's treatise as an uneasy gloss
on Max Weber's differentiation of autonomous value spheres. Recall that
for Weber, modernity is characterized by the conflict among these self-
legitimating, nonhierarchically proliferating, and increasingly rationalized
spheres, such as religion, economics, politics, aesthetics, science, and even
erotic love. Schmitt apparently accepts this order—at least tentatively or
heuristically—when he attempts to articulate the distinction that should be
used to isolate the nature of the political. If we assume, he states, that morality operates by way of the good/evil distinction, aesthetics by beauty/ugli-
ness, and economics by profitability/unprofitability, then we can also identify the political as the capacity to distinguish friend from enemy (Schmitt
1976, 26). In passages that echo Weber's "Science as a Vocation," Schmitt
stresses the incommensurability or nonisomorphic nature of these distinctions, thereby clearly differentiating—emancipating, one might say—the
political from these other domains. "The political enemy," he argues, "need
not be morally evil or aesthetically ugly; he need not appear as an economic
competitor" (26) or as a "debating adversary" (28). We are enjoined, then,
not to interpret this distinction symbolically or psychologically, but rather to
see in friends and enemies the alignments of political groups. "An enemy exists only when, at least potentially, one fighting collectivity of people confronts a similar collectivity. The enemy is solely the public enemy" (28).
Hence, "the enemy in the political sense need not be hated personally," but
neither can one love him as one's neighbor, for one can never lose sight of
the enemy for what he is—"the enemy of one's own people" (29).

One might be tempted to read Schmitt here as endorsing the liberal thesis of the autonomy of value spheres. After all, how else is one to understand the political notion of a public, collective enemy that is differentiated from the realm of moral judgments, especially when this enemy is said to threaten one's own collective existence? Strauss most emphatically says that one cannot make this separation and sets out to "save" Schmitt both from superficial liberal appropriation and from his own imprecision. A notion of the political enemy that is not linked to a substantive notion of the good—which, in turn, is a notion that can be rationally derived from the almost instinctive exercise of moral judgments (Strauss 1988, 10) —becomes, in Strauss's view, a simple, amoral bellicosity. This *procedural* view of the friend/enemy grouping is as neutral as the liberalism it is designed to combat, "as tolerant as the liberals," Strauss notes,

but with the opposite intention. Whereas the liberal respects and tolerates all "honestly held" convictions, so long as these respect the legal order or acknowledge the sanctity of *peace*, whoever affirms the political as such, respects and tolerates all "serious" convictions, in other words, all decisions leading up to the real possibility of *war*. Thus the affirmation of the political as such proves to be liberalism preceded by a minus-sign. (Strauss 1976, 103)

If the peace of classical liberalism is devoid of meaning, so, says Strauss, is Schmitt's invocation of war. Indeed, Strauss's critique of Schmitt finally centers on the latter's neutrally anthropological, "innocent" notion of evil, evil not as moral corruption but as Hobbesian instinct, as vital, irrational, animal power. "In order to launch the radical critique of liberalism that he has in mind," Strauss contends, "Schmitt must first eliminate the conception of human evil as animal evil, and therefore as 'innocent evil,' and find his way back to the conception of human evil as moral depravity" (Strauss 1976, 97). Implicitly claiming to understand Schmitt better than he understood himself (to use a time-honored hermeneutical trope), Strauss claims that Schmitt in fact did operate out of this stronger sense of evil. The latter's critique of liberal, humanitarian, pacifist morality, the masterly critique of "humanity" and the world state found in section 5 (Schmitt 1976, 53–58), is itself, Strauss insists, a *moral* critique (Strauss 1976, 102), directed by the "nausea" one feels when confronted with the lack of seriousness in the world of interest and entertainment (Strauss 1976, 99). Hence, the Straussian Schmitt wishes to return us to the state of nature, a Straussian state of nature that is not, despite Hobbes, a state of war but the state of the correct order of human affairs. In this reading of Schmitt, our escape *to* nature is an escape *from* the illusions and false security of the pluralist status quo (Strauss 1976, 101). In short, the state of nature to which this Straussian version of Schmitt would return us is the opposite of the play of shadows that coarsens our sensibilities in the cave of modern culture.

Clearly, the premodern notion of human nature articulated here is Strauss's, not Schmitt's; it is political philosophy in a classic vein, not the type of quasi-Weberian, political "realism" indicated above. Of course, Schmitt is conventionally identified not as a hardheaded realist but rather as a political theologian, and a strong reading of Schmitt as a particularly *Catholic* political theologian, such as the one offered by Heinrich Meier (Meier 1995; 1998), arrives at the same identification of the moral and the political as Strauss does. If, as Strauss notes, "political philosophy is limited to what is accessible to the unassisted human mind," political theology is based on divine revelation (Strauss 1988, 13). What is revealed is not the law that is to be followed but a choice that is to be made: Believe or be damned. The choice is between God and Satan, between the order that comes with belief and the chaos that comes with anarchy, and no evasion, no neutralization of the necessity to choose is possible. Political theology thus refutes the autonomy of the spheres and conflates morality, theology, and politics. The evil to be denied is primordial; it is the evil given at the beginning of time; it is Original Sin. Consequently, one must distinguish choice based on revelation from the type of existential decisionism with which Schmitt is usually associated (Wolin 1992, 85–86). If theological choice is based on belief in revealed and transcendent truths, existential decisionism is commitment to a position in spite of the inability to ground one's choice. Weber's famous articulation of the polytheistic modern predicament states: "So long as life remains immanent and is interpreted in its own terms, it knows only of an unceasing struggle of these gods with one another. Or speaking directly, the ultimately possible attitudes toward life are irreconcilable, and hence their struggle can never be brought to a final conclusion." What, we may ask, are we to do? Weber answers, "it is necessary to make a decisive choice" (M. Weber 1946, 152). From the point of view of the strict political theologian (as well as from Strauss's standpoint), Weber's universe is the universe of liberal tolerance, in which commitment commands respect and must therefore respect the commitment of others. The struggle of the gods who "ascend from their graves" and "resume their eternal struggle with one another" (M. Weber 1946, 149) becomes, in parliamentarian liberalism, the point-counterpoint of a debating club, devoid of epistemological or moral meaning. And so the strict moralist has to see Weber, with his plural gods, as a heathen living in a world of ultimate and dark disorder. When faced with evil and forced either to turn the other cheek or to resist, Weber can only say:

> And yet it is clear, in mundane perspective, that this is an ethic [i.e., the ethic of the Sermon on the Mount] of undignified conduct; one has to choose between the religious dignity which this ethic confers and the dignity of manly conduct which preaches something quite different; "resist evil—lest you be co-responsible for an overpowering evil." According to our ultimate standpoint, the one is the devil and the other the God, and the individual has to decide which is God for him and which is the devil. And so it goes throughout all the orders of life. (M. Weber 1946, 148)

Which is God, which is the devil—*for him*?! The political theologian cannot treat the question of evil as just one of a variety of questions "throughout all the orders of life." The political theologian cannot say, "*In my opinion*, Satan is the devil." This way, the political theologian will warn, can only lead to the dark disorder of nihilism.

## Two Types of Pluralism

If the Straussian reading and the reading of Schmitt as a strict Catholic political theologian were the only readings possible, one would be hard-pressed to understand his appeal within the ranks of those who are attempting to reconfigure liberal democracy. More to the point, if Good and Evil, God and Satan, were the models on which his friend/enemy distinction is based, it would be hard for us pluralist, polytheistic, "morally depraved" moderns to see it as a useful concept. But Schmitt's positions are more elusive and intricate than either Strauss or Meier want them to be.

Schmitt, of course, is a notorious and inveterate foe of modern, liberal pluralism, a position he definitively stakes out in his *The Crisis of Parliamentary Democracy*. In this work, democracy, as a homogeneously defined equality, achieved by way of exclusion, is pitted against liberalism, the concern with indiscriminate and heterogeneously defined liberty (Schmitt 1985; Mouffe 1993, 105–9, 117–34). In Schmitt's view, equality—understood as the sovereign will of the people, potentially incorporated in such varied ways as a plebiscitary democracy or a dictatorship—and liberty are mutually exclusive. Liberal pluralism, based on the neutralization of politics and the primacy of private rights, hobbles the clear and unambiguous exercise of sovereignty that defines the state. In section 4 of *The Concept of the Political*, concentrating on the writings of Harold Laski and G. D. H. Cole, Schmitt takes the Anglo-Saxon pluralist tradition to task. Based ultimately on Otto von Gierke's association theory (Schmitt 1976, 41–42 n. 17), pluralism believes that "the individual lives in numerous different social entities and associations," from religious institutions to labor unions to sporting clubs and the like (41), and that within this scheme, the political appears as just one association among others. "The state simply transforms itself," he observes, "into an association which competes with other associations; it becomes a society among some other societies which exist within or outside the state" (44). As one might expect, Schmitt focuses on what he takes to be the disastrous consequences of pluralism for the idea of the state. The pluralist account, he claims, cannot determine what the nature of the political is, whether it should, in classically liberal fashion, simply be the servant of the economy, or whether it should serve as an "umbrella association of a conglomeration of associations." In either case, the state would not be able to act decisively out of a clear knowledge of its sovereignty.

Although pluralism as a *theory* of modernity is found to be contemptible, the annihilation of the pluralist structure of modern society does not seem to be the purpose of Schmitt's critique. He explicitly states that he does not mean to "imply that a political entity must necessarily determine every aspect of a person's life or that a centralized system should destroy every other organization or corporation" (Schmitt 1976, 38–39), a concession that George Schwab (intro. to Schmitt 1976) may overemphasize and that Strauss and Meier ignore, but nonetheless, a point worth noting. Schmitt seems willing to tolerate the plurality of associations provided that he can guarantee that the political will be regarded as something *qualitatively*, not just quantitatively, different from the other value spheres. It is the deneutralization of politics, not the dedifferentiation of society, that seems to be his main concern, keeping in mind, of course, that within any differentiated structure, the primacy of the political must be assured. Emphasizing the supposed "political meaning" of Hegel's "often quoted sentence of quantity transforming into quality," Schmitt wants us to realize that "from every domain the point of the political is reached and with it a qualitative new intensity of human groupings" (Schmitt 1976, 62). In cases of dire emergency (*Ernstfall*), when conflicts trigger the ultimate friend/enemy distinction, the political emerges as a qualitatively different set of circumstances and a qualitatively different set of human associations; hence, the political supersedes all other concerns.

One can understand Strauss's frustration with Schmitt's residual liberalism. On the one hand, Schmitt does not see the state as a mere umbrella for a conglomeration of liberally defined associations; on the other hand, he tolerates these associations. It is as though Schmitt were thoroughly infected with the germ of liberal indecisiveness. But the picture becomes clearer once one realizes that Schmitt attacks the liberal theory of domestic or internal pluralism in order to assure another form of pluralism, that of international or interstate rivalry (Schmitt 1976, 45). To the extent that domestic pluralism threatens international pluralism, the former is suspect, which is to say that to the extent that domestic pluralism threatens the unity of the state, the structure of international pluralism loses its basis. Indeed, his entire discussion of pluralism is governed by a dialectic, so to speak, of unity and difference. One can have, in Schmitt's view, a plurality only of unities. Thus, in deciding which form of liberalism one prefers, one must not only decide which plurality one desires but also bear in mind the "atomic" unity on which it is based. Whereas Schmitt opts for external plurality based on internal unity, the liberalism he argues against endorses internal plurality based on a nebulous, yet highly threatening, universal foundation.

"As long as a state exists," Schmitt asserts, "there will thus always be in the world more than just one state. . . . The political world is a pluriverse, not a universe" (Schmitt 1976, 53). To insure *this* form of pluralism, the unity of the individual, particular, and determinate state, defined as a democratic homogeneity based on the primacy of the political, has to be affirmed. In opposition to this view of the particularity of the political stands the liberal, universal concept of humanity. Schmitt charges that despite its purported emphasis on the equilibrant differentiation of associations, the pluralism of a Laski or a Cole is in reality a monism, based on "an all-embracing, monistically global, and by no means pluralist concept, namely Cole's 'society' and Laski's 'humanity'" (44). What apparently frightens Schmitt about the universality of humanity as a concept is the consequent inability to apply the necessary, and necessarily political, friend/enemy distinction without condemning the enemy to total exclusion from the system. "Humanity as such," he stresses, "cannot wage war because it has no enemy, . . . because the enemy does not cease to be a human being." The enemy of "humanity" can only be the inhuman, or the dehumanized; therefore, if a war is waged in the name of humanity, it is still not a war waged "for the sake of humanity, but a war wherein a particular state seeks to usurp a universal concept against its military opponent." Such a concept, then, becomes "an especially useful ideological instrument of imperialist expansion," one with "incalculable effects, such as denying the enemy the quality of being human and declaring him to be an outlaw of humanity; and a war can thereby be driven to the most extreme inhumanity" (54).

Granted, Schmitt is engaged in some special pleading here. His venom, loosed on Versailles and the League of Nations, originates in part in his bitterness over the treatment accorded post–World War I Germany by the victorious Allies; and one also has to note that the regime that utilized the human/inhuman distinction to greatest effect was the regime he aligned himself with after 1933.[2] Nevertheless, the theoretical problem, the quasi-logical problem of sameness and difference, is worth exploring here. Schmitt claims that liberal, domestic pluralism is based on a monism, on a universal, if infinitely divisible, substance called "humanity." One can account for human and social difference, it seems, only by way of an underlying unity. We are all different, but we can respect our differences, because when it comes down to it, we are all the same. If, however, one deviates from this postulated foundational sameness, one is ostracized. By starting this way, with difference, we end with bland, deceptive, and potentially dangerous unity. So, following Schmitt, we reverse the order. Within a democratic, homogenized state, we are domestically the same so that we may be internationally different, and internationally respect our differences, even as we fight about them. For this to be assured, states, regarded as moral persons embodied in the unquestioned authority of the sovereign, must confront each other on a "horizontal" plane governed by equal rights in peace and war. There can be no higher "third term," no international court of law, to adjudicate disputes between nation-states, and, equally important, no dissension or disunity on the micro level, no disloyalty or rebellion that could threaten the authority of the sovereign. In order for sovereign nation-states to contest each other internationally, the sovereignty of the political cannot be contested domestically. Or, to put it another way, only by asserting the political as the third term on the domestic level, as the sphere that overrides the economic or the religious or the aesthetic, can the third term—"humanity," say—be avoided on the international scene.[3]

Schmitt, however, rarely asks about the corresponding danger. If the monism of liberalism leads to inhuman wars of extermination in the name of humanity, then should we not also be worried about the monism of a democratically homogenized state, especially when we begin to ask about the criterion that is to be used to define sameness? Is that criterion language? Tradition? Class? Race? Even if Schmitt does not ask these questions, we should. And this means that if we find aspects of Schmitt's critique of liberalism useful for a reconfiguration of liberalism, we will still need to be particularly careful concerning his claim about the primacy of the political.

## Politics as a Structure of Conflict

If one starts with international heterogeneity, or, more precisely, if one starts with a structure that allows for interstate heterogeneity and rivalry, can one duplicate that structure on a domestic level and at the same time translate the friend/enemy distinction into one that will exclude civil war while retaining the legitimacy of conflict? Can one, in other words, propose domestic antagonism, domestic friend and enemy groupings, and simultaneously limit conflict within acceptable channels? We are looking for a structure that allows for the inclusion of irreducible antagonism and the exclusion of any ultimate resolution of antagonism, though individual conflicts will always find tentative solutions. Thus, we are looking for a structure that deploys the friend/enemy distinction on two levels. On the one hand, the distinction should delimit the political system and preserve it from annexation. The "friend" is the political sphere; the "enemy" all that which seeks to identify the political with the moral or the religious or any other domain. On the other hand, within the political system thus delimited, the friend/enemy distinction should define political oppositions (parties, ideologies, interest groups, etc.). One might say that on the first-mentioned level, the homogeneity of the political, its autonomy, is preserved, while on the second, the heterogeneity of the political, its internal differentiation, is guaranteed.

Of course, in framing the question in these terms, I am evoking, however obliquely, Luhmann's systems-theoretical model of functionally differentiated modernity. According to his quasi-evolutionary scheme, the structural change that occurred no later than the end of the eighteenth century is best described *not* as the emergence of bourgeois capitalist society but rather as the shift from social stratification, in which the unity of society is represented by a unity at the "top" (the court), to a plurality of functionally differentiated social systems, with no one system able to represent the unity of the whole, and certainly with no "lifeworld" serving as a watchtower overseeing and disciplining the individual function systems (Luhmann 1982, 229–54; 1997, 707–76). Each autonomous system directs its activities via communication, which is to say, via binary coding. Science, for example, operates according to the true/false distinction, religion by immanence/transcendence, economics by profitability/unprofitability, and so on for the other differentiated systems and subsystems of society (Luhmann 1989a, 36–105). Within this systems-theoretical model, then, the "political," too, must be conceived of as one social system among many, standing in a "horizontal" or nonhierarchical relationship to the others; the political system operates by a particular refinement (or, if you will, "domestication") of Schmitt's friend/enemy distinction, the distinction between government and opposition.[4] What is important to understand is that this internal differentiation or structural bifurcation and resultant contestation of power is possible only if the political itself is functionally differentiated from the other spheres of society. As Luhmann puts it:

As long as society as a whole was ordered hierarchically according to the principle of stratificatory differentiation, such a bifurcation of the top was inconceivable or had been associated with experiences like schisms and civil wars, i.e. disorder and calamity. Only if society is structured so that, as society, it no longer needs a top but is arranged non-hierarchically into function systems is it possible for politics to operate with a top that is bifurcated. In this, at present, unavoidable situation politics loses the possibility of representation. It cannot presume to be—or even to represent—the whole within the whole. (Luhmann 1990c, 233)

One can read this passage as a direct critique of Schmitt's "premodern" notion of the homogeneity of the state. Indeed, from Luhmann's remarks it follows that sovereignty, Schmitt's crucial category, becomes problematical, in that it no longer resides in a unity—not in the single person (monarch or dictator), nor in the collectivity as a personified whole (general will), nor in the state as moral subject. Rather, sovereignty, defined as the ability to make binding decisions, lies now in an essential bifurcation of power. Perhaps one can talk of the self-differentiation of sovereignty, sovereignty based on difference and the plurality of competing wills, not on the general will. Thus, the modern solution to the political problem destabilizes authority, "and it would be a self-deception to confer it now, as the covert sovereign, on public opinion or even the people. The structural gain lies rather in the instability as such and in the sensibility of the system that is created by it" (Luhmann 1990c, 234). On this view, rather than threatening sovereignty, pluralism becomes its new form.

In a similar fashion, within the realm of politics, the true and the good (not to mention the beautiful) are banned. Here one can observe, perhaps, a certain affinity between Luhmann and Schmitt, an affinity that can be traced back to Weber. However, the political, for Schmitt, is not localizable; it can arise anywhere that difference "qualitatively" transforms itself into conflict. As Strauss gleefully maintains, it is at these moments that politics participates in the great moral antagonisms of an age and the liberal becomes a superfluous nuisance. "The struggle," Strauss writes,

is fought out alone between mortal enemies: the "neutral," who seeks to act as intermediary between them, who seeks some middle way, is pushed aside by both of them with unqualified contempt—with rude insults or under maintenance of the rules of courtesy, according to the character of the individuals in question. The "contempt," the disregard, is to be taken literally: they do not "regard" him; each seeks only a view of the enemy; the "neutral" obscures this view and obstructs the line of fire; he is gestured aside: the enemies never look at him. The polemic against liberalism can therefore have no meaning other than that of a subsidiary or preparatory action. It is undertaken only to clear the field for the decisive battle between the "spirit of technology," the "mass faith of an antireligious, this-worldly activism" and the opposite spirit and faith, which, it seems, does not yet have a name. (Strauss 1976, 103–4)

Luhmann, on the other hand, targets precisely those types of "politicians with Mosaic pretensions" who, by operating with the distinction between "how things are and how they ought to be" or "immanence and transcendence" (Luhmann 1990c, 233), inflate the political into a metaphysical substance. Rather than identifying the messianic impulse with the political, Luhmann, like Weber, finds those "drunk with morality" (237) to be a threat to the autonomy and operation of the political system.

Indeed, this critique of Mosaic pretensions is crucial for an understanding of a possible pluralist politics. Luhmann's view might be represented roughly in the following way. If one lives by a fundamental "is/
ought" distinction, bemoaning the way things are and promulgating a
utopic vision of the way things ought to be (a socialist utopia, say, that
seeks to revolutionize material conditions, or a Straussian neoconservatism
aimed at reestablishing the natural, moral order), then one will be tempted
to coordinate this distinction with the political distinction, condemning
those who oppose one's own "ought" as representing not a politically different position but rather the morally indefensible status quo. In this way,
the political will transform itself into the type of moral Armageddon that a
Strauss longs for, and only one side can win such a final battle. But if one's
vision is less than apocalyptic, a transformation of this type would represent the end of politics.

But what alternative offers itself? "Only chatter," would be the un-
charitable answer. This is, in fact, Schmitt's answer in his critique of parliamentarism, written during the years of the Weimar Republic. In this work
he claims that discussion, as the conflict of opinions and the willingness to
be persuaded, has lost its epistemological ground (if it ever legitimately had
one) and has been replaced in modern mass democracy by the conflict of
special interests (Schmitt 1985, 5–6). With the dissolution of its epistemological foundation, Schmitt goes on to maintain, parliamentarism can only
posit a contingent, pragmatic, social-technical justification for its own continued existence, a justification, Schmitt holds, that will not succeed in preserving the institution (8). History, however, seems to have proven him
wrong, at least so far. Even if no one any longer (except, perhaps, Habermas and his followers) believes in discourse as the epistemological (and ethical) ground of parliamentary democracy, the social-technical efficacy of
such democracy continually proves itself, even as it generates perennial dis-
satisfaction, especially among those who long for the conflation of the true
and the good with the political. Indeed, discussion is the means by which
the political system reproduces itself, not, *pace* Habermas, because consensus is reached but precisely because each political decision produces both
consensus and dissensus simultaneously and thus allows for multiple linkages. The political, it might be said, operates precisely because it finds itself
without a determinate ground. That is, in Kantian terms, the political is the
realm not of determinative judgment but rather of reflective judgment

(Arendt 1982; Mouffe 1993, 14, 130). The political, as the realm of opinion, is distinguished from science and religion or morality. Therefore, if one opposes a political decision, one does not find oneself outside the political system because one opposes what is true or what is good; rather, one finds oneself in the "opposition," as a politically legitimate "enemy" of the governing majority, an "enemy" who manipulates the power of those out of power to influence future decisions.

## The Limits of Pluralism

Luhmann rejects, then, a vision of the good life that could be said to direct our actions toward the promised land of harmony, social solidarity, and emancipation. Or, to put it in terms Luhmann would perhaps favor, his vision of the good life consists in just this rejection of a vision of the good life. Such a position, of course, leaves him open to the charge that he is much too comfortable with the social-technical justification of a differentiated and limited political sphere. Mouffe, for instance, sees in Luhmann the type of technocratic neoconservative who wishes to "transform political problems into administrative and technical ones" and "restrict the field of democratic decisions by turning more and more areas over to the control of supposedly neutral experts" (Mouffe 1993, 48).[5] Opposed to this technocratic "neutralization" of politics, she suggests that we "reestablish the link between ethics and politics" (Mouffe 1993, 112). In calling for this linkage, Mouffe clearly does not want to overturn the modern achievement, the distinction between politics and morality. On the contrary, her critiques of communitarians and Kantian liberals (e.g., Rawls) alike center on their conflation of political philosophy with moral philosophy and their inability to perceive the specificity of the two discourses (112–13). Indeed, recognizing the specificity of the political means, for Mouffe, rehabilitating political philosophy and (in marked distinction to Strauss) strictly differentiating it from moral philosophy. This distinction echoes the public/private split that marks modernity and precludes a politics derived from a "private" vision of the morally good life (113–14). However, an "ethics of the political," a "type of interrogation which is concerned with the normative aspects of politics, the values that can be realized through collective action and through common belonging to a political association" (113), remains an inherent component of Mouffe's political philosophy. Perhaps

her effort to configure an ethics of the political resembles Jean Cohen's reception of Habermasian discourse ethics as a political "ethics of democra-
tization" that would allow for a "plurality of democracies" while excluding
"domination, violence, and systematic inequality" (Cohen 1990, 101, 100).
But whereas Cohen rediscovers civil society—albeit a politicized civil society—as the haven for pluralism,[6] Mouffe, rather surprisingly, turns to the
notion of the state for conceptual clarity.

What is at stake for Mouffe is pluralism, an antagonistic pluralism
not founded on the rationalist fundamentalism of traditional (and, one
might add, Habermasian) liberalism. To achieve such a pluralism, one
must, she contends, limit pluralism itself. "Schmitt is right," she claims, "to
insist on the specificity of the political association, and I believe we must
not be led by the defense of pluralism to argue that our participation in the
state as a political community is on the same level as our other forms of social integration" (Mouffe 1993, 131). On this view, the *specificity* of the political must be thought in terms of the *primacy* of the political, and thus in
terms of the primacy of the state.

Antagonistic principles of legitimacy cannot coexist within the same political association; there cannot be pluralism at that level without the political reality of the
state automatically disappearing. But in a liberal democratic regime, this does not
exclude their being cultural, religious and moral pluralism at another level, as well
as a plurality of different parties. However, this pluralism requires allegiance to the
state as an "ethical state" which crystallizes the institutions and principles proper
to the mode of collective existence that is modern democracy. (Mouffe 1993, 131)

Mouffe is correct in insisting on the limits of pluralism, on the *paradox* of
a pluralism requiring a structure that cannot itself be pluralistically relativized. Pluralism is not self-justifying; hence it requires allegiance. But to
what is allegiance owed if pluralism is to flourish?

Though Mouffe certainly does not call for a Schmittian "total state,"
her stress on the primacy of the political and her seeming identification of
the political with the state do, I believe, succumb to Schmitt's insistence
that pluralism can be based only on some sort of homogeneity. This
Schmittian tendency can perhaps best be seen in Mouffe's reliance on the
traditional state/civil society distinction. Within this distinction, as she
uses it, the state serves a dual purpose: it is both *part* of the distinction,
standing over against civil society as its other, and the overarching and all-
encompassing *unity* of the distinction. Herein lies the danger. If the state,

as the self-description of the political (Luhmann 1990b, 166), is not one as-sociation (one system) among many, then it does not stand in a pluralist relationship to the other social systems. Mouffe wants to remove the state surgically from the body in which it is embedded and insist that the polit-ical, as a "quality" (one is tempted to say: as a metaphysical substance), exists independently of society, or at least preexists the historical phenom-enon of modern social differentiation. As such, the political serves a tran-scendental function. The state, therefore, as "container" of this universal quality or substance, must be simultaneously divisible, as an empirical rep-resentation of the political among the differentiated spheres, and indivisi-ble, as the transcendental unity that sets limits to pluralism. On this view, modernity is still marked by a hierarchical structure in which the political enjoys a preeminent status not enjoyed by, say, morality and religion, which are, it seems, discourses or systems that enjoy only an empirical status and can be easily delimited.

But why should this be the case? Why should the political, but not the divine, or the good, or for that matter the beautiful, "determin[e] our very ontological condition" (Mouffe 1993, 3)? It is easy to see how the po-litical is perverted when religion or morality enjoy preeminent status. In such cases, the political either disappears or threatens to become the servant of the church or of a potentially oppressive moral code. We see increasing pressure along these lines in the rise of conservative religious fundamental-ism in the United States, in the Arab world, in Israel, and elsewhere. But why is not the reverse also true? Why would not the primacy of the politi-cal threaten religious or moral autonomy, just as ascendant religious move-ments threaten the autonomy of the political? The true and the good may be subordinated to the politically efficacious in the political sphere, but how can one entertain a legitimate pluralism if the true and the good do not stand in a symmetrical relationship with the political in society as a whole? If they do, then the state cannot be conceived as the unity of the difference between state and society, but rather must be conceived as the location, in-deed, the self-description of the political within a society seen as differenti-ated, symmetrically ordered social spheres. My point here is merely cau-tionary: Championing the primacy of the political would seem to establish an asymmetry between the moral and the political, one that mirrors the asymmetry originally combated. "The relegation of religion to the private sphere," Mouffe notes, "which we now have to make Muslims accept, was only imposed with great difficulty upon the Christian Church and is still not completely accomplished" (Mouffe 1993, 132). But if the relationship between the state and the civil society—the "private sphere"—is to be thought of as hierarchical, the "relegation" will never be "accomplished," because Muslims and Christians (and Jews and others, for that matter) will continue to fight "relegation" to the "private sphere" if the latter becomes nothing but the code for the hegemony of the state. The antagonism of antagonistic pluralism lies precisely in the symmetry of the structure that precludes ultimate victory. Without symmetry, no conflict, only conquest and colonization.

It would seem, then, that the structure to which advocates of pluralism should show allegiance, if allegiance must be shown, would be the structure of modernity itself, modernity as pluralist differentiation. Rather than conceiving of pluralism as the result of a necessary and sovereign homogeneity, especially the homogeneity of the state as a moral or ethical agent, one would, on this view, think of pluralism as the correlation of internal and external differentiation. If the system of modernity is the plurality of autonomous, incommensurable, and therefore horizontally ordered systems, then the threat to modernity is *de*differentiation, the supervision of society from one central watchtower, or worse, the collapsing of all systems into one overarching totality. Consequently, if one finds differentiation and the pluralism it brings with it worthy of preservation, then one must think the preservation of modernity as the self-preservation of the autonomy of systems, the fierce battle of systems to preserve their own self-reproduction by way of specialized communication and binary coding. In effect, Luhmann suggests that communication about society should give up its habitual recourse to the is/ought distinction and reorient itself according to a distinction that is fundamentally based on the opposition of preservation and extinction. In his eyes, "the critique of functional differentiation reaches the limits of alternativity. A society can imagine a change in its principle of stability, in its pattern of differentiation or of drawing systemic boundaries as nothing but catastrophe" (Luhmann 1990b, 141). Change is not thereby precluded, only stripped of its messianic quality. Change occurs, and can occur, only as a consequence of preservation, as the accommodation of perturbations and the reiteration of the same that can never be the same. Self-preservation, of course, has a nasty ring to it, evoking as it does the Social Darwinism of the late nineteenth century and the performativity of the system so feared by the likes of Horkheimer, Adorno, and Lyotard in the twentieth century. But if the ideal of moral or political control of the social system is to be eschewed—and how can one seriously entertain an antagonistic pluralism if one also wants to reserve the right to regulate or predetermine outcomes—then reproduction of differentiation as the condition of possibility for pluralism becomes the goal. Hence, if Luhmann wields the friend/enemy distinction, he does so on behalf of differentiation, for it is differentiation, not homogeneity, that defines the type of pluralism that would, as Mouffe claims, go beyond the fundamentalism of traditional liberalism.

# Appendix: Two Interviews

The two interviews that follow were conducted in September 1994, while Niklas Luhmann was a Fellow of the Institute for Advanced Study at Indiana University, Bloomington. Both were conducted in English.

"A Theory of a Different Order," which was conducted on September 21, included Katherine Hayles. To prepare for the interview, Hayles had reviewed in advance Luhmann's essay "The Cognitive Program of Constructivism and a Reality That Remains Unknown" (Luhmann 1990a), and Luhmann had reviewed Hayles's "Constrained Constructivism: Locating Scientific Inquiry in the Theater of Representation" (Hayles 1991). The conversation was organized and moderated by Eva Knodt, William Rasch, and Cary Wolfe.

"Answering the Question: What Is Modernity?" was conducted approximately ten days earlier. It was organized and conducted by Eva Knodt and William Rasch.

To avoid breaking the flow of the conversation, no footnotes or parenthetical citations are included in the two interviews. Bibliographic information regarding the texts referred to in the interviews can be found in the Works Cited. For bibliographical information on the "Macy conference transcripts" referred to by Hayles, see Hayles 1999, 300–304. The second interview mentions two essays that are not listed by title in the Works Cited but are included in listed source volumes: Luhmann's "The Future of Democracy," in Luhmann 1990c, 231–39; and Max Weber's "Politics as a

Vocation," in M. Weber 1946. Interested readers who wish to investigate Luhmann's writing on functional and other forms of differentiation, on morality and its relation to politics, and on theory design (the main topics of conversation on this date) should consult Luhmann 1997, 595–865, and the literature cited in the present volume in Chapter 6 note 6, and Chapter 4 note 7.

# Theory of a Different Order: A Conversation with Katherine Hayles and Niklas Luhmann

CARY WOLFE: I'd like to begin with a general question. In your different ways you have both explored a second-order cybernetics approach to the current impasse faced by many varieties of critique. And that impasse, to schematically represent it, seems to be the problem of theorizing the contingency and constructedness of knowledge without falling into the morass of relativism (as the charge is usually made), or, to give it a somewhat more challenging valence, without falling into philosophical idealism. You both have worked on this, and I'm wondering if each of you could explain, in whatever order you'd like, what makes second-order theory distinctive, and how it might help move the current critical debates beyond the sort of realism versus idealism deadlock that I've just described.

KATHERINE HAYLES: Would you care to go first?

NIKLAS LUHMANN: OK. Well, I reduce the general term "second-order" to second-order observing, or describing, what others observe or describe. One of the distinguishing marks of this approach is that we need a theory of observation which is not tied to, say, the concept of intelligence, the mind of human beings, but a more general theory of observation that we can use to describe relations of social systems to each other, or minds to social systems, or minds to minds, or maybe bodies to neurophysiological systems, or whatever. So, it needs to be a general theory of observing—and I take some of these things out of *The Laws of Form* of George Spencer Brown—to think of observing as an operation that makes a distinction and is then bound to use one side of the distinction, and not the other side, to continue its observations. So we have a very formal concept of observation. And the problem is then, if you link different observing systems, what can be a cause of stability, how can—in the language of Heinz von Foerster and others—*eigenvalues*, or stable points or identities, emerge that both sides of a communication can remember? And I think this is the idea which goes beyond the assumption that relativism is simply arbitrary: every observation has to be made by an observing system, by one and not the other, but if systems are in communication, then something emerges which is not arbitrary anymore but depends on its own history, on its own memory.

KH: For me, second-order theory would be distinct from first-order theory because it necessarily involves a component of reflexivity. If you look at first-order cybernetics, it's clear that it has no really powerful way to deal with the idea of reflexivity. In the Macy conference transcripts, reflexivity surfaced most distinctly in terms of psychoanalysis, which was threatening to the physical scientists who participated in the Macy conferences because it seemed to reduce scientific debate to a morass of language. When they would object to Lawrence Kubie's ideas, who was the psychoanalyst there, he would answer with things like "Oh, you're showing a lot of hostility, aren't you?" To them, that was almost a debasement of scientific debate because it kept involving them as people in what the conference was trying to do. As Steve Heims's book makes clear, there were strong voices speaking at that conference in favor of reflexivity—people like Gregory Bateson and Margaret Mead from an anthropological perspective. But because reflexivity was tied up with psychoanalysis and the complexities of human emotion, it seemed to most people at the Macy conferences simply to lead to a dead end. When Maturana and Varela reconceptualize reflexivity in *Autopoiesis and Cognition*, they sanitize reflexivity by isolating the observer in what they call a "domain of description" that remains separate from the autopoietic processes that constitute the system as a system. I think Professor Luhmann's work is an important refinement of Maturana's approach, because he has a way to make the observer appear in a non-ad hoc way; the observer enters at an originary moment, in the fundamental act of making a distinction. Nevertheless, I think that the history I've just been relating is consequential—the point that you can get to is always partly determined by where you've been. The history of second-order cybernetics is a series of successive innovations in which the taint that reflexivity acquired through its connection with psychoanalysis has never completely left the theorizing of the observer as it appears in that tradition. This is quite distinct from how reflexivity appears in, say, the "strong program" of the Edinburgh School of Social Studies of Science, where they acknowledge that the act of observation is grounded in a particular person's positionality.

Reflexivity has been, of course, an ongoing problem in both science and the history of science. When reflexivity enters relativity theory, for example, it has nothing to do with a particular person's personality, cultural history, or language; it has only to do with the observer's physical location in space and time. Relativity theory is not reflexive; it is only relative. To try to arrive at a theory of reflexivity which would take into account the full force of the position of the observer, including personal history, language, a culture, and so forth, has been, I think, a very important and extremely difficult problem to solve. To me, it's essential to talk about the observer in terms that would take account of these positional and locative factors as well as the theoretical question of how it is that we can know the world.

CW: To what extent do you think that, in their recent work, Maturana and Varela have tried to move in this direction? I'm thinking now of the collaboration of Varela, Thompson, and Rosch in *The Embodied Mind*, but more broadly of the whole concept of embodiment in second-order cybernetics, which has certain affinities with Donna Haraway's work on this problem, which is very much in the register that you were emphasizing. I'm thinking, too, of the explicit derivation of an ethics at the end of *The Tree of Knowledge* from second-order cybernetics. To what extent, then, do you see much of this work moving in that direction? And is it moving in the way that you would like?

KH: You know, it's difficult to try to coordinate all these works, because they seem to me all significantly different, maybe because I'm geared to thinking about texts, and therefore about the specific embodiment of these ideas in the language they use. But to compare just for a moment *Autopoiesis and Cognition* with *The Tree of Knowledge*. In the latter the authors write for a popular audience, and in the process the work changes form. It goes from an analytical form into a circular narrative. And with that shift come all kinds of changes in their rhetorical construction of who the observer of that work is, as well as of themselves as observers of the phenomena that they report. In this sense, *The Tree of Knowledge* is more positioned. But it does not solve a problem also present in *Autopoiesis and Cognition*—that is, using scientific knowledge to validate a theory which then calls scientific knowledge into question. Autopoiesis leads to a theory of the observer in which there is no route back from the act of observing to the data that was used to generate the theory in the first place. The problem is exacerbated in *The Tree of Knowledge*. Even as they move from a "domain of description" to a more capacious idea of a linguistic realm in which two observers are able to relate to each other, there arise other problems having to do with the work's narrative form.

WILLIAM RASCH: What is your reaction to this?

NL: Well, there are several reactions. One is that I have difficulties, regarding the later work, comparing Maturana and Varela. Maturana advanced in the direction of a distinction between the immediate observer and the observer who observes another observer. The "objective reality" is that there are things, or niches, which are not reflected in the immediate observer's boundaries. But on the other hand, if you observe that observer, then you see how he or she sees the world by making this distinction. But the limit of this type of thought is the term "autopoiesis" itself as a system term. Autopoiesis was another term for circularity; that was its beginning. Maturana talked about cells in terms of circular reproduction and then, after some contact with philosophers, used "autopoiesis," finding the Greek term more distinctive. But there remains in Maturana the idea that circularity is an objective fact, and so the problem of self-reference is not really confronted in the theory—not in the sense of, for example, the cyberneticians who would say that a system uses its output as input and then becomes a mathematical cosmos with immense amounts of possibilities which cannot be calculated anymore, as in Heinz von Foerster or Spencer Brown's discussion of a "reentry" of the distinction into the distinguished. And there are, within these more mathematical theories, possibilities which are not visible, I think, in the writings of Maturana and Varela. They are too empirically tied to biology. And then of course we have always this discussion of whether one can use biological analogies in sociology or in psychology or not, which doesn't lead anywhere.

WR: I have a question. Professor Luhmann, you said that you wanted to find a definition of observation that is on a very formal basis, that does not only apply to consciousness but to systems of a sort. When you, Professor Hayles, talked about observation, the sense of an individual came out more because you were talking about the person's locality, the observer's situation. Do you have a sense that observation is tied strictly to consciousness? Or is observation also for you a more formal definition that can be applied to systems other than consciousness?

KH: For me, observation is definitely tied to consciousness. In Professor Luhmann's article "The Cognitive Program of Constructivism and a

Reality That Remains Unknown," you have a paragraph where you're talking about the observer, and you list a series of things like a cell, a person, and so forth. On my own copy of that article I put a big question mark in the margin: can a cell observe? Of course, I realize that it's partly a matter of definition, and you're free to define the act of observation however you want. But, for me, a cell could not observe in the way I use the term.

EVA KNODT: Could you maybe clarify...

WR: Let's let Professor Luhmann clarify how a cell can observe.

NL: Well, it makes distinctions. It makes a distinction with input/ output, what it takes in or what it refuses to take in, or a distinction about its own internal reproduction, to do it in a certain way and not in another way. I'm not sure whether making distinctions implies the simultaneity of seeing both sides, or whether it is just discrimination. The immune system discriminates, of course, but does it know against what it is discriminating? And if you require for a concept of observing that you see both sides simultaneously, and the option becomes an option against something, then I would not say that cells are observing or immune systems are observing. They just discriminate. But for me this is not very important. It would be very important for Maxwell's Demon, for example, that he can distinguish —or it, whatever it is—can distinguish what belongs on which side. But it is hardly thinkable for us, because we are always using meaning in constructing reality. So the problem is to think of distinction, of observation, without the idea of seeing out of the eyes, out of the corner of the eyes, the other thing which we reject or give a negative value. So we, psychologically and socially, use the idea of meaning, so that "observing" becomes a distinct characteristic. And there is a question, of course, of whether we should extend it. But this is I think a terminological...

EK: I have a follow-up here, because I also was puzzled in the beginning when I started reading your work about this use of observation, and how it is different from this metaphorical idea that one thinks one sees with the eyes. It's very hard to separate oneself from it. Where exactly do you see the advantage of widening this concept of observation to an extent that it is no longer located in consciousness?

NL: For me, the advantage is to make possible a kind of interdisciplinary commerce, a kind of transference of what we know in cybernetics or biology into sociology or into psychology. Saying that there are very general patterns which can just be described as making a distinction and crossing the boundary of the distinction enables us to ask questions about society as a self-observing system. What happens in a self-observing, self-describing system? This is not only a question for conscious systems. I mean, there are five or more billion conscious systems, and you cannot make any theory of society out of adding one to another or dissolving them all into a general notion like the transcendental subject. But you can make some headway, perhaps, by using the formal idea of observing, and of making distinctions, to understand a system that has a recursive practice of making distinctions and guiding its next distinctions by previous distinctions, using memory functions, and all this. There are formal similarities between psychic systems and social systems, and this is for me important in trying to write a theory, a social theory, of self-describing systems, in particular of society.

wr: Shall we move on to a topic that is perhaps broached more directly in the two articles, and that is the topic of reality? Based on your reading of each other, how would each of you distinguish your notions of reality from the other? Both of you use the term "reality," and yet strict realists would not recognize the term as each of you uses it. But how do you observe each other using the term "reality"? Either one of you start.

kh: I'll be glad to start. In Professor Luhmann's article I alluded to before, the sentence that I found riveting was this: "Reality is what one does not perceive when one perceives it." It was when I got to that sentence that I thought I was beginning to grasp his argument, because I fully agree with that, with one important reservation. I, too, agree that whatever it is that we perceive is different, dramatically different, than whatever is out there before it is perceived. If you want to call what is out there before it is perceived "reality," then we do not perceive it, because the act of perception transforms it. Where I would differ is with the distinction between reality and nonreality, the binary distinction which he uses so powerfully in a theoretical way. I am concerned about a fundamental error that has permeated scientific philosophy for over three hundred years: the idea that we know the world because we are separated from it. I'm interested in exploring the opposite possibility, that we know the world because we are connected to it. That's where I would distinguish the approach I take. It is not really even a disagreement; it's more a matter of where you choose to put the emphasis. Do you choose to emphasize the interfaces that connect us to the world, or do you choose to emphasize the disjunctions that happen as distinctions are drawn?

cw: Professor Luhmann, I imagine you would like to respond.

NL: This formulation has a kind of ancestry, and in former times was associated with the idea of existence, with the idea, to put it another way, that I see trees, but I don't see the reality of trees. And if reality refers to *res*, and *res* is the thing, then you have visible and invisible things—and that's the world. In this philosophical tradition, the problem simply was not possible to formulate. But the formulation that reality is what you don't see if you see something can be phrased in different ways. And one of these other possibilities is to say that reality emerges if you have inconsistency in your operations; language opposes language, somebody says "yes," another says "no," or I think something which is uncomfortable given my memory, and then you have to find the pattern of resolution. Reality is then just the acceptance of solutions for inconsistency problems, somewhat as, in a neurophysiological sense, space is just produced by different lines of looking at it, by internal confusion and then a solution to the internal confusion which is in turn produced by memory that could not remember if it could not make differences in time. I am here now, but before I was in the hotel, and before that I was in the restaurant, and were this everything at the same moment, then I could not have any kind of memory. So time is real because it tries to create consistency and solve inconsistency problems. And this explains why reality is not an additional attribute to what you see, but is just a sign of successful solutions. This also helps us to see the historical semantics of reality. For example, "culture" at the end of the eighteenth century is a term which is able to organize comparisons—regional ones (French, German, and so on, or Chinese or European) and historical ones —so that there is a new pattern, some striking insight that is possible because the compared things are different. And "reality," as a result of functional comparisons, is just this kind of insight. You needn't have a more abstract notion of culture or identity or society, or whatever, to be able to handle contradictions which otherwise would obstruct your cognition.

cw: Let me just ask, for clarification, is this reality to which you are referring here different from the reality which is a kind of a creation or accumulation of what you elsewhere call *eigenvalues*, or is that in fact what you are describing?

NL: No, I think that is just another formulation.

cw: OK, all right. I'd like to come back to something you said, Professor Hayles, and ask you about this issue of connection versus separation that you're interested in. One of the things that's distinctive to me about second-order cybernetics—its central innovation, I think—is that it theorizes systems that are both closed *and* open: in Maturana and Varela, the attempt to theorize closure on the level of operations or organization, but openness to the environment on the level of structure. So, in a sense, isn't that a theory of self-referential systems which are nevertheless connected to the reality in which they find themselves?

KH:  Well, for Maturana and Varela, systems are connected by structural coupling. What that gets you in explanatory power is a way to explain the plasticity of systems and changes in structure. Where I have a fundamental difference with Maturana and Varela is in their assumption that there is no meaningful correlation between stimuli that interact with receptors and information that the receptors generate. This may finally come down to religious dogma: I am of one faith, and they are of another. I have studied the articles on perception which Maturana and his co-authors published on color vision in humans and on the visual system of the frog. I do not believe the data support his hypothesis that there is no correlation between inside and outside. It was a bold and courageous move to make that assumption, because it allowed them to break with representation and to avoid all of the problems that representation carries with it. It did get them a lot of leverage. But it's one thing to say there is no correlation, and another to say that the transformations that take place between the perceptual response and outside stimulus are transformational and nonlinear. The latter, I believe, is more correct than the former. I think it's important to preserve a sense of correlation and interactivity. This is primarily where I differ from them.

WR:  I will follow up, and then maybe both of you could comment. You mentioned before that where you had differences with Professor Luhmann's work was with the assumption that knowledge of the world is attainable because of separation from the world. If now you're saying that there is some way of thinking of a correlation between an outside and an inside, doesn't that ontologize separation from the world, and doesn't that get you back into what you were trying to get out of—that is, the idea that we can only know the world because it is outside of us and it has causal effects on us through sensory perception? Doesn't that solidify the inside/outside distinction? Why not talk instead about closure and knowledge coming from the inside, where the inside/outside distinction is made in the inside, and there is thus a more fluid relationship between the two, where you know the world because you are the world?

KH: Well, if you allow the distinction to fall into an inside/outside, as it certainly can, then you're back essentially to realism in some form and also representation. What I was trying to do in my article on constrained constructivism was to move the focus from inside/outside into the area of interaction, where inside and outside meet. That precedes conscious awareness, but it is in my view an area of interaction in which, precisely, a correlation is going on between stimuli and response. So...

EK: Could you elaborate a bit? I have a problem here because you said a little earlier that whether or not you accept the idea of closure comes down to dogma or faith, and now you're referring to some observations that seem to confirm the model that you're proposing. Could you say a little bit more about what kind of evidence leads you to your particular choice?

KH: If we start from the frog article of Lettvin and Maturana, which was the beginning for Maturana, what the article concludes (this is a near quotation) is that the frog's eyes speak to the frog's brain in a language already highly processed. It does not, however, show that there is no correlation between the stimuli and the response.

EK: Yes, but what is the status of this correlation? I mean, that's what the observer constructs as the frog's reality.

KH: Yes, that's right—that is, what is constructed is the frog's reality.

EK: From the human point of view.

KH: Yes. From the experimental point of view, to be more precise.

NL: But then you have the question: Who is the observer? If it is a scientist, he or she can make theories and can see correlations, but if it's a frog itself, then things are different. Maturana talks about structural couplings and so on, but the frog as such constructs his reality as if it were outside, to solve internal conflicts. So, in this sense, the question is, why does a closed system like a brain need a distinction inside/outside to cope with its own problems, and why does it construct something outside that externalizes the internal problems of the workings of the brain, just to order his world, in which he himself is, of course, given?

WR: Can I follow up on that? This brings us to the notion of consistency, which Professor Hayles talks about in her article. And if I understand that correctly, the fact is that each one of us in this room would probably open that door to try to walk out of this room. We're all constructing the world based on internal contradictions, but it all happens to be the same world with reference to this room and these five people. How is that possible?

NL: Well, I think it would be—to take an example from the article of Professor Hayles—that if we jump out of the window we would contradict our own memory. We have never seen someone stop before they hit the ground, so we simply sort out our contradictions, as long as it is not necessary to change it, within the old pattern. So we go through the door and take the elevator, and this is reality as a solution of formal contradictions. Maybe we try once to jump from too high a place, but we never see apples or something stopping in the middle of the fall.

WR: So it's strictly experiential?

NL: It is just the solution of an internal conflict of new ideas or of variations within your memory.

WR: So, in a sense, you both believe in constraints. If I understand you correctly now, Professor Luhmann, you would phrase constraints in terms of internal operations, especially memory, in this case. How do you, Professor Hayles, see the constraints that would prevent us from walking out of this window or trying to walk through that door? If you don't want to be a realist, and say because it's a door, or because of gravity, how do you define what the constraints are?

KH: Well, the way I think about it is that "reality" already carries the connotation of something constructed, so I prefer to use the term "unmediated flux." The unmediated flux is inherently unknowable, since by definition it exists in a state prior to perception. Nevertheless, it has the quality of allowing some perceptions and not others. There is a spectrum of possibilities that can be realized in a wide range of different ways, depending on the perceptual system that's encountering them, but not every perception is possible. Therefore, there are constraints on what can happen. We can all walk out the door together because we share more or less the same perceptual system—more importantly because we share language, which has helped to form our perceptual systems in very specific ways.

WR: How does that differ from memory as Professor Luhmann described it? In other words, I'm being very devious here in trying to coax the word "physical" out of you. How can you describe what you're describing without using the term "physical constraints"? Or are the constraints strictly in the way the brain is structured?

KH: I believe there are constraints imposed by our physical structure; I have no doubt of that. I think there are also constraints imposed by the nature of the unmediated flux itself.

WR: What one would conventionally call the actual physical structure of the unmediated flux?

KH: Yes, that's right.

NL: Then, if you use for a moment the idea that reality is tested by resistance—that's Kant—how can you have external resistance if you cannot cross the boundary of the system with your own operations? You cannot touch the environment with your brain, and even if you touch it you feel something here [points to his head] and not there, and you make an external reality just to explain that you feel something here [points again] and not in other places on your body. So, finally, it's always an internal calculation; otherwise, you should simply refuse the term "operational closure." But if we have operational closure, we have to construct every resistance to the operations of a system against the operations of the same system. And reality then is just a form—or, to say it in other terms, things or objects outside are simply a form in which you take into account the resolution of internal conflicts.

EK: If that model holds, can you account for the historical emergence of this idea that there is, and ought to be, a difference between the reality as unmediated flux—what we do not perceive when we perceive—and the world of objects that we encounter in everyday life. I mean, does this idea itself have a similar function?

NL: I'm not sure...

EK: Starting with Kant, we find the distinction between the unknowable noumena and phenomena, where you locate some sort of reality outside and then you talk about constructed phenomenological reality. Could one apply this idea that you just mentioned—that reality has the function of neutralizing contradictions—to account for the emergence of this historical distinction?

NL: The emergence of this kind of internal distinction between inside and outside is even earlier. A system makes a distinction because it couples its own operations to its environment over time and has to select fitting operations, or it simply decays: Then, if it makes such a distinction, it has no way to handle the environment except by reconstructing or copying the difference between system and environment into the system itself, and then it has to use an oscillator function to explain to itself something either as an outcome of internal operations or as the "outside world." In Husserl, it's clearer than in Kant that you have noesis and noema, and you have intentions, and you can change between the two and put the blame on your own thinking or be disappointed with the environment. And to explain how our system copes with this kind of distinction, instead of just checking out how it is out there, we need an evolutionary explanation of how systems survive to the extent that they can learn to handle the inside/outside difference within the system, within the context of their own operation. They can never operate outside of the system.

WR:  Do you have a response?

KH:  This is not really so much a response to the thought that Professor Luhmann was just developing as a more or less independent comment. For me the idea of closure as reproduction of the organization of the system is perfectly acceptable. It seems like a wonderful insight. But I don't share the feeling Maturana and Varela have that organization is a discrete state. According to them, if a system's organization changes, the system is no longer the same system—it is a different system if its organization changes. It seems to me organization exists, on the contrary, on a continuum and not as a discrete state. Consider for example evolution, in which all kinds of small innovations and mutational possibilities are tried out in different environments. It's problematic when these mutational possibilities constitute a new species. Drawing distinctions between species is to some extent arbitrary, especially when there is an extensive fossil record. There are many instances in contemporary ecologies where it is impossible to say if an organism falls within the same species or constitutes a different species. Clearly the organizational pattern of that system has changed in a substantive way, enough to allow one to make a distinction, but the change falls along a spectrum. It is not black and white—either no change, or a completely different system. While it's an important insight to see that the living is intimately bound up with the reproduction of a system's organization, I don't see that it's necessary to insist there is a definitive closure in what constitutes an organization.

CW:  The way I read Maturana and Varela's point is in a more cognitive or epistemological register, which is to say that if you observe something, you either call it $X$ or not-$X$, $X$ or $Y$, and that to cognize at all is to engage in the making of that distinction. Your description, it seems to me, is talking as if all these things are going on out there in nature, and then the question is, do our representations match up with them or not? That seems to me to be the pretty strongly realist and representationalist premise of the scenario you just described.

KH:  Yes, but in this I don't differ in the least from Maturana and Varela, who are constantly using arguments based on exactly the kind of natural history case studies that I just mentioned in order to demonstrate the closure of the organism. I grant your point, that I'm assuming there is some way to gain reliable knowledge about these things. And of course it's always possible to open up scientific "facts"—or, as Bruno Latour calls them, "black boxes"—and bring them into question again. But one has to argue from some basis.

WR:  Can I ask you, Professor Luhmann, about your black box? In a sense, your black box is operational closure, beyond which you will not go. You do not want to dispense with it; it's the fundamental element of your system or your theory. As we discussed before, if we are talking about leaps of faith, that's your leap of faith. What is at stake in retaining operational closure? Why is it so important for your theory?

NL:  Certainly, in sociological theory, or in social theory in general, you have the problem of how to distinguish objects or areas of, say, law, the economy, and so on. You can say that the economy is essentially coping with scarcity, or something like this. And to avoid these kinds of essentialist assumptions, I try to say that the law is what the law says it is, and the economy is just what the economy in its own operation produces out of itself. This is, I think, the alternative, in which I try to opt for a tautological definition. And then I'm obliged to characterize how the operations of the system—say, communication as the characteristic operation of society— follow a certain binary code, like legal versus illegal, to be able to reproduce, say, the legal system. Recursive decision-making reproduces an organization. But then I have this problem: I do not share the opinion of Maturana and Varela that outside relations are cognition, that you have already a cognitive theory if you say "operational closure." Maturana and Varela present structural coupling, structural drift, and these terms as cognitive terms. But I would rather think that a system is always, in its operation, beyond any possible cognition, and it has to follow up its own activity, to look at it in retrospect, to make sense out of what has already happened, to make sense out of what was already produced as a difference between system and environment. So first the system produces a difference of system and environment, and then it learns to control its own body and not the environment to make a difference in the system. So cognition then becomes a secondary achievement in a sense, tied to a specific operation which, I think, is that of making a distinction and indicating one side and not the other. It's an explosion of possibilities, if you always have the whole world present in your distinctions.

WR:  OK, maybe we should move on to the topic of negation. Could you summarize for us, Professor Hayles, your use of the semiotic square in your notion of double negation in your article on constrained constructivism?

KH:  I don't know how to give a short answer to this, so I'll have to give the long answer.

WR:  Good.

KH:  As I understand Greimas's work, he developed the semiotic square in order to make simple binaries reveal complexities that are always encoded in them but that are repressed through the action of the binary dualism. The idea is to start with the binary dualism and then, by working out certain formal relationships, to make it reveal implications that the operation of the binary suppresses. To give you an example, consider Nancy Leys Stepan's article about the relation between race and gender in physiognomic studies in the late nineteenth and early twentieth centuries; Stepan notes the circulation within the culture of expressions like "women are the blacks of Europe." To analyze this expression, consider a semiotic square that begins with the duality "men and women." What implications are present in that duality which aren't fully explicit? Some of those implications can be revealed by putting it in conjunction with another duality, white/black. By using the semiotic square and expanding the men/women duality, it is possible to demonstrate, as Ronald Schleifer and his coauthors have done, that "men" really means "(white) men" and "white" really means "white (men)." By developing formal relationships of the semiotic square, one can make the duality yield up its implications. It is important to remember that there is no unique solution to a semiotic square. Any duality will have many implications encoded into it, connotations which are enfolded into that duality but which are not formally acknowledged in it. So there are many sets of other dualities that can be put in conjunction with the primary one. If they're doing the work they should do in a semiotic square, each second pair would reveal different sets of implications. This is a preface to explain what

I think the semiotic square is designed to do. Beyond this, the semiotic square is formally precise. It is Greimas's hypothesis that there are certain formal relationships that dictate how dualities develop. So it's not arbitrary how the relationships within the square are developed.

In the semiotic square I used, I wanted a binary which is associated with scientific realism: true and false. If a hypothesis is congruent with the world, it's true. Popper argued that science cannot prove truth, only falsity. According to him, a hypothesis must be falsifiable to be considered scientific. The true/false binary is rooted in scientific realism. In order to have the "true" category occupied, you have to be in some objective, transcendent position from which you can look at reality as it is. Then you can match your hypotheses up with the world and see if the two are congruent. Thus the true/false binary comes directly out of realist assumptions. The binary I proposed to complicate and unravel the true/false dichotomy with was "not-false" and "not-true." I claim that the "true" position cannot be occupied because there is no transcendent position from which to say a hypothesis is congruent with reality. The "false" position *can* be occupied, because hypotheses can be falsified, as Popper argued. More ambiguous is the "not-false" position. This position implies that within the realm of representations we construct, a hypothesis is not inconsistent with the unmediated flux. Notice it is not true, only consistent with our interactions with the flux. Even more ambiguous is the "not-true" position; it represents the realm of possibilities which have not been tested, which have not even perhaps been formulated, and which may never be formulated because they may lie outside the spectrum of realizable experiences for that species. It is this position on the lower left of the square, the negative of a negative, that is more fecund, for it is the least specified and hence the most productive of new insights. Hence Shoshana Felman's phrase for it, "elusive negativity."

cw: It's very important to you, it seems to me, to insist that those other possibilities that are opened up are not solely possibilities dependent upon the context of inquiry. This goes back to what you were talking about earlier with the unmediated flux containing or acting as a constraint, a finite set of possibilities—that's what these constraints finally are. So it's important to you to insist, versus say Maturana, that these unfolding possibilities do not tell us only about the *context* of inquiry, but about the *object* of inquiry. Would that be fair to say?

kh: Yes. That would be true to say.

WR:  What is your reaction to the schema?

NL:  Well, again, a long one. The first is that I would distinguish between making a distinction and positive/negative coding, so that negation comes into my theory only by the creation of language, and with the special purpose of avoiding the teleological structure of communication, its tendency to go by itself to a fixed position, to a fixed point, to a consensus point. So, if we have a situation in which every communication can be answered by "yes" or by "no"—I accept or I reject your proposal—then every selection opens again into either conformity or conflict. So, negation in this sense comes into my theory of society only by coding language, or doubling language so to speak, in a "yes" version and a "no" version. And of course it is important that you have the identity of the reference, the possibility to say "yes" or "no" to the same thing, and not to something else. I say "this is a banana," and you can say "yes" or "no," but if you think that maybe it is an apple, then you have to make a distinction to talk about this. So this concerns negation. But I have also, independently of this, thought about an open question concerning distinction: distinction from what? And there are in principle, I think, two possibilities: distinction of an object from an unmarked space, from everything else (again, this is not a glass of wine, and not a tree, and so on). So, one type of distinction is that you create an unmarked space by picking out something. But then there is another type of distinction where you can cross the boundaries— male/female, for example, or in this example, true/false. And then you can oscillate between the two, and say, well, this is a job for a man or a job for a woman, this is good or this is bad, this is expensive, given our budget, and so on. But if you *can* indicate both sides by this distinction, then you also create by this very distinction an unmarked space, because then you can change from the distinction true/false to the distinction good/bad. Or to the distinction male/female. And then you can make a kind of correlation or coupling between different distinctions. But this always creates the world, creates an unmarked space, a kind of thing which you cannot indicate. Or if you indicate the unmarked space, then you have two marks, marked and unmarked.

WR:  Then you'll have another unmarked space...

NL:  Yeah, yeah, then you create another unmarked space beyond this distinction. And if I look at this four-fold scheme of Greimas's, I think that first it is quite clear that false/true is a specifiable distinction, specifiable on both sides. You can give arguments for true and you can give arguments for false, and you can have true arguments that something is false and false arguments that something is true. In this sense, it is complete. But then, when you make this distinction you also specify the unity of this distinction—which is, I would say, the code of science—and then you do not use, say, a political code (powerful or less powerful), or the gender code, or the moral code, or the legal code, or the economic code, or whatever. And when I look at this enlargement, I wonder whether it would be possible to say that indeed the false/true distinction is not a complete description of the world, that it leaves out the unmarked space, or it leaves out what you do not imagine, what you do not see, what you do not indicate, if you operate within this kind of framework. And this is important for my theory of functional differentiation, because if I identify codes and systems, then of course I need always a third value or third position: the rejection of all other codes. So, if I am in the legal code, then I am not in the economic code; the judge doesn't make his decision according to what he is paid for his decision...

cw: Sometimes! [general laughter]

nl: Well, yes, but then that's a problem of functional differentiation. And if I look at Greimas's table with its four positions, I think first that the lower line, the "not-true" and "not-false" line, is simply representing the unmarked space. Then I would change the positions: in other words, I would make the distinction between "false" and "not-false." "False" is something which is verified as "false"; "not-false" is everything else. Or "true" and "not-true." I don't know whether this makes any sense, but the essential point is that for my theory, especially for the theory of functional differentiation, we need something which Gotthard Günther would call "transjunctional operation"—that means, going from a positive/negative distinction to a meta-distinction, rejecting or accepting this kind of distinction. And you can, of course, have a metadistinction, then a metametadistinction, and that would always mean "marked/unmarked." And at that point, of course, you are in the middle of the question of how systems evolve by marking, by making marks in an unmarked space, and then you can have a history of possible correlations between structural developments and semantic developments in the history of society.

ek: Now your reinterpretation of this scheme, Professor Hayles, makes it look like it can no longer fulfill the function that, as I understand you, it's supposed to fill: namely, as far as I understand it, it's supposed to somehow assure us that we can somehow reach out of language and get language into contact with some sort of physical constraint. And when you interpreted the scheme...

WR: Negation is simply part of...

EK: ...part of the inside. Then you don't need a constraint anymore. I mean...

NL: ...self-imposed constraint...

EK: ...in your reinterpretation of the scheme you get rid of the external constraints, and I think I have trouble really understanding how we can reach, with the square, the idea of an external constraint.

WR: I guess the question is, how? What evidence does double negativity give? What evidence not only of the outside world, but in a sense what evidence does double negativity give that it does deal with...

KH: It does not give any evidence, I think. I did not intend to say that it gave evidence. But Professor Luhmann was, I think, exactly right in identifying something in that second line with what he calls the unmarked, that which lies outside distinction, and that's exactly the category that I meant to designate by "not-true." "Not-true" is absence of truth, which is not to say that it's untrue; it's to say that it is beyond the realm in which one can make judgments of truth and falsity. It's an undistinguished area in which that distinction does not operate. So his idea of distinctions is very applicable to what I was trying to do there. What I was trying to ask was, is there a place in language that points toward our ability to connect with the unmediated flux? This does not prove that the unmediated flux exists; it does not prove that the unmediated flux is consistent; it does not prove that the unmediated flux operates itself through constraints. It's simply asking the question, if we posit the unmediated flux, then where is the place in language that points toward that connection? That place is "not-true" or "elusive negativity," because that's the area in language itself which points toward the possibility I'm trying to articulate as "unmediated flux." It's no accident, I think, that in Greimas's article on the semiotic square he talks about this position emerging through the constraints that are present in the structure of language itself. In other words, his idea is that the structure of the semiotic square is not arbitrary; it's embedded in the deep structure of language. That, of course, is a debatable proposition. But just say for a moment that we accept the proposition. Then my argument is that the structural possibilities offered to us by language contain logically and semantically a category which points toward something we cannot grasp but is already encoded into our language.

cw: Can I jump in here at this specific point? What I hear you saying is that language as such does not presuppose any particular referent, but it does presuppose reference as such, right? Would that be fair?

kh: Well, I don't know that I was saying that. I thought I was saying that language has a logical structure, and part of that logical structure is to provide for a space for the unknowable and the unspeakable, even though paradoxically that space has to be provided within the linguistic domain.

cw: Right, but it's presupposed that it could be knowable and could be speakable, and moreover that that knowable and speakable is finite, right?

kh: The knowable and the speakable...

cw: ...or contains a finite set of applications in language.

kh: What is in the category "absence of truth" could always be brought into the category of either "not-false" or "false." It would be possible to have a scientific theory which brings something which was previously unthought and unrecognized into an area of falsifiability. But no matter how much is brought into the area of falsifiability, it does not exhaust and cannot exhaust the repertoire of those possibilities. So, this goes back to Professor Luhmann's idea that there is a complexity outside systems which is always richer than any distinction can possibly articulate.

cw: I guess the difference that I'm trying to locate here is that, in Professor Luhmann's scheme, this outer space is automatically produced by the deployment of distinctions—marking produces an unmarked space—but the difference is, in principle it seems to me, your claim about constraint, as we talked about it earlier: that it depends upon this set being finite. For you, it's not possible in principle to just go on and on and on deploying yet another distinction.

kh: Right.

cw: Because otherwise the claims about reality and the constraints that it imposes seem to me to fall apart at that point.

kh: Well, here maybe I can invoke some ideas about mathematics and say that I'm not sure the range of things that can be brought into the realm of "not-false" and "false" is finite. It may be infinite, but if it is infinite, then it is a smaller infinity than the infinity of the unmediated flux, and as you know, Cantor proved the idea that one infinity can be smaller than another. So, if it's an infinity, it is a smaller infinity than the set of all possibilities of all possible constructions.

NL: In my terms, you would then have the question, what do you exclude as unmarked if you make the distinction between infinite and finite? [laughter] But that's a book of Phillip Herbst from the Tavistock Institute entitled *Alternatives to Hierarchies*, where he refers to Spencer Brown and raises somewhere the question, what is the primary distinction? You could have the distinction finite/infinite; you could have the distinction inside/outside; you could have the distinction being/not-being to start with; and then you can develop all kinds of distinctions in a more or less ontological framework. And I find this fascinating, that there is no exclusive, one right beginning for making a distinction. The classics would of course say "being" and "not-being," and then the romantics would say infinite/finite, and systems theory would say inside/outside. But how are these related? If you engage in one primary distinction, then how do the others come again into your theory or not? This is part of the postmodern idea that there is no right beginning, no beginning in the sense that *you have* to make one certain distinction and you can fully describe the start of your operations. And that's the background against which I always ask, "What is the unity of a distinction?" or "What do you exclude if you use this distinction and not another one?"

CW: For me at least, the interest of your work, both of you, is that it is trying to take that next step beyond the mere staging or positing of incommensurable discourses. It seems to me that both of you—in finally somewhat opposed ways—are trying to move beyond this paradigmatic type of postmodern thought and move on—in your case, Professor Luhmann—to what you call a universally applicable or valid description of social systems. And in your case, Professor Hayles, that effort is revealed in your attempt to work out this problem of constraints—in a way, to try to rescue some sort of representationalist framework—to say that in fact there is a reality out there that does pose constraints and, moreover, can be known.

KH: Yes, though I would not say—this sounds like a nitpicking correction, but to me it's the essence of what I'm trying to say—I wouldn't say that what is out there can be known; I would say our interaction with what is out there can be known.

CW: Then I think the question has to be for me at least, in what sense are you using the term "objectivity," at the end of the "Constrained Constructivism" essay? A point that Maturana makes in one of his essays is that to use the subjective/objective distinction is to automatically presuppose or fall back on representationalist notions, which immediately recasts the problem in terms of realism and idealism.

KH: I don't use the word "objectivity."

CW: I have the *New Orleans Review* version...

KH: I don' t think I use it in that essay...

CW: "In the process,"—this is about three paragraphs from the end...

KH: ...oh, OK...

CW: "...in the process, objectivity of any kind has gotten a bad name. I think this is a mistake, for the possibility of distinguishing a theory consistent with reality, and one that is not, can also be liberating"—and you go on to talk about how this might be enabling politically, which is, I think, interesting because it does accept the challenge of moving beyond just saying, "well it's all incommensurable."

KH: Here, I accept the kinds of arguments that have been made by Donna Haraway and Sandra Harding about "strong objectivity," that to pretend one does not have a position is in fact not being "objective," in the privileged sense of "objective," because it ignores all those factors that are determining what one sees. And to acknowledge one's positionality, and explore the relationship between the components that go into making up that position and what one sees, in fact begins to allow one to see how those two are interrelated, and therefore to envision other possibilities. Sandra Harding's formulation of "strong objectivity" takes positionality into account, and is therefore a stronger version of objectivity than an objectivity that is based on some kind of transcendent nonposition.

CW: Let me follow up here. I guess the problem I have, and this is the case with Harding's work, is that what you're describing is inclusion. I see how that means more democratic representation of different points of view, but I don't see how it adds up to "objectivity" in the sense that it's usually used. Unless the sense of objectivity here is procedural, that we all agree to follow certain rules of a given discourse.

KH: As a philosopher, Harding doesn't want to relinquish the term "objectivity."

CW: Yes, that's quite clear.

KH: I don't have any vested interest in keeping the word "objectivity," but I think the idea of what she's pointing to, whether one calls it "objectivity" or not, is no matter how many positions you have, they will not add up to a transcendent nonlocation.

CW: Right. The God's-eye view.

KH: $P_1$ plus $P_2$ plus... $P_n$ is not God.

CW: Right.

WR: So actually what you're talking about is what you mentioned in the very beginning, the word "objectivity" basically means "reflexivity"— the reflexivity that you were missing in the early cybernetic tradition?

KH: Yes. I don't know if anybody's used the word "strong reflexivity," but I would like to. Strong reflexivity shows how one can use one's position to extend one's knowledge. That's part of what is implied in the idea that we know the world because we are connected to it. Our connection to it is precisely our position. Acknowledging that position and exploring precisely what the connections are between the particularities of that position and the formations of knowledge that we generate is a way to extend knowledge. There is a version of reflexivity that, in the early period of science studies, was like an admission of guilt: "Well, I'm a white male, and so therefore I think this." There was a period when you couldn't write an article without including a brief autobiography on who you were. But that really missed the point, because the idea is to explore in a systematic way what these correlations are and precisely why they lead to certain knowledge formations, and therefore to begin to get a sense of what is not seen.

NL: Then my opponent should be not so much for the term "objectivity" but for the term "interaction," and who sees the interaction.

WR: Interaction between us and an environment...

NL: Yeah, yeah. I have no trouble in posing external observers, a sociologist who sees an interaction between the capitalistic economy and the political system, or between underdeveloped countries—center/periphery, and so on—but how could we think that the system that interacts with its environment is itself observing the interaction as something which gives a more or less representational view of what is outside? How can we see this without seeing that this is a system which does the observing? How could we avoid involving the system—which means a radically constructivist point of view—when we ask the question, "Who is the observer?" We say, "The outside observer, of course." He sees interactions of any kind, causal or whatever, as objective reality in *his* environment, because *he* sees it. But if the system in interaction tries to *see* the interaction, how could we conceive this?

KH: There may be many ways to use the word "interaction," and I'm not sure I'm using it in the sense you mean. For me, when I say the word "interaction," it already presupposes a place prior to observation, whether self-observation or observation by someone else. It's the ultimate point that we can push to in imagination; it's the boundary between the perceptual apparatus and the unmediated flux, and as such it is anterior to and prior to any possible observation. So, I would say that the interaction is not observable.

NL: Then you can drop the concept.

KH: You could drop the concept, except then you have a completely different system. What interaction preserves that I think is important is the sense of regularities in the world and the guiding role that the world plays in our perception of it. If representation and naive realism, with their focus on external reality, only played one side of the street, Maturana's theory of autopoiesis, with its focus on the interior organization of systems, only plays the other side. I am interested in what happens at the dividing line, where one side meets the other side. Maturana's theory is important for me because it shows, forcefully and lucidly, how important perception and systemic organization are in accounting for our view of the world. It also opens the door to a much deeper use of reflexivity than had been possible before—an insight significantly extended by your positioning of the observer as he (or she) who makes the distinctions that bring systems into existence as such. But for me, this is not the whole picture. If it is true that "reality is what we do not see when we see," then it is also true that "our interaction with reality is what we see when we see." That interaction has two, not one, components—what we bring to it, and what the unmediated flux brings to it. The regularities that comprise scientific "laws" do not originate solely in our perception; they also have a basis in our interactions with reality. Omitting the zone of interaction cuts out the very connectedness to the world that for me is at the center of understanding scientific epistemology.

WR: Well, I think that we've hit that outer limit right here, where we are redefining boundaries. Do we have any other general questions? Maybe the system in question ought to be dinner...

CW: Let me just ask one more very general question, since we're on this point, and it's something we've touched on. At the end of the "Constrained Constructivism" article, Professor Hayles, you make it clear that this rethinking you're engaged in has pretty direct ethical imperatives. Objectivity, for you and for Sandra Harding and for Donna Haraway, is an ethical imperative as well as an epistemological or theoretical one, and you go on to specify what those imperatives are. I take it for you, Professor Luhmann, that you want to be very careful to separate ethics as just one of many social systems from other types of social systems, all of which can be described by systems theory. So what I'm wondering is, could you all talk a little bit about what you see as the ethical and political imperatives, if there are any, of second-order theory, to reach back to where we started?

KH: I don't know that I really have anything to add beyond what you just said, but it is clear for me that there are ethical implications of strong reflexivity and strong objectivity. I'm not really versed in ethics as a kind of formal system, so I'll defer that to Professor Luhmann.

NL: Well, for me ethics or morality is a special type of distinction, and a particularly dangerous one, because you engage in making judgments about others—they are good or bad. And then if you don't have consensus, you have to look for better means to convince them or to force them to agree. There is a very old European tradition of this: the relation between standards and discrimination. If somebody is not on your side, then he is on the wrong side. And I think my work is a sociologist's way to simply reflect on what we engage in if we use ethical terms as a primary distinction in justifying our cognitive results: terms like, "If you accept this you are good, and if you don't you have to justify yourself."

# Answering the Question: What Is Modernity?
## An Interview with Niklas Luhmann

EVA KNODT: It is obvious especially from your most recent work that you don't like the term "postmodern." In *Observations on Modernity* you dismiss it as a mere catchword. At the same time, your own observations of modernity seem to concur with much of what contemporary theorists take as evidence for the fact that we do live in a postmodern society. For example, the theoreticians of the postmodern speak of the end of metanarratives, the absence of a center, of a crisis of the subject. You speak of the crisis of the external observer and of a "polycontextual" world that can no longer produce the single, all-encompassing representation of itself. To what extent are these descriptions intertranslatable? And if they are, what are your objections to the term "postmodern"?

NIKLAS LUHMANN: I think my primary objection to the term "postmodern" is the confusion of distinctions it implies, by which I mean the distinction between an operational level, where communication just happens, and a semantic level, or an observational level, where communication describes itself. You could also say that there is a lack of distinction between the structural and operational continuities in modern society, on one hand, and the change of semantic descriptions or self-descriptions of society, on the other hand. And in a theory of society I think the most important distinction is between structure, as the *form* of differentiation of modern society, and semantics.

EK: Are you saying that basically the self-description of society in terms of postmodernism is somewhere inadequate to its principle of operation? In other words, is there a discrepancy between this kind of self-description that calls itself postmodern and the principle of functional differentiation?

NL: Yes, that's already the next distinction. I mean first, postmodernity is only a self-description, that's one thing, and not just a representation of the reality. But then we have to admit that all kinds of self-descriptions are selective, focusing on something and rejecting other things. So, postmodernity can be criticized, or the discourse of postmodernity can be criticized, as not being adequate, because it doesn't take continuing tendencies of modernity into account, and it can also be described as inadequate in terms of its own version of modern society, its own way of describing society. For example, that it focuses on a temporal difference, a historical difference—first modern and then postmodern—but we can ask the question why we have to choose a historical difference as characterizing the present society.

WILLIAM RASCH: As a follow-up to that, Lyotard, whose name is most often mentioned with the notion of postmodernity, has tried *not* to come up with a temporal definition of postmodernity and in different ways has said that what is described as postmodernism is the originary moment of modernism, that first you have postmodernity, in a certain sense, and then you sink into modernism. And I think he's talking about it in terms of developing these grand narratives, that postmodernity is a recognition of the lack of grand narratives, and then modernism is the sort of papering over that gap. How would you react to that as a definition of postmodernity?

NL: I think I would accept this, but then for us the question is why it is called "*post*modernity," and second, what kind of information does it give? Just to say a lack of principle, or a lack of unifying identities, or a lack of metanarratives in the self-description of modernity—in general, "lack of" doesn't say very much about the situation in which we now find ourselves.

EK: In other words, you object to the semantics of negation on some level, that it seems to be characteristic...

NL: That's why—it is maybe good, in historical terms, that we negate expectations that we would have if we come from history into modern conditions, but this doesn't give much information, for example, about what we can expect from an autonomous economic, capitalistic, monetary, or whatever system, or what we can expect from science as a system of its own.

WR: Perhaps we should address the issue of temporality one more time. The notion of postmodernity implies some sense of chronology, which we've just talked about. In like manner, Marxists like Fredric Jameson speak of "late capitalism," again implying a qualitative change from the capitalism that Marx himself diagnosed. In your analysis of modernity, there seems to be no significant change over the past two hundred years, at least at the structural level. Is that true? Would you still hold to that assessment, that there has been no structural change over the course of what we call "modernity"? And, a related question: Is it possible to perceive structural change when you're in the middle of structural change? Can we say that something is going on now that is structural change?

NL: Well, I would make a distinction between a change in the form of differentiation—in this respect I actually don't see anything which goes beyond functional differentiation—and change within function systems. Within function systems there are enormous changes—for example, in science, in politics, in family life, in religion...

EK: But the changes you notice are to be described as happening within the framework of functional differentiation? And then you look at each subsystem, at how each system gets more complex and changes...

NL: Functional differentiation is the frame of the changes, but it doesn't change itself—at least I cannot see any kind of post–functional differentiation type or form of society.

EK: Now, your notion of modernity implies that functional differentiation—that is, a horizontal form of differentiation as opposed to a hierarchical one, such as stratification or segmentation—is the predominant form, or primary form of differentiation in modern society. At the same time, I think, one cannot deny that there are relics of stratification, or perhaps even segmentation, in modern society, and if that is true, why do they seem to be so persistent?

NL: Well, they have to be explained as a consequence of functional differentiation. You have a change from the legitimacy of a hierarchical, stratificatory differentiation into a class society which is no longer legitimate. I mean, we do not currently think that class structure maintains order, as people once thought about hierarchy in the late middle ages or in early modern times. So, I think the increase, even, of inequalities in a stratificatory sense, and also the increase in the use of segmentary differentiation—for example, the plurality of states as a segmentary differentiation of the political system to achieve a closer relation between consensus and violence, consensus and state force on a territorial and traditionally cultural level... If we have, in this case, functional differentiation of politics against religion, science, the economy, and whatever, then the system needs for its own optimal running a kind of segmentary, a secondary segmentary differentiation. So, in this sense, one could say that functional differentiation achieves or allows for a complexity which is then able to use, to have new uses for, inequalities—center-periphery differentiation, say, or stratificatory differentiation, or segmentation.

EK: If I may just follow up some—you seem to say that functional differentiation, by virtue of its own principle, will always, on some level, require these other forms of differentiation, and it's not necessarily so that we will eventually get rid of all traces of stratification, say. The real difference, then, seems to be that people no longer believe that these residual forms of differentiation are legitimate.

NL: Well, yes, I don't know what it is to believe...

EK: Well, I mean, their legitimacy...

NL: I cannot communicate as if... there are no successful ways to communicate, to say "I'm rich, because I'm born rich. And you're... "

EK: ...and that's part of the world order.

NL: "...poor because you're born poor," and believe that that's part of the world order in an Aristotelian sense, that all kinds of composed units have to have a dominating and a subordinating part—that's Aristotle. And this was of course the ideology of early modern times, and we can no longer use this kind of description in communication, because persons believe they operate on their merits, that their merits are on a high or a low level. But whether a highly complex, functionally differentiated society needs stratification, needs center-periphery differences, or needs segmentary differences, that's a very difficult question, and I'm not sure whether I can answer it because it would mean that we could look into the future and say there would never be a society without center-periphery differentiation, or without stratification.

EK: Since, as you just said, functional differentiation allows for a mixture of different forms of differentiation, my question would be: What is the status of differentiations like class—no, no—like race and gender, as opposed to, for instance, class or functional differentiation. What particular status would they have?

NL: First of all I think that race and gender are forms of communication which don't need an intention and which don't need to be conveyed, which are present in reciprocal perception, so they are universals, in the sense that you cannot avoid, in interaction, and you don't need to say "I'm a man" because this is evident. And, of course, you do not need to say, "I am Afro-American," but this is evident, and the question is then how this evidence, or this obviousness of type of natural outfit of humans, natural makeup of humans, can adapt to different forms of differentiation. I think in functional differentiation the most important development is a delegitimization of race and gender as a distinction—I mean it doesn't make, if you invent something scientifically, it doesn't make a difference if you are a woman or a man, and the same also holds if you are Chinese or an African—the question is whether the invention or the discovery is "true" or not, and the same thing, of course, in the economy. And then this means that referring to race or gender is no longer legitimate, and this is the reason we can have feminist movements and antiracist movements, because we don't need this distinction, and if you refer to it, you are not quite on the level of what is required under the regime of functional differentiation.

WR: Then why the persistence of exclusion? For instance, why, in the sciences, are there so few women? Or, in the United States, in the participation in the economy, why is there, or has there been, a systematic exclusion of blacks? Or in Germany, on the level of citizenship, why does there seems to be a systematic exclusion of German-born Turks, whereas ethnic Germans, who have lived for centuries in Russia or other parts of Eastern Europe, have immediate German citizenship? Why the persistence of these distinctions, if these distinctions have no function anymore?

NL: I think this a matter of interest, in defending interest.

EK: Whose interest?

NL: Well, the interest of males to hold their position against females, and the interest of whites to hold their position against other races. So I think there is a kind of conflict, a kind of difference between what is legitimate and rational, with respect to the working of the function systems, or what kind of distinctions function systems can use and what kind of distinction disturbs or limits the capacity of function systems, on one hand, and the traditional interest of a position you have from old times, on the other.

WR: When I hear you say this, it sounds as if the idea of functional differentiation is at least an implicit political critique of the politics of interest. In other words, you can marshal the argument "modernity is functionally differentiated" to argue against racism, against gender hierarchy, etc. Is that true?

NL: Yeah, that's true, but it is difficult to generalize it as a kind of critique of interest. There can be interests which are—for example, to reinvest capital and not to consume it—which are completely legitimate in the order of functional differentiation. It cannot serve as a kind of total dele-gitimization of interest, but as a kind of trivialization of interest conflicts. At the end of this century we see very clearly, at least in Europe, that the state, or the welfare state, which was based on handling interest conflict, is at the end of its possibilities, and we now have conflicts, identity conflicts, or fundamentalist conflicts, or simply conflicts which arise out of formu-lating an identity—as Islam, or as Turk or as Serb, and so on—which are not able to be mediated by financial incentives or by legal regulation. The interest point of view seems to be a point of view which emerged in the seventeenth or eighteenth century and became the focus of state organiza-tion, the reason for the expectation that the economy would increase wel-fare and not lead to unsolvable conflict. But now we can already observe that the interest point of view is not the only problem we have to solve in modern society. And then, of course, the question of what kind of interests are supported by, or support themselves within, functional differentiation becomes important, and what kinds of interest simply prevent functional differentiation from being realized.

EK: This is a little bit out of order now, but when first this question came up about the status of race and gender, you mentioned that it's some-thing that's obvious and quasi-natural, and I have some problems with that, because, especially as these questions have been reflected upon in recent the-ories, the assumption seems to be that gender categories are precisely not natural, they are at some level socially constructed. So where do you see—for instance within a functionalist framework—where would there be the necessity to construct these distinctions in ways that historically were insep-arable with hierarchical organization. In other words, why is it that within premodern society, the hierarchy was constructed in such a way that at the center it was the male point of view and not the female—I mean, why was it constructed such that women were excluded?

WR: And then why in the eighteenth century, when the hierarchies were shifting to functional differentiation, why do you have a naturaliza-tion of gender characteristics, in Rousseau, in Humboldt, in Kant, that persists? In fact, there is a great regeneration of the attempt to naturalize gender distinction, and naturalize it not just on a physical level.

NL: Well, first of all I think the role of the male in traditional society, I mean in late medieval and early modern times, reflects the fact that society was based on stratification, and stratification was based on the household, or on "houses," that is, on families in the old sense. So then you need a link which bridges over this kind of differentiation based on families. And the trouble of course was political. Political society was a society which connects households; it has nothing to do with the internal workings of families. And I think for this link you needed a decision, namely, whether husband or wife should have this kind of linking function. And it was of course then the man. I don't know why I say of course [laughter]. You had to make a choice, and the tradition did indicate that it would be the male. And when society changes, and it uses the individual as a natural framework from which to rebuild families by organizing marriage around love relations, by organizing the economy around careers, and the political system around elections and a kind of political career—then you have the individual as a base, which, at the same time, criticizes the old society as an artificial construct that forces individuals into fixed positions. However, you have a chance to rebuild society, yet you do not know what kind of society that will be. And I think the tendency, around 1800 and later, to rely on a "natural" difference between men and women—"women are such and such, and men are such and such"—had to do with this focusing on the individual and not going beyond this, not asking whether the individual is itself a social construction. Because it was felt that you needed the individual as a reference point in order to undermine the traditional order. But now we are beyond this stage of reflection, and we have just the question which you asked: what is the relation between social construct and the clear, natural identity which you cannot avoid conveying in communication. For example, the answer to the question "Is it a boy or a girl?" will be clear; there is no *tertium quid*, no other possibilities. But then this doesn't predict very much—what kind of boy and what kind of girl, and how "girlish" the boy or how "boyish" the girl. So the security of the natural basis is at the same time the openness of social definitions. So you could not do without them, but you can reconstruct it and adapt it to all kinds of, not so much personal needs, but social organizational needs.

EK: So you are basically distinguishing here between biological sex and gender as a construct, and when you talk about natural and obvious you mean this realm of biological determination.

NL: It is very difficult for a woman to maintain she is a man, but it is possible for her to take over "male" roles.

WR: When you talk about functional differentiation being a frame for modernity that hasn't changed, and that this frame has allowed for the withering away of interest-based politics, for instance, or has provided the basis for the critique of stratifications based on class or on race or on gender, then it seems that functional differentiation is, in a certain sense, a normative, if not an optimistic, concept for you? How would you respond to that?

NL: I don't think that it is normative because norms only make sense if there is an alternative. But I see no alternative to functional differentiation, and if we propose functional differentiation as a normative rule, then we should think that there are other possibilities to organize society in a better way, for example in the socialist-communist organizational way, and I don't see the point in establishing norms on such a fundamental level of the society. This of course collides with the Frankfurt School, who take this to be an affirmative attitude toward society, and not a critical one, and a conservative, not a progressive one, but I really don't see in any kind of critique of modern society an idea of how we could do without functional differentiation. So, norms have to be adapted to the given regime, the given order of functional differentiation, and then, of course, the main, important thing is that we destabilize norms to cope with the dynamic stability of function systems. But this is a secondary phenomenon, not something which says functional differentiation is good. This would amount to saying that complexity is good. Of course, there is a relation between functional differentiation and higher complexity. And there is a kind of evolutionary tendency to say that more highly complex systems can adapt, have better capacities to adapt, to the environment, and therefore they are better. But we may have many reasons to doubt this, given the ecological problems in modern society, or the way modern society handles individuals. So I'm not sure whether complexity, the argument of complexity, is a way to give functional differentiation a normative priority over other things. But then, on the other hand, and this is of course related, I don't have a very optimistic idea about functional differentiation, and I may almost repeat opinions which came about early in the eighteenth century, that European society at that time would be dynamic and therefore give reasons for more optimistic and more pessimistic expectations with regard to the future. And I think also we have reasons to be very pessimistic about our society and at the same time have confidence, or not have confidence, in our abilities to cope with all kinds of problems. Therefore, we are not sure whether we can solve our problems or not, and this will be partly a question of time. We start with seeing, defining, and handling problems. All this tends neither to a pessimistic nor to an optimistic view but to a view that tries to adapt a mix of optimism and pessimism to a more realistic description of function systems.

WR: I'd like to follow up on that. Your theory always starts off with distinctions, and when you talk about functional differentiation, or when you talk about the differentiation of society, there has to be a counter-term, and that counter-term is dedifferentiation. It seems as if functional differentiation is a positive term and dedifferentiation would be a negative term. In that sense, is it possible to talk about functional differentiation, if not as a norm, then as something that is positive in distinction to, say, the type of dedifferentiation that characterized Eastern European communism. Is it possible to talk about functional differentiation as a positive value in your system in that sense?

NL: Well, the question of differentiation is much more complicated than simply talking of differentiation and dedifferentiation. First of all, if we have forms of differentiation we can distinguish these forms in the sense that we distinguish functional differentiation from stratification. And then of course we see easily that it would be a catastrophe for modern society if we go back to a stratification or segmentation. This could only be the outcome of a technical catastrophe, or an environmental catastrophe, or whatever. So, in this sense, the facts, how we evaluate them is a different question, but the facts of modern life, the huge population increase and everything, force us to prefer functional differentiation as a question of survival. So, in this sense, there is a distinction which indeed makes it necessary to cope and to accept functional differentiation. And then, of course, you have the difference of, the distinction between, forms of differentiation and differentiation as such. And then we see that all kinds of forms of differentiation dedifferentiate former types of distinctions, for example, the one between the nobleman and the commoner. Here we perceive a kind of dedifferentiation of distinctions which were appropriate for other forms of social differentiation.

WR: Do you describe the—however you want to call it—the communist experiment of the twentieth century as an attempt to go back to a stratified society? Was there an attempt to restratify society even though the ideology was egalitarian?

NL: I think they did not make the important distinction between society and organization, and their differentiation was simply an organizational one. Their problem was that they could not identify their organization—the party—with society, so they had to use techniques of extinguishing boundaries in a society. For example, in interpersonal interaction you never knew who was present and who was absent. I mean you had the pictures of Stalin or Khrushchev or whomever on the wall, and you had somebody who could hear or not hear, so they had to eliminate the boundaries of interaction, and there was a kind of dedifferentiation on the level of interaction, organization, and society. They started simply to see everything from the point of view of organization. And this is, I think, one necessity, a necessity, if you start to eliminate the distinctions between the economy and the political system, the family life and religion, or whatever, and to fuse it into a question of resources and interest which could be handled by organization. In this sense, it is dedifferentiation. And the other thing is, of course, corruption. Corruption is also a dedifferentiation. You have a network of relations, of favors, and of legitimate or illegitimate maneuvering of resources that is dominant in society, then you decide, within this network, whether you should use legal or illegal means, or whether you should favor this one or that one, or whether the big families of the country use their own network to integrate their firms or not. There are, I think there are these two forms of dedifferentiation which are not able to use the possibilities of functional differentiation. The one is already gone; the other, corruption, is still with us—what we call corruption, from a normative point of view, but from the insider point of view it is, of course, not corruption but just preferring friends over enemies.

EK: Just a follow up to this: so do you think that the failure of the socialist-communist experiment has to do with the fact that it dedifferentiated more than it differentiated within the context of a global, what do you call it, a global world society? That it became an anachronism that couldn't be reconciled with the general development of things on a world scale?

NL: Yeah, I think the last explanation is the more important one. If the world were one large organization, it could survive; there would not be an outside question to it. What was most important, I think, in this relation between the international economy—mostly the financial system, because the international economy operates in a way in which the financial market is the center of the system, and what you can have as production, or labor, depends on the financial market—and the Eastern or socialist societies which depended on international credit, was the fact that they had no information about their own economy, they could not know what is economically rational or not, because everything was a kind of outcome of politics. And then they could not link this kind of lack of information with the outside financial conditions.

WR: Just another little follow-up question. Do you see the same problem, then, in those areas where what we've normatively called "corruption" prevails. Are they also on the verge of extinction because they can't operate in a world economy? Or what...

EK: Which ones are you...

WR: The ones...

NL: Mexico or Brazil or whatever...

EK: ...or the Mafia and these...

NL: Yeah, Mafia relations, but...

WR: They seem to be surviving, this is my question.

NL: But how long? And the question is, there is a kind of opening of these societies to the international market, and then there will be a dominance of financial and economic problems which probably cannot be solved very well by this kind of network politics. They have—one indicator of this is that they cannot have any military government anymore. So Brazil, the militarists could not go on because the financial situation, the public state debts and the national debts, were so overwhelming, and so they could not create an autonomous economic system in Brazil. And similar things are happening in Argentina and Mexico now. So there are signs of opening. On the other hand, we have very successful economies in, for example, Taiwan, in which in fact large families dominate the economy as families. And this, by the way, may mean that the power of women is more important in this context, to establish relations, to marry, then, in our context. So, it is very difficult to say that the corruption network collapsed like socialist politics collapsed. At least we have to take into account that there are functional equivalents—the functional equivalents of family relationships and financial networks is one thing we should observe more clearly, to see whether there is really a functional equivalent and what this means with respect to the differentiation of, say, the political system and the legal system, the legal system and the family system, or what it doesn't mean in terms of religion.

EK: According to neo-Marxist accounts of modern society, commodification presents a threat to the principle of functional differentiation, in the sense that it restricts the autonomy of function systems. The systems of science, art, education, and politics can be autonomous as long as their autonomy is compatible with economic demands. But if it is true, as some argue, that today in science the question of truth becomes a question of money, of having or not having a research grant or a laboratory, do you insist on the principle of functional differentiation?

NL: Well, I think commodification, if it means that you can buy something for money, is less general now than in the middle ages. In the middle ages, you could buy everything, including salvation or state positions, and so on. Then the movement was to restrict the economy and to save religion from money, or to marry for love and not for commercial or for family reasons. I mean large, rich families. So, the tendency is not increasing commodification but on the contrary, limiting the range of economic evaluations and establishing something which is, which functions on its own right—love or political power; you should not be able to buy the presidency. There are some problems, but in general I think the tendency is not as the Marxists say, but, on the contrary, is more towards differentiation and to let function systems work with their own media, their own codes, drawing their own boundaries. But then we have the question of whether this leads to an equilibrium, or whether the economic system is nevertheless the dominant system. And this becomes a very complicated question, whether for example the political system can operate without a growing economy anymore. Or whether families in fact can survive unemployment. Can love survive unemployment is one of these questions, so we have to look very closely to see what kind of inequalities or what kind of disruptive causalities are built into the system of autonomous self-reproducing, autopoietic systems. And it is very difficult to sum this thing up in a statement which would say that the economy is the dominant system, because in many senses the economy depends, of course, on the legal system. And you could not have an economy without legally valid contracts, and in modern ecological problems, in Germany at least, we have the experience that the economy asks for state rules, because otherwise competition would favor people who have an ecologically unsound business. So state rules establish again the equality of competition, because everybody has to pay attention to some ecological constraints. And then the educational system —what is the relation between the educational system and the economic system? The economic system depends, of course, on a sufficiently educated populace; it needs, at least if it is a technologically sophisticated system, it needs some basic knowledge given in the universities. So, one way to put this question is, how could society survive the collapse, more or less, of one of these function systems? The collapse of art, for example, would not be very harmful for the total society...

EK: Which means maybe it's already collapsed. I mean...

NL: Well, we would not...

EK: Maybe it's already disappeared...

NL: Well, there is some kind of...

EK: ...has lost its function.

NL: ...some kind of news about society that you can get only in art; at least in the nineteenth century this is clear; in the twentieth century you can discuss it, but... So, the collapse of the economy, if you cannot buy anything for your money, would mean the death of almost the total population. If you can, what can you do if you cannot buy anything anymore, because nobody accepts money. And we could survive the lack of state rules—well, for some time.

WR: Does that mean that the economic system has a certain primacy?

NL: Well, this is a question of the point of view. It does not, it cannot work without a sufficient level of other systems, without a legal order, or without education, and without political power to enforce legal decisions.

WR: The argument of commodification that comes primarily from the left argues that it's not just dependent on these systems, but precisely because it needs these systems it determines these systems; it determines their type of operation. More and more in the United States, for instance, we've moved away from this so-called Humboldtian ideal of science for its own sake or knowledge for its own sake to knowledge for business's sake. Even in the public school sector there are some communities that have given the financing of public schools over to business interests, and therefore, there is the claim that business interests are determining the pedagogical system. How do you talk about this?

NL: I think there is a symmetrical relationship, and it's difficult to make an asymmetrical one out of it, to say, for instance, that the economy determines the educational system. This would... well, then you have to explain the surplus of output of the education system as a strategy for selecting the best prospect from the worst. But then you would still have the educational system to make the selections, which it doesn't do in any kind of reliable sense, at least not in Germany. So, I'm not sure whether there is a reason to interpret a symmetrical, reciprocal interdependence as a dependence of one system on the other, and not vice versa. Also, in legislation— I mean we have, of course, business influence on legislation, and lobbies in the United States, perhaps even more so than in Germany, but on the whole, of course, this is because the economy depends on the law and not as a kind of independent variable economy which then makes the law as it would like to have it; this is empirically simply not true.

WR: So, if we can identify differences, say, in the pedagogical system or in science, between, say, the year 2000 versus the year 1800, that's not because one system has caused science to change but because all of the systems have been coevolving in a different direction? Is that how you would.,.

NL: Yeah, then the question becomes much more concrete, and it is very difficult to generalize it into a dependence of the total society on one subsystem. Science, of course, has invented things, which devaluates a lot of investments in the economy. You have simply to change the investment to be able to cope with small competitors which use ... which start in a new way. And, of course, technology is, science is one thing, but technology is something else—the invention of the computer, the invention of atomic energy production, the invention of biogenetic engineering—then you have to change the law to protect *Urheber*...

EK: Copyright.

NL: ...copyright, or the patent. You have to change the law because science has made some invention, or some technologies are developing. Does this mean that science dominates the law? Or simply that the legal system recognizes that it would not be able to cope with its environment if it does not have the instruments to react to changes in the environment?

EK: You've used the term structural coupling to describe interrelationship. How does that term "structural coupling" enable you to describe the complexity of these relationships?

NL: Well, the term "structural coupling," if you use it the way Maturana uses it, has the advantage of making clear that there is no causal determination of the state of one system by the other, but there is simply a channel of reciprocal irritation, or also one-way irritation. There is a structural coupling between the medical system and the economy, because you need a doctor to confirm that you are sick, and the writing is a kind of structural coupling between the economy and the medical system. And there may be some kind of playing with this kind of structural coupling. If you know the doctor very well, you can have an easier way to get off and begin your vacations earlier. And also the constitution as a structural coupling between the political system and the legal system means, on the one hand, that political operations can only have a large-scale effect if they use the law, and the legal system can make a kind of asymmetric move of its own to the "outside" when it says, "Well, I'm dependent on the law, and if there is no law, then the judge has to make his own decisions." So...

EK: So, could one say that maybe the university would enable a structural coupling between the economy and the educational system, on the one hand, and a system of science, on the other?

NL: Well, I'm not sure whether you can restrict this to the university, because high-school graduates also find jobs. But within the educational system there are ways of marking persons; the output of the educational system is marked: "this is a biologist, this is a high school student, this is... And then also "good" or "bad." But the marking, of course, doesn't predict careers.

WR: To broach another theme: According to your own words, systems theory offers descriptive analyses of society, not prescriptions or recommendations. You have used the word "value-neutral" or "value-free" (*wertfrei*) in conjunction with scientific discourse, especially systems theory. Could you explain what you mean by that?

NL: I think so, but I'm not sure to what statement in my work you are referring. In general...

EK: *Social Systems.*

NL: *Social Systems?*

EK: From that kind...

NL: Uh huh. *Wertfreiheit,* "value neutrality," can only mean that you have to restrict yourself to the values of your subsystem, and that means to the code. If we have no value whatsoever, we have no selection. A selection requires an orientation: "This is better than this," or "We prefer this and not that." And so we prefer truth against falsity, but this you cannot avoid in science, otherwise you would not do science. But then *Wertfreiheit* in the Max Weber sense could only mean that you should avoid mixing the values of different function systems, for example, not to give religious reasons for preference in scientific theories.

EK: Now, in Lyotard's *The Differend*, there is an incommensurability between language games such as the prescriptive and the descriptive. Do you agree with Lyotard's analysis? Do you see some sort of parallel between Lyotard's description in terms of language games or discourses, and your idea of function systems, such that you would say that there is an "incommensurability" between a descriptive function system, science, and a prescriptive function system, morality?

NL: I make the distinction between prescriptive, or normative, expectations on one side and descriptive, or "commentive," expectations on the other side. And I think that some systems, like a legal system, have to start with normative expectations—norms—and then use cognitive expectations only to see whether a norm can be applied or not, whether somebody has killed another or not. This is, of course, a cognitive question and not a value or a normative question. And in science, vice versa. You have to start with cognitive expectations; that means the expectation will have to be corrected and changed if they are not true. If you meet disappointments, you don't change your normative expectations, but you do change your cognitive expectations. And this is, I think, a very central distinction, but I don't see a reason to use the term "discourse" or "language game" and generalize this and similar distinctions to a general idea of different language games. This is one distinction that is important, but there may be other distinctions in discourse analysis which are not so important, and which are simply on the level of programs or concrete structures. So, for this distinction I think I would agree with Lyotard.

EK: Just to follow up: Assuming there is a kind of reverse symmetry between the legal system, which starts with normative expectations and then moves to cognitive reasoning, and the science system, which starts with the cognitive. Where does the normative appear in science?

NL: I think methodology or logic becomes normative, gets a normative marking, which is difficult to reverse, because you can have a correct use of methodology or not, a correct use of logic or not—and then you are supposed to use methodological rules correctly, even if they produce results which you do not want.

WR: Moving on to another topic: What is the status of morality in modern, functionally differentiated societies? In your essay "Ethik als Reflexionstheorie der Moral," you state that morality is a binary code—good/bad—but not a function system. My question is: How is that possible?

How can you have a binary code not attached to a function system? True/false is attached to science, to have or not to have is attached to the economy, etc. But somehow good/bad does not have its own system. How is that possible?

NL: The first questions is: Why should it be impossible? Or, what are the conditions that allow the code to be free from the consequence of producing a known system. In traditional societies, there was a tendency to think of morality as the central code of all society. Then you have different moralities or different programs for moral judgment in the nobility and the lower class. But, under this condition, morality was coupled with manners, with good manners, and with the clear distinction of inside and outside, almost the kind of generalized village concept—"we and the others"—and under this condition you could describe society as a moral, naturally moral unit, an entity, an entity which has, by nature, a morality. But this broke down in the eighteenth century, and I think that this must have to do with the shift from stratificatory or segmentary, family-oriented societies towards functionally differentiated ones. And now I think we can no longer produce a functional subsystem within society which uses the moral code. Either morality has to be *the* society—and Durkheim thought in these terms—but then you have, of course, the question of what to do with the people who have different opinions and object to the consequences of moral judgment. So, my characterization of the present situation is that we have a distinction between good and bad, mostly because we can evaluate, according to rules, in such a way as to make clear what kind of people we would accept as persons and what kind of people we would reject, would refuse to interact with, or would not trust, and so on and so forth. But on the level of the program, that means on the level of the criteria that indicate what is good and what is bad, we don't have consensus anymore. And we try to change moral programs, or to differentiate moral programs, according to what function system we have in view. So there is a certain morality in the family, or in intimate relations, and a different one in politics. You could not use the moral program—there is always a good/bad or good/evil distinction—but we could not use the program adequate for intimate relations in politics, and vice versa.

WR: Following up on that, you have indicated in that same essay as well as in other essays that the moral code acts like a bacterial infection—you use that phrase—and that this can have good consequences, as bacterial infections can have good consequences. But you really emphasize the negative consequences. Specifically, you insist on what you call the orthogonal relationship between codes. And that the danger of the moral code is that it does not respect that orthogonal relationship. In other words, in politics, the binary code that operates is government/opposition, and the danger of the moral code is that it overlays that distinction with good/bad, such that government equals good and opposition equals bad, or the other way around, government equals bad, opposition equals good, and that you see this as a threat. Could you comment on that?

NL: Well, the description is OK. I mean, I think that functional differentiation requires the differentiation of codes. You could not reintegrate them by a metacode of good and bad, or good and evil. Otherwise we would simply collapse functional differentiation. And in fact we have empirical reasons to see that there is a resistance against the moralizing of codes—for example, resistance against thinking "Rich people are good." We can, of course, think of rich as good, and poor as bad, but also vice versa, as Christians would tend to think; for example, poor people have a better start into salvation than rich people because they are inherently prevented from doing bad things. So, in this sense, the moral code cannot be congruent in its positive and negative values with any kind of other codes, not even with the legal code, because we cannot think of a criminal who has to go into prison for a limited time as morally bad, because then he stays morally bad when he gets out of prison. To destroy a person morally is much more severe than to give a fine, or to give a prison sentence. So, this is one thing, but this does not mean that the codes and programs of function systems are completely indifferent or immune from moral evaluations. And I think that function systems use the moral code to fight disintegrative or pathological cases in their own codes. So, if we tend to think that the governing party is morally good, and if we tend to think that the opposition party is morally bad, and if we have election campaigns which use moral evaluations, if we fight with moral terms within the political campaign, then this is not acceptable for moral reasons. Politically it may work, but morally you think: "I want to be able to choose the opposition party, but if these are the bad guys, then I am prevented, and I don't like this."

WR: So you introduce a paradox here. In other words, your intention is to restrict the use of moral discourse in function systems, and the reason why is, in a certain sense, a moral imperative. It's moral; there is a moral or ethical imperative to restrict the use of morality.

NL: Not the reason why but the form in which. I mean the reason why is of course maintaining the code.

WR: Maintaining the code is, in a sense, almost a moral imperative. Otherwise you have dedifferentiation.

NL: You have problems only in pathological cases. If you try to collapse the code, then this case becomes a moral problem. The moral code is evoked, so to speak, if somebody intends to collapse the code of the function system, either to integrate the function code into a moral scheme, or just to say, "I'm the only possible leader of this country, and the other ones are bad." This may be politically successful, but it endangers the political system.

WR: It's being used right now in the United States by those on the Right who identify themselves as Christian, and say only Christian morality, only Christians are patriots, only Christians are moral—and their definition of Christianity is very narrow, which excludes most Christians.

EK: But not just by... When Clinton campaigned for a health care bill he invoked...

WR: Right, he was trying to tap in—you have to—there is sort of an obligatory—you have to believe in God if you're a politician in this country. So Clinton has to demonstrate ostentatiously that he believes in God; he has to invoke God's name. This has become part of American politics. And it's being really fueled by the so-called Christian Right. What is your perspective on this?

NL: I think that's a dangerous thing, like the McCarthy campaign in the '50s. "We are not communists; the others are communists." And there is maybe a tendency just to... it may be politically successful, depending on the electorate, and... but there are, I think, in a developed... in a morality which is appropriate to functional differentiation we should morally object to this. In Brazil, for example, there is now, for the first time, an electoral campaign where the president doesn't show himself with the Cross in the background. And Cardoza is the first... even he used to make much out of his relationship to the church. But Cardoza now doesn't do this, and this is a very interesting development, given a largely illiterate population which has close ties to the church. But the main point is that we need what I call a polycontextural logic or way to make distinctions, and we should be able to switch from one distinction to another by what Gotthard Günther would call transjunctional operations. And this would be a requirement of functional differentiation. My skepticism about morality is that it is very strong on the level of interaction and in the media, on television...

EK: Your objection?

NL: Normally moralists think that to make a distinction between good and bad is good.

WR: You're willing to say that at times to make that distinction is bad?

NL: Yeah, sometimes it is bad, and you have to look at the consequences. I'm not going from Kant to the Marquis de Sade, but I think ethics and other moral conditions should be able to warn against an unreflected use of moral judgment.

WR: In this way, are you like Max Weber? In other words, in Max Weber's "Politics as a Vocation," he made a distinction between, well, it's translated into English as the "ethics of ultimate ends" and the "ethics of responsibility." Leaving the word "responsibility" aside for a moment, is your objection to morality similar to his objection to the ethics of ultimate ends?

NL: Well...

WR: Within the political system?

NL: The translation is not good, by the way. *Gesinnung* is not an end in the sense which I have in mind, but a principle. I would translate "ethics of principles" and "ethics of consequences or results," and the problem with this distinction, of course, is that it is difficult to know results. So, if you stick to an ethics of responsibility, you have to suppose that you can know the outcome of your actions, which is more or less fictional, or utopian. And also there is normally a change of preferences; you see the outcome of your action, you change your preferences, and neither the principled ethics nor the Weberian ethics of responsibility can cope with the problem of changing your preferences.

WR: But on the other hand, when you say that you at times want to apply the value "bad" to the good/bad distinction, in a sense you're applying a sort of ethics of consequences, because you fear the consequences of employing that distinction here in this area.

NL: But then I think I have a kind of help in judging functional incompatibilities, and if I start with the idea that we should not fuse the codes—this of course is a theoretical argument—but if this is correct, then the consequences are a secondary question. You can condemn the collapse of distinctions, but then you are obliged to give reasons for this condemnation, and then you have to show what kind of trouble would emerge out of this. But I rely on structural reasons, and not only on empirical consequences.

WR: I guess this brings up another question. You place a great reliance on theory. In other words, most of your reasoning comes from theory, and most of your critiques—what I've seen in print and more recently in conversation with you—come from the notion of theory deficit. That is, you find other analyses of society theoretically deficient, too unsophisticated. So, all the empirical evidence that you use is somehow filtered very explicitly through theory. Is there a danger in this, in existing too much on this theoretical level? Or do you find this a great clarifying procedure for you? I'm not sure whether I've phrased my question clearly enough.

EK: I agree that... I have this impression too that somehow your observations of modernity and of specific situations are somehow mediated or filtered through your theoretical framework. And that seems also true, on some level, for direct normative evaluations. And so the question—let's see if I can get this right: What is the relationship between a theory, or a theory deficit, and a particular evaluation or political action? OK, this idea... OK, yet another way to phrase this: On the one hand, you say, for instance, it's totally irrelevant what science and theory say about the facts of daily life, how one should act, what one buys for dinner, and these normal, everyday activities; it's also completely indifferent, let's say, to politics; and at the same time it seems irrelevant to, let's say, ecological communication, where you say "I'm not going to recommend any courses of action; I just want to get a better view of the relationship between society and the ecology." But at the same time you critique environmentalist movements for their theory deficit, which seems to suggest that you would recommend that these movements adopt a more sophisticated theory which will then result in a changed politics. So, how do you see the relation between theory, on the one hand, and what is often called praxis or action, on the other?

NL: Well, first of all I go back to the theory of functional differentiation. If we have functional differentiation, this means that there is no technocratic, scientific government of the country or of the world. That is, we cannot make political decisions as an outcome of theoretical or methodological programs within sociology or any other kind of science. So, I reflect my theory in my theory, insofar as I refrain from any kind of political consultancy. If I go to talk with politicians or with business consultants, I'm aware that I'm under another code and just use my theory to ask questions, to find problems. And also in relation to social movement, I think that I would say that if they want to be political parties, and if they want to have a say in political decisions which are not just decisions about ecological problems or new paved roads or enlarged airports or something like this, then they need to understand what logic, or what kind of self-descriptions, exist in other function systems. So, if I say they suffer from a theory deficit, that means that they have a problem in recruiting or in drawing attention to their own goals, or—and this is really a problem with the German Green movement, the internal division between fundamentalists and realists— they have to be able to cope with a world in which other kinds of descriptions prevail.

EK: Just to follow up: It seems that your notion of the political system has been governed by a code of government/opposition, that the primary interest in maintaining the autopoiesis of the political system according to your definition would be simply to remain in power, which seems to have the effect that people, rather than acting according to these particular self-descriptions or acknowledging them, or taking them seriously—taking seriously, for instance, what systems theory, or any theory, says—would prefer much more simplified self-descriptions that are made simply for the sake of remaining in power. You address this in *Ecological Communication.*

WR: And also in the essay "The Future of Democracy," you emphasize the high improbability of politics precisely because what works politically, in the narrow sense (staying in power), at times works against the whole political system at large—as we mentioned before about the use of morality or religion and the like.

NL: I think there are two codes in the political system: one is having power/not having power; the other is holding office/not holding office. If we collapse these distinctions, we would collapse the separation of the political system from the economy, for example, or the system of powerful families. And only if we preserve this difference between having power and being in office can we have the distinction government/opposition, because then it makes sense to go into office, to redefine policies. So this is one complication. And theory can somehow focus on the improbability of maintaining these distinctions. If you collapse the power distinction then you will also collapse the attractiveness of having an office in the political system. Of course, we can play with this idea of evolutionary improbability, in the sense that we see that it is more probable that the system would collapse than it can be maintained. We can focus on problems of the autopoiesis of the political system by just seeing developments which would be dangerous in the long run.

EK: OK, maybe to formulate this differently: At least according to my understanding, there seem very few ways in which, let's say, theory or science can really irritate the political system. And just, for instance, one example: Sometimes one hears that there have been studies, scientific studies, that have been put into the drawer because they seem to be inopportune. And so it seems that the way science and theory work as a system and the way politics works as a system—I don't really see how there can be a real productive irritation between the two.

NL: I think if you use science as adapted to political frameworks, for example, collecting data in some sense, then you could irritate the political system, but not so much in the sense of a theoretical advance.

EK: For example, to justify programs.

NL: Yeah. But there is a kind of structural coupling which is not applied theory, where you have the fantasy of looking for alternatives or to redefine problems. My experience with politics is always this: That I come to problems which are unsolvable for the political system, so I can irritate them in the sense that they cannot pursue their old definitions, even when they have no useable new ones. But I should... but can I make a few more remarks about the addiction to theory? I think that science, or sociology in particular, has two ways of making programs: methods and theories. Theory refers to the outside, to something which you describe as the object of research. Methodology is another type of program which articulates self-reference. To get to true and not to false statements, you have to obey the rules of logic or methodology. And, in fact, I'm aware that I use far more theory than methodology—partly in reaction to the situation in which I find sociology, because they, sociologists, normally mediate theory by methodological, almost subconscious methodological requirements, so that it comes out as a prediction of a relation between variables or something like this. I think that we have gone too far in this direction, and what we need is in fact to have theories which are, in a sense, designed with a technique specified for theories, specific for theories, so that you can make the steps transparent in order to incite or provoke critique. Then you can say, "This step is not correct"; or you can then know what would happen in your theory if you reject the term "autopoiesis," or the term "self-reference," or the term "evolution," or the term "adaptation," or the term "representation," or whatever. The idea is to make a theory transparent so that it is easier to criticize it and, at the same time, more difficult, because you then can see what happens in the theory. If you take this stone out of it, will it crumble; can the stone be replaced; can this argument, this concept be replaced or not? What does it mean in Hegelian theory if distinctions are formulated as contradictions, and contradictions are thought of as inherently unstable. So...

EK: So, is that what you mean by "technique"?

NL: Yeah, theory technique is... we had a lot of seminars on theory technique, and they were really well attended by students, just to see what kind of critique is possible within the framework of theory, or whether the way a theory is built—via cross-tabulation, or functionalism, didactics, or a more humanistic approach, developing everything out of the nature of human beings, whatever—is limiting.

EK: So, technique—I'm not quite sure whether I understand the term "technique" as opposed to "methodology"—technique, what would that be in your theory? Would that be the premise, like the idea of autopoiesis, and then everything that follows out of it? Or the idea of system differentiation and everything that follows out of it?

NL: Well, it could mean, in fact, that you could use undefined terms but only to limit the range of other terms, and not to refer to the outside. So, if people talk about "action," they refer to something which they suppose exists as action. I don't know what an action is, where the beginnings and the limits or the boundaries of one unit called action are, but when someone uses "action theory" to say what action is, then I have, of course, an observer in the background, and I have to be clear on what kind of observing system makes what kind of causal attributions. But then I need a theory of the observer, and I have to work on it, otherwise my idea of causality and action would collapse. And this process tends toward abstraction and toward a kind of structural coupling, if I may say so, between sociology and traditional philosophy, because these are then problem areas in which philosophers normally work. But the essential point is that you can make decisions in building up a theory, and you can be aware of the consequences of decisions, not in the world, but in your own framework. And I can see, for instance, that if I use autopoiesis, I cannot use representation in the traditional sense. How then do I replace reality, representation, adaptation...

EK: ...or consensus...

NL: ...or consensus, or whatever.

EK: These things are incompatible.

NL: Incompatible, but I can't simply say that it's wrong, but I have to find a place for what we have so far described as consensus. And I think this type of work, well, this is a speciality; not everybody is supposed to do it. And this has a special kind of fascination, and it is something which I suppose would be a possible scientific contribution to the self-description of modern society. Not the only one; I think the mass media do that job in general. They describe what kind of society, what kind of world is ours— but to have a little bit of distance from the results of mass-media descriptions, we could use this kind of theory...

EK: ...supplement.

NL: Yeah, supplement, or parasite. But the essential point is that in our historical situation I think we have neglected... partly perhaps because we have deconstructed all these possibilities within philosophy, within analytic philosophy, or historical philosophy in Germany, the Ritter school, and so there is the terrible pedantry of analytic philosophists, on the one hand, and the historical relativistic tendency in Germany, on the other hand—and so that I see an area of a kind of work, a kind of need which could be fulfilled in a better way, at least relative to what I find.

EK: One final topic: You claim that modernity, namely functional differentiation, is a worldwide phenomenon today (*Weltgesellschaft*). First of all, could you explain what you mean by a global society or a *Weltgesellschaft*? And secondly, where does that leave the Third World? Is the Third World included in world society?

NL: There are two answers or two problems implied in this question. First, nobody doubts that there is a global system or that there are strong globalization tendencies in the economy, science, the mass media, and also in international politics. So, the question is only whether we talk about this global system as *the* society, or whether we maintain the concept of society on a local level. But since it is very difficult to distinguish local societies from each other, to know whether Paraguay is a different society than Uruguay, or whether before German unification there were two societies and then suddenly there is one—no sociologist can seriously elaborate this kind of concept. So, in this sense, world society is the only choice we really have. But sociology has not produced a sufficient concept of society that could be elaborated on the world level, and this is exactly my ambition, to reformulate the concept of society and to get rid of classical notions like consensus or sociability, etc. And the Third World, or the developing countries, or the periphery is of course included in world society, and this fact is the starting point—to see why and how long and under what conditions they remain underdeveloped, or whether they have a different kind of future than the centers of modernity have. If you start with a local concept of society, and you say the Serbs are Serbs and therefore they act in a certain way, and the Brazilians are Brazilians, therefore... then you have to bring all the particularities of local conditions in as unexplained variables, and I rather tend—and I think this is more adequate, at least at the end of this century—to see the structures of undeveloped, underdeveloped, developing countries as a consequence of world society, as a consequence of its own type of rationality, a type of rationality which tends to reinforce distinctions or differences: the rich get more rich and the poor more poor; or technological know-how develops in close relation to the research centers, such that those on the periphery can only copy, come late, and have to pay for it; or that demographic control is easier in rich countries than in poor countries; and so on and so forth. So that I start with the world society and then see how the degrees of realization or the structural dynamics in different regions are different, and then I have to explain this by the historical situation, which is already the product of the operations of the world society, and local conditions.

EK: When you talk of world society, you say that world society includes the Third World; that does not mean that the Third World is going to be totally integrated in the world society? Does it mean that?

NL: Oh, this is different because the power of integration—we need a concept of integration that means something. Integrated cannot mean consensus, or uniform standards, or something like this. Integration—I would like to say that integration is the limitation of the degrees of freedom of subsystems. Then you can see, for instance, that Europe or Japan are strongly limited by the existence of world financial markets, by international politics, by increasing awareness, via mass media, of human rights and things like this. So, the real question is whether we could use this kind of loose coupling which is a requirement of integration... reciprocal limitation of freedoms... whether we could find this kind of loose coupling in all kinds of regions of the world or whether there are some types of couplings which prevent the differentiation of function systems in developing countries. The whole world may be negatively integrated, but I would rather say that we would have a distinction between positive integration and negative integration. Positive integration means loose coupling; negative integration means simply that one exclusion reinforces all other ones, and so we will have a...

WR: So, undereducated means unemployed.

NL: ...means unemployed, means poor health, means no access to police, means...

WR: ...which is certainly a feature not just in the Third World but in the United States, where you have a class of people who are virtually excluded in these ways.

NL: And the question is whether we get this kind of ghetto building in cities in Europe, too—if we have a strong migration movement and strong resistance to newcomers of different races.

REFERENCE MATTER

# Notes

INTRODUCTION

1. The reference, of course, is to Jürgen Habermas's use of the phenomenological concept of *Lebenswelt*. See Habermas 1984–87, 2: 119–97.

2. On the influence of Strauss on American conservatism, see Drury 1997.

3. See, for instance, Strauss 1953, 1–8, 81–97.

4. The reference is to Habermas 1992, 115–48.

5. Reference here is to Lyotard 1984.

6. I have stolen this delightful image from my colleague Jonathan Elmer. See his reference to Luhmann's "discursive mitosis" in Elmer 1995, 121.

7. For an overview of the debate on the so-called Duhem-Quine thesis, see the introduction by Sandra G. Harding in Harding, ed., 1976, ix–xxi.

8. The term is Werner Heisenberg's and comes from his "Der Begriff 'abgeschlossene Theorie' in der modernen Naturwissenschaft" (Heisenberg 1973, 87–94; originally published in 1948). Hacking refers to his own thesis as a "gloss on Heisenberg's 'closed systems'" (Hacking 1992, 31) as well as an extension of Duhem's work.

9. "Something is contingent," Luhmann writes, "insofar as it is neither necessary nor impossible; it is just what it is (or was or will be), though it could also be otherwise. The concept thus describes something given (something experienced, expected, remembered, fantasized) in the light of its possibly being otherwise; it describes objects within the horizon of possible variations" (Luhmann 1995b, 106).

10. For a historical overview of the technical, theological, and logical uses of the term, see Blumenberg 1959 and Ritter, ed., 1971–98, vol. 4, cols. 1027–38.

11. For a comparison of Rorty's pragmatism with Luhmann's constructivism, see Wolfe 1994.

12. See, for instance, Habermas 1987b, 126–30, and Strauss 1953, 26–27.

CHAPTER I

1. The piece is contained in Lyotard 1984. For the 1980 Habermas essay, titled "Modernity Versus Postmodernity," see Habermas 1981. Lyotard's title is ironic be-

cause Lyotard, as a modern-day Kantian, replaces Kant's "Enlightenment" ("An Answer to the Question: 'What Is Enlightenment?'"), which is territory now occupied by Habermas, with "Postmodernism," a term conventionally seen as critical of Enlightenment thought.

2. Marquard et al. 1995, 32–33. See also Cassin 1998.

3. From the way he describes order, chaos, and that middle range in between, it is clear that Pagels's order is Weaver's simplicity and Pagels's chaos is Weaver's disorganized complexity. What lies in between for Pagels is equivalent to Weaver's organized complexity.

4. See Gleick 1988, 14, on von Neumann and Laplace's dream.

5. Used by Weaver for a somewhat different purpose (Weaver 1948, 537–38).

6. Some complex systems, in the words of Pagels, "cannot be simulated by anything simpler than the system itself" (Pagels 1989, 12).

7. See Dyke 1988, 39–40, for a discussion of constituting and sealing off an object of investigation.

8. Rosen uses the example of a seemingly simple stone to make this point: "For instance, most of us would regard a stone, say, as a simple system; an organism, on the other hand, is clearly complex. Why do we believe this? Clearly, this intuition rests in the fact that we typically interact with a stone in only a few ways, while we can interact with an organism in many ways. As we multiply the number of ways with which we interact with a stone, its complexity appears to grow; to a geologist, who interacts with a stone in many distinct ways, it can appear infinitely complex. Conversely, as we circumscribe the number of ways we interact with an organism, its complexity accordingly appears to diminish. Thus in this intuitive sense, our characterization of complexity is a reasonable one" (R. Rosen 1985, 322).

9. For two sympathetic accounts of the motivations informing Habermas's reconstructive activities, see Jay 1984, 462–509, and White 1988, 1–6.

10. Habermas had already made this distinction in 1971 in a new introduction to his *Theory and Practice*. See Habermas 1973, 22–24.

11. For his account of the difference between strategic and communicative action, see Habermas 1987b, 294–326; see also White 1988, 44–47.

12. See Gleick 1988, 250–52, and Pagels 1989, 75–76, 83, for the notion of determined but unpredictable phenomena.

13. Luhmann is indebted to Humberto R. Maturana's notion of autopoiesis and cites his definition of observation: "The basic cognitive operation that we perform as observers is the operation of distinction. By means of this operation we define a unity as an entity distinct from a background, characterize both unity and background by the properties with which this operation endows them, and define their separability" (Maturana 1981, 23, cited in Luhmann 1995b, 506 n. 69). The definition of observation as the ability to designate distinctions has been elaborated primarily by George Spencer Brown (Spencer Brown 1979), of whom more will be said in subsequent chapters.

14. Luhmann distinguishes himself here from Maturana, who sees an outside observer as necessary for the construction of a system (Luhmann 1995b, 37).

15. For a critique of Luhmann's reliance on observation and its purported inability to escape a subject-centered philosophy, see Habermas 1987b, 368–85.

16. In fact, Luhmann thinks no longer in terms of simplicity but only in terms of complexity: environmental complexity, disorganized or organized, and system complexity, disorganized or organized (1995b, 27).

17. This is to say not that there are no real or natural objects in the world but only that in order for them to become objects of scientific study, they must be constituted as such by some system, discipline, or discourse. See Canguilhem 1979, 29–30.

18. That question is a qualified form of the more general question "How is order possible?" This question, in turn, is a concretizaton of "How is————possible?" See Luhmann 1981, 195–200.

CHAPTER 2

1. I emphasize Luhmann's critique of the transmission model of information in part to counteract Barbara Herrnstein Smith's (mis?)characterization of Luhmann's position in Smith 1997, 179 n. 24. The interested reader should consult Luhmann's chapter on "Communication and Action," in Luhmann 1995b, 136–75, esp. 139–45; the chapters on "Complexity and Meaning" and "The Improbability of Communication" in Luhmann 1990b, 80–98; Luhmann 1990d, 11–67; Luhmann 1994a; and Luhmann 1970–95, 6: 113–24.

2. The influence of the theoretical biologist Henri Atlan is apparent. In his attempt at a formal definition of organization, Atlan relies on two definitions of order: on the one hand, repetitive or redundant order, and on the other, nonrepetitive order, "which is measured by an information content in Shannon's (1949) sense, *i.e.* a degree of unexpectedness directly related to variety and unhomogeneity. Therefore, the ideas leading to a formal quantitative definition of organization should involve a kind of optimization process so that any optimum organization would correspond to a compromise between maximum information content (*i.e.* maximum variety) and maximum redundancy" (Atlan 1974, 296). On Atlan and his influence on Michel Serres, see Hayles 1990, 56, 205–6.

3. *Mitteilungsverhalten* is Luhmann's term in German. It implies an utterance as well as a type of "conduct" or "attitude" that is distinguished from and implied by that utterance. See especially Luhmann 1995b, 139–45; in German, Luhmann 1984, 193–201.

4. Luhmann mentions the "differentiation between evolutionary mechanisms for variation and for selection, *i.e.*, between language and the media of communication." Language he understands to be the "linguistic freedom to introduce deviations and variations," while the "symbolically generalized media of communica-

tion" are "particular codes (such as truth, political power and law, property and money, love and art) which provide institutionalized rules for determining *when* attempts at communication will probably be successful" (Luhmann 1982, 266).

5. Specifically, the "distinction between artful and artless interpretation . . . is based on the fact that we want to understand with precision some things and not others" (Schleiermacher 1977, 108).

6. Or, in Serres's bleaker vision: "A new obscurity accumulates in unexpected locations, spots that had tended toward clarity; we want to dislodge it but can only do so at ever-increasing prices and at the price of a new obscurity, blacker yet, with a deeper, darker shadow. . . . The shadow brought by knowledge increases by one order of magnitude at every reflection" (Serres 1982b, 18).

CHAPTER 3

1. See, for example, Schmidt, ed., 1987.

2. The original German is as follows: "Das Erkennen kann nicht ohne Erkennen zur Außenwelt kommen. Es ist, mit anderen Worten, Erkennen nur als selbstreferentieller Prozeß" (Luhmann 1970–95, 5: 33).

3. Perhaps the turf is more neo-Kantian. One could profitably trace the view of an infinite and irrational reality back to Rickert. See, for instance, Oakes 1988, esp. 53–72. "Attribution of interest" (see below) might then be seen as an updated version of "value relevance."

CHAPTER 4

1. Acknowledging that in *his* analysis he starts from a description, Lyotard denies that he draws any prescriptions from it. Referring to the Kantian notion of "Idea" (of reason, as opposed to the concept of the understanding), he writes: "I start with a description, and what one can do with a description . . . is to extend, or maximize, as much as possible what one believes to be contained in the description. . . . And the idea that emerges is that there is a multiplicity of small narratives. And from that, 'one ought to be pagan' means 'one must maximize as much as possible the multiplication of small narratives'" (Lyotard and Thébaud 1985, 59). One can see that Lyotard, somewhat like Hannah Arendt (Arendt 1982), wishes to rehabilitate a form of "indeterminate" political judgment, akin to Kantian aesthetic judgment, that is not grounded in (or "terrorized" by) rationally derived norms. Nevertheless, though the imperative to "maximize" is not rationally grounded, it unavoidably remains a prescription that is paradoxically "based" on a description—even if (or precisely because) that description claims that no prescription can be based on a description.

2. For Derrida's critique of a reconstituted "we" in Lyotard, and for the general nervousness shared by Derrida and Lyotard over the issue of nostalgia, see Lyotard 1989, 386–89. See also Alain Badiou's critique and Lyotard's response in

Labarrière, ed., 1989, 109–13, 118–21. The most thoroughgoing critique of Lyotard in the Habermasian vein can be found in Frank 1988, but see also McGowan 1991, 180–91.

3. The model is provided by Popper 1994, but see also Bartley 1984. Here Bartley "solves" the problem by making reason criticizable (in the Popperian sense) but finds that he must exempt logic from that critique.

4. For a brief survey of this silencing tactic in contemporary philosophy (Apel, Habermas, Rorty), see Cassin 1998.

5. See Kainz 1988, 22–34 and 109–10, where he refers to Hegel's philosophy as "the most massive and sustained instance in the history of philosophy of the systematic dialectical development of a conceptual paradox."

6. See also, for example, Luhmann 1990b, 125, and Luhmann 1997, 20, 866–67, 1118.

7. Luhmann 1995b, xlvii–xlviii, 15–16, 481–83; Luhmann 1990d, 412–13.

8. On Luhmann's ambitions regarding the possibilities of a general theory, see Luhmann 1995b, xlv–lii, and Luhmann 1997, 11–15. For a moment of self-deprecating irony regarding the necessary abstraction and complexity of such a general theory, see Luhmann 1995b, xxxvii. On the inexorable turn toward epistemology and its paradoxes in modern thought, see, for instance, the interesting opening passage of Luhmann 1990a, 64–65; Luhmann 1991b, 58–63; and Luhmann 1995a.

9. It must be stressed again that Luhmann equates observation with making a distinction (between self- and hetero-reference), a "cut in the world" that allows observation to "see" itself, but only partially. For a brief overview in English, see Luhmann 1989a, 22–27, and Luhmann 1998, 46–50. For a more comprehensive view, see Luhmann 1990d, 68–121, and Luhmann 1970–95, 5: 228–34.

10. Though Luhmann relies on Spencer Brown's mathematical calculus, Maturana's biology, and Heinz von Foerster's second-order cybernetics for his operational vocabulary, his affinity with certain strains of poststructural thought is apparent. The terminology of "blind spots" calls Paul de Man immediately to mind, but see also Fish 1989. On Luhmann's affinities with Derrida, see Platt 1989. For Luhmann's own reading of Derrida, see Luhmann 1993.

11. Hawking provides the following ironic image of the increase in *disorder* that accompanies every increase in order: "The progress of the human race in understanding the universe has established a small corner of order in an increasingly disordered universe. If you remember every word in this book, your memory will have recorded about two million pieces of information: the order in your brain will have increased by about two million units. However, while you have been reading the book, you will have converted at least a thousand calories of ordered energy, in the form of food, into disordered energy, in the form of heat that you lose to the air around you by convection and sweat. This will increase the disorder of the universe by about twenty million million million million units—or about ten million million million times the increase in order in your brain—and that's if you re-

member *everything* in this book" (Hawking 1990, 152–53). If you remember everything in *this* book, however, the increase in order and disorder will be considerably smaller.

12. Luhmann would seem to concur with Lyotard's assessment. See Luhmann, Bunsen, and Baecker 1990, 66.

CHAPTER 5

1. Also note Lyotard's equation of Luhmann and Habermas in *The Postmodern Condition* (Lyotard 1984, 66) as opposed to the distinction he makes in the essay "Oikos" (Lyotard 1993, 101).

2. Speaking in the language of Luhmann's *Social Systems*, one can say that choice, as structure, is reversible; what is excluded remains accessible as potentiality. As process, however, the irreversible aspect of time enters the picture. One chooses, and then one can never return to the spot where the original choice was made, but must continue to choose in a way that is conditioned by previous choices. See, for instance, Luhmann 1995b, 41–45; for a further complication of these themes, see the discussion of expectations in Chapter 8, "Structure and Time," in Luhmann 1995b, 278–356. The image of the doors marked "male" and "female" comes from Lacan 1977, 151. Clearly, similar examples from other areas can be found: a rational theory of the irrational, for instance, or the inner-worldly rejection of the world. For further discussion, see the essays in Luhmann and Fuchs 1989; and for a far more detailed and challenging examination of the trope of observation in both Lacan and Luhmann, see Elmer 1995.

3. That we could go on to infinity is clear, but that would add nothing to our analysis of the situation.

4. Here, both Luhmann and Lyotard are in agreement with Derrida. As Beardsworth has recently put it, "a decision is always needed because there is no natural status to language, and . . . given this irreducibility of a decision, there are different kinds of decisions—those that recognize their legislative and executive force and those which hide it under some claim to naturality *qua* 'theory' or 'objective science'" (Beardsworth 1996, 12). Theory or objective science here would be equivalent to synthesis, i.e., theory seen as the resolution of, and not as a participant in, a differend.

5. For a fuller discussion of "the jews," see Lyotard 1990, esp. 3–48.

6. See Derrida's response to Lyotard, which contains the following: "He [Lyotard] lays this inexplicability of Auschwitz (which ought at the very least to invite brevity) to the account of 'Verdrängung,' the 'originary repression,' of which it would serve, in sum, as an example or particular instance. This can leave some perplexity, and says nothing at all about that singularity, if there is one, not to mention those quotation marks around some 'jews.' Who died at Auschwitz, the 'jews,' or some Jews? . . . What is the referent of this proper name, Auschwitz? If, as I sus-

pect, one uses this name metonymically, what is the justification for doing so? And what governs this terrible rhetoric? Within such a metonymy, why this name rather than those of all the other camps and mass exterminations? Why this heedless and also troublesome restriction? As paradoxical as it may seem, respect is due equally to all singularities" (Derrida 1992, 212).

7. For a more detailed reading of the "ethical" Lyotard from a systems-theoretical perspective, see Stäheli 1996. See also Bonacker 1997.

8. As Dirk Baecker pointed out to me in personal correspondence, Lyotard's "fable" perfectly describes autopoiesis. Entropic dissipation of elements leads to the negentropic emergence of new elements, with the effect that a "constitutive outside" (Derrida's term) is produced as the source of shock and irritation.

9. That a relatively high level of integration or "consensus" occurs within the "negative" space of exclusion, while the "positive" space of inclusion is marked by a relatively low level of integration, is an anti-Habermasian irony that would appeal to Lyotard.

CHAPTER 6

1. For Maturana's own account of the genesis of the concept of autopoiesis, see his introduction to Maturana and Varela 1980, xi–xxx. See also the interview in Riegas and Vetter 1990. A description of the color-perception experiments can be found in Maturana and Varela 1992, 18–23. For a critical assessment of Maturana's use of the empirical evidence, see Riegas 1990.

2. On Luhmann's appropriation of autopoiesis, see Luhmann 1990b, 1–20; Luhmann 1995b, 34–36; and Luhmann 1997, 65–68. For Maturana's critique of Luhmann's "misuse" of his concept, see Riegas and Vetter 1990, 39–41. For a discussion of Maturana, Varela, and the second wave of cybernetics, see Hayles 1999, 131–59; for "Maturana and Varela with Luhmann," see Wolfe 1998, 41–84.

3. Wittgenstein 1961, 6.421. In citations of this Wittgenstein work, numbers refer to paragraphs, not pages.

4. Operational closure need not be synonymous with homeostasis. On the contrary, the *resilience* of a system, to use C. S. Holling's terminology, depends on its ability to "absorb" and accommodate itself to environmental disturbances, to "keep options open," to "emphasize heterogeneity," and not on its ability to take instructions (Holling 1973, 21). Only by formally rigorous and self-referentially operative closure can the system (indirectly and unpredictably) accommodate environmental perturbations, including the perturbations of an ethical call.

5. On binary codes, see Luhmann 1989a, 36–50; Luhmann 1980–95, 2: 301–13; Luhmann 1970–95, 4: 13–31.

6. On morality, see Luhmann 1989a, 127–32; Luhmann 1989b; Luhmann 1991a; Luhmann 1994b; Luhmann 1997, 241–49, 396–405, 1036–45.

7. The imperative to preserve any particular system's code is the "micro" equiv-

alent of the "macro" imperative to preserve functional differentiation—i.e., modernity—as such.

CHAPTER 7

1. For the "post-Soviet" Marxist perspective on liberal values, see, e.g., Laclau and Mouffe 1985. For the poststructuralist perspective, see, e.g., the influence of Nietzsche and Foucault in Connolly 1991 and Connolly 1993.

2. For general discussions, in English, of the Weimar and Third Reich contexts of Schmitt's thought, see Bendersky 1983 and Schwab 1989.

3. See Schmitt 1988 for elaboration.

4. It should be noted that differentiation, as Luhmann understands it, does not deprive the political of its "universality," but this is also true of all the other realms as well. From within the political system, anything can be viewed as politically relevant, just as from within the economic system, for instance, anything can be seen as potentially profitable, and so on for science, religion, etc.

5. For a more favorable assessment, see Mouffe's reference to Luhmann in her introduction (Mouffe 1993, 4–5).

6. Cohen explicitly questions the public/private distinction Mouffe relies upon (Cohen 1990, 86), and critiques theories like Luhmann's for their "denormatization of politics and law" and "depoliticization of morality" (Cohen, 1990, 87). The point I would stress is not Luhmann's depoliticization of morality (though that, too) but his demoralization of politics.

# Works Cited

Arendt, Hannah. 1982. *Lectures on Kant's Political Philosophy*. Chicago: University of Chicago Press.

Ashmore, Malcolm; Dereck Edwards; and Jonathan Potter. 1994. "The Bottom Line: The Rhetoric of Reality Demonstrations." *Configurations* 2: 1–14.

Atlan, Henri. 1974. "On a Formal Definition of Organization." *Journal of Theoretical Biology* 45: 295–304.

Bartley, W. W., III. 1984. *The Retreat to Commitment*. 2d ed. La Salle: Open Court.

————. 1987a. "Philosophy of Biology Versus Philosophy of Physics." In *Evolutionary Epistemology, Rationality, and the Sociology of Knowledge*, ed. Gerard Radnitzky and W. W. Bartley III, 7–45. La Salle, Ill.: Open Court.

————. 1987b. "Theories of Rationality." In *Evolutionary Epistemology, Rationality, and the Sociology of Knowledge*, ed. Gerard Radnitzky and W. W. Bartley III, 205–14. La Salle, Ill.: Open Court.

Beardsworth, Richard. 1996. *Derrida and the Political*. London: Routledge.

Beiser, Frederick C. 1987. *The Fate of Reason: German Philosophy from Kant to Fichte*. Cambridge, Mass.: Harvard University Press.

Bendersky, Joseph W. 1983. *Carl Schmitt: Theorist for the Reich*. Princeton, N.J.: Princeton University Press.

Benhabib, Seyla. 1995. "Feminism and Postmodernism: An Uneasy Alliance." In Seyla Benhabib et al., *Feminist Contentions: A Philosophical Exchange*, 17–34. New York: Routledge.

Blumenberg, Hans. 1959. "Kontingenz." In *Handwörterbuch für Theologie und Religionswissenschaft*, cols. 1794–95. Tübingen: Mohr, Paul Siebeck.

Bohm, David. 1981. *Wholeness and Implicate Order*. London: Routledge.

Bonacker, Thorsten. 1997. *Kommunikation zwischen Konsens und Konflikt: Möglichkeiten und Grenzen gesellschaftlicher Rationalität bei Jürgen Habermas und Niklas Luhmann*. Oldenburg: Bibliotheks- und Informationssystem der Universität Oldenburg.

Butler, Judith. 1995. "Contingent Foundations: Feminism and the Question of 'Postmodernism.'" In Seyla Benhabib et al., *Feminist Contentions: A Philosophical Exchange*, 35–57. New York: Routledge.

Canguilhem, Georges. 1979. "Der Gegenstand der Wissenschaftsgeschichte." In *Wissenschaftsgeschichte und Epistemologie: Gesammelte Aufsätze*, ed. Wolf Lepenies, trans. Michael Bischoff and Walter Seitter, 22–37. Frankfurt: Suhrkamp.

Cassin, Barbara. 1998. "Speak, If You Are a Man, or The Transcendental Exclusion." In *Terror and Consensus: Vicissitudes of French Thought*, ed. Jean-Joseph Goux and Philip R. Wood, 13–24. Stanford, Calif.: Stanford University Press.

Chomsky, Noam. 1965. *Aspects of the Theory of Syntax*. Cambridge, Mass.: MIT Press.

Cohen, Jean. 1990. "Discourse Ethics and Civil Society." In *Universalism vs Communitarianism: Contemporary Debates in Ethics*, ed. David Rasmussen, 83–105. Cambridge, Mass.: MIT Press.

Connolly, William E. 1991. *Identity and Difference: Democratic Negotiations of Political Paradox*. Ithaca, N.Y.: Cornell University Press.

———. 1993. *Political Theory and Modernity*. Ithaca, N.Y.: Cornell University Press.

Cornell, Drucilla. 1992. *The Philosophy of the Limit*. New York: Routledge.

Cornell, Drucilla; Michel Rosenfeld; and David Gray Carlson, eds. 1992. *Deconstruction and the Possibility of Justice*. New York: Routledge.

Derrida, Jacques. 1978. *Writing and Difference*. Trans. Alan Bass. Chicago: University of Chicago Press.

———. 1989. "Three Questions to Hans-Georg Gadamer." In *Dialogue and Deconstruction: The Gadamer/Derrida Encounter*, ed. Diane P. Michelfelder and Richard E. Palmer, 52–54. SUNY Series in Contemporary Continental Philosophy. Albany, N.Y.: SUNY Press.

———. 1992. "Canons and Metonymies: An Interview with Jacques Derrida." Trans. Richard Rand and Amy Wygant. In *Logomachia: The Conflict of the Faculties*, ed. Richard Rand, 197–218. Lincoln, Nebraska: Nebraska University Press.

Dretske, Fred I. 1981. *Knowledge and the Flow of Information*. Cambridge, Mass.: MIT Press.

Drury, Shadia B. 1997. *Leo Strauss and the American Right*. New York: St. Martin's Press.

Dyke, C. 1988. *The Evolutionary Dynamics of Complex Systems: A Study in Biosocial Complexity*. New York: Oxford University Press.

Elmer, Jonathan. 1995. "Blinded Me with Science: Motifs of Observation and Temporality in Lacan and Luhmann." *Cultural Critique* 30: 101–36.

Engelmann, Paul. 1968. *Letters from Ludwig Wittgenstein: With a Memoir*. Trans. L. Furtmüller. New York: Horizon.

Felman, Shoshana. 1983. *The Literary Speech Act: Don Juan with J. L. Austin, or Seduction in Two Languages*. Trans. Catherine Porter. Ithaca, N.Y.: Cornell University Press.

Fish, Stanley. 1989. *Doing What Comes Naturally: Change, Rhetoric, and the Practice of Theory in Literary and Legal Studies*. Durham, N.C.: Duke University Press.

Foerster, Heinz von. 1981. *Observing Systems*. Seaside, Calif.: Intersystems.

Frank, Manfred. 1988. *Die Grenzen der Verständigung: Ein Geistergespräch zwischen Lyotard und Habermas*. Frankfurt: Suhrkamp.

Fuchs, Peter. 1989. "Die Weltflucht der Mönche: Anmerkungen zur Funktion des monastisch-aszetischen Schweigens." In Niklas Luhmann and Peter Fuchs, *Reden und Schweigen*, 21–45. Frankfurt: Suhrkamp.

Gadamer, Hans-Georg. 1976. "On the Problem of Self-Understanding." In *Philosophical Hermeneutics*, trans. and ed. David E. Linge, 44–58. Berkeley: University of California Press.

———. 1988. *Truth and Method*. Trans. Garrett Barden and John Cummin. Ed. Donald G. Marshall and Joel C. Weinsheimer. Revised ed. New York: Continuum.

Gleick, James. 1988. *Chaos: Making a New Science*. New York: Penguin.

Gray, John. 1996. *Isaiah Berlin*. Princeton, N.J.: Princeton University Press.

Greimas, A. J. 1987. "The Interaction of Semiotic Constraints." In *On Meaning: Selected Writings in Semiotic Theory*, trans. Paul J. Perron and Frank H. Collins, 48–62. Minneapolis: University of Minnesota Press.

Günther, Gotthard. 1979. "Life as Poly-Contexturality." In *Beiträge zur Grundlegung einer operationsfähigen Dialektik*, 2: 283–306. Hamburg: Meiner.

Habermas, Jürgen. 1971. "Vorbereitende Bemerkungen zu einer Theorie der kommunikativen Kompetenz." In Jürgen Habermas and Niklas Luhmann, *Theorie der Gesellschaft oder Sozialtechnologie: Was leistet die Systemforschung?*, 101–41. Frankfurt: Suhrkamp.

———. 1973. *Theory and Practice*. Trans. John Viertel. Boston: Beacon.

———. 1979. "What Is Universal Pragmatics?" In *Communication and the Evolution of Society*, trans. Thomas McCarthy, 1–68. Boston: Beacon.

———. 1981. "Modernity Versus Post-Modernity." Trans. Seyla Benhabib. *New German Critique* 22: 3–14.

———. 1984–87. *The Theory of Communicative Action*. Trans. Thomas McCarthy. 2 vols. Boston: Beacon.

———. 1987a. *Knowledge and Human Interests*. Trans. Jeremy Shapiro. Cambridge, Eng.: Polity.

———. 1987b. *The Philosophical Discourse of Modernity: Twelve Lectures*. Cambridge, Mass.: MIT Press.

———. 1992. *Postmetaphysical Thinking: Philosophical Essays*. Cambridge, Mass.: MIT Press.

———. 1996. *Between Facts and Norms: Contributions to a Discourse Theory of Law and Democracy*. Trans. William Rehg. Cambridge, Mass.: MIT Press.

———. 1997. "Kant's Idea of Perpetual Peace, with the Benefit of Two Hundred Years' Hindsight." In *Perpetual Peace: Essays on Kant's Cosmopolitan Ideal*, ed. James Bohman and Matthias Lutz-Bachmann, 113–53. Cambridge, Mass.: MIT Press.

Hacking, Ian. 1992. "The Self-Vindication of the Laboratory Sciences." In *Science as Practice and Culture*, ed. Andrew Pickering, 29–64. Chicago: University of Chicago Press.

Haraway, Donna J. 1988. "Situated Knowledges: The Science Question in Feminism as a Site of Discourse on the Privilege of Partial Perspective." *Feminist Studies* 14: 575–99.

Harding, Sandra. 1994. "Introduction: Eurocentric Scientific Illiteracy—A Challenge for the World Community." In *The "Racial" Economy of Science*, ed. Sandra Harding, 1–22. Bloomington: Indiana University Press.

Harding, Sandra G., ed. 1976. *Can Theories Be Refuted?: Essays on the Duhem-Quine Thesis*. Dordrecht, Holland: Reidel.

Hartsock, Nancy C. M. 1987. "The Feminist Standpoint: Developing the Ground for a Specifically Feminist Historical Materialism." In *Feminism and Methodology: Social Science Issues*, ed. Sandra Harding, 157–80. Bloomington: Indiana University Press.

Hawking, Stephen. 1990. *A Brief History of Time: From the Big Bang to Black Holes*. New York: Bantam.

Hayles, N. Katherine. 1984. *The Cosmic Web: Scientific Field Models and Literary Strategies in the 20th Century*. Ithaca, N.Y.: Cornell University Press.

———. 1990. *Chaos Bound: Orderly Disorder in Contemporary Literature and Science*. Ithaca, N.Y.: Cornell University Press.

———. 1991. "Constrained Constructivism: Locating Scientific Inquiry in the Theater of Representation." *New Orleans Review* 18, no. 1: 76–85.

———. 1999. *How We Became Posthuman: Virtual Bodies in Cybernetics, Literature, and Informatics*. Chicago: University of Chicago Press.

Heims, Steve Joshua. 1993. *Constructing a Social Science for Postwar America: The Cybernetics Group, 1946–1953*. Cambridge, Mass.: MIT Press.

Heisenberg, Werner. 1973. *Schritte über Grenzen: Gesammelte Reden und Aufsätze*. Erweiterte Neuausgabe. Munich: Piper.

Herbst, Phillip. 1976. *Alternatives to Hierarchies*. Leiden: Nijhoff.

Holling, C. S. 1973. "Resilience and Stability of Ecological Systems." *Annual Review Ecology and Systematics* 4: 1–23.

Holmes, Stephen. 1993. *The Anatomy of Antiliberalism*. Cambridge, Mass.: Harvard University Press.

Horkheimer, Max, and Theodor W. Adorno. 1972. *Dialectic of Enlightenment*. Trans. John Cumming. New York: Seabury.

Hübner, Kurt. 1983. *Critique of Scientific Reason*. Trans. Paul R. Dixon, Jr., and Hollis M. Dixon. Chicago: University of Chicago Press.

Jameson, Fredric. 1991. *Postmodernism, or, The Cultural Logic of Late Capitalism*. Durham, N.C.: Duke University Press.

Jay, Martin. 1984. *Marxism and Totality: The Adventures of a Concept from Lukács to Habermas*. Berkeley: University of California Press.

Kainz, Howard P. 1988. *Paradox, Dialectic, and System: A Contemporary Recon-struction of the Hegelian Problematic.* University Park: Pennsylvania State University Press.

Kant, Immanuel. 1965. *Critique of Pure Reason.* Trans. Norman Kemp Smith. New York: St. Martin's Press.

Kierkegaard, Søren. 1962. *Philosophical Fragments, or, A Fragment of Philosophy.* Trans. David Swenson. Trans. revised by Howard V. Hong. Princeton, N.J.: Princeton University Press.

Labarrière, Pierre-Jean, ed. 1989. *Témoigner du différend: Quand phraser ne se peut.* Paris: Osiris.

Lacan, Jacques. 1977. *Ecrits: A Selection.* Trans. Alan Sheridan. New York: Dutton.

Laclau, Ernesto, and Chantal Mouffe. 1985. *Hegemony and Socialist Strategy: Towards a Radical Democratic Politics.* London: Verso.

Larmore, Charles. 1996. *The Morals of Modernity.* Cambridge, Eng.: Cambridge University Press.

Lawson, Hilary. 1985. *Reflexivity: The Post-Modern Predicament.* La Salle, Ill.: Open Court.

Lessing, Gotthold Ephraim. 1957. "On the Proof of the Spirit and of Power." In *Lessing's Theological Writings: Selections in Translation,* ed. Henry Chadwick, 51–56. Stanford, Calif.: Stanford University Press.

Lettvin, J. Y.; H. R. Maturana; W. S. McCulloch; and W. H. Pitts. 1959. "What the Frog's Eye Tells the Frog's Brain." *Proceedings of the Institute for Radio Engineers* 47: 1940–51.

Luhmann, Niklas. 1970–95. *Soziologische Aufklärung.* 6 Vols. Opladen: Westdeutscher Verlag.

———. 1980–95. *Gesellschaftsstruktur und Semantik: Studien zur Wissenssoziologie der modernen Gesellschaft.* 4 vols. Frankfurt: Suhrkamp.

———. 1981. "Wie ist soziale Ordnung möglich?" In Niklas Luhmann, *Gesellschaftsstruktur und Semantik: Studien zur Wissenssoziologie der modernen Gesellschaft,* 2: 195–285. Frankfurt: Suhrkamp.

———. 1982. *The Differentiation of Society.* Trans. Stephen Holmes and Charles Larmore. New York: Columbia University Press.

———. 1984. *Soziale Systeme: Grundriß einer allgemeinen Theorie.* Frankfurt: Suhrkamp.

———. 1987. *Archimedes und wir: Interviews.* Ed. Georg Stanitzek. Berlin: Merve.

———. 1989a. *Ecological Communication.* Trans. John Bednarz, Jr. Chicago: University of Chicago Press.

———. 1989b. "Ethik als Reflexionstheorie der Moral." In Niklas Luhmann, *Gesellschaftsstruktur und Semantik: Studien zur Wissenssoziologie der modernen Gesellschaft,* 3: 358–447. Frankfurt: Suhrkamp.

———. 1990a. "The Cognitive Program of Constructivism and a Reality That Remains Unknown." In *Selforganization: Portrait of a Scientific Revolution,* ed.

Wolfgang Krohn, Günter Küppers, and Helga Nowotny, 64–85. Dordrecht: Kluwer.

———. 1990b. *Essays on Self-Reference.* New York: Columbia University Press.

———. 1990c. *Political Theory in the Welfare State.* Trans. John Bednarz, Jr. Berlin: de Gruyter.

———. 1990d. *Die Wissenschaft der Gesellschaft.* Frankfurt: Suhrkamp.

———. 1991a. "Paradigm Lost: On the Ethical Reflection of Morality. Speech on the Occasion of the Award of the Hegel Prize 1989." Trans. David Roberts. *Thesis Eleven* 29: 82–94.

———. 1991b. "Sthenographie und Euryalistik." In *Paradoxien, Dissonanzen, Zusammenbrüche: Situationen offener Epistemologie,* ed. Hans Ulrich Gumbrecht and K. Ludwig Pfeiffer, 58–82. Frankfurt: Suhrkamp.

———. 1993. "Deconstruction as Second-Order Observing." *New Literary History* 24: 763–82.

———. 1994a. "How Can the Mind Participate in Communication." In *Materialities of Communication,* ed. Hans Ulrich Gumbrecht and K. Ludwig Pfeiffer, trans. William Whobrey, 370–87. Stanford, Calif.: Stanford University Press.

———. 1994b. "Politicians, Honesty and the Higher Amorality of Politics." Trans. Josef Bleicher. *Theory, Culture and Society* 11, no. 2: 25–36.

———. 1994c. "Speaking and Silence." Trans. Kerstin Behnke. *New German Critique* 61: 25–37.

———. 1995a. "The Paradoxy of Observing Systems." *Cultural Critique* 31 (1995): 37–55.

———. 1995b. *Social Systems.* Trans. John Bednarz, Jr., with Dirk Baecker. Stanford, Calif.: Stanford University Press.

———. 1996. *Protest: Systemtheorie und soziale Bewegung.* Ed. Kai-Uwe Hellmann. Frankfurt: Suhrkamp.

———. 1997. *Die Gesellschaft der Gesellschaft.* Frankfurt: Suhrkamp.

———. 1998. *Observations on Modernity.* Trans. William Whobrey. Stanford, Calif.: Stanford University Press.

Luhmann, Niklas; Frederick D. Bunsen; and Dirk Baecker. 1990. *Unbeobachtbare Welt: Über Kunst und Architektur.* Bielefeld: Haux.

Luhmann, Niklas, and Peter Fuchs. 1989. *Reden und Schweigen.* Frankfurt: Suhrkamp.

Lyotard, Jean-François. 1984. *The Postmodern Condition: A Report on Knowledge.* Trans. Geoff Bennington and Brian Massumi. Minneapolis: University of Minnesota Press.

———. 1988. *The Differend: Phrases in Dispute.* Trans. Georges Van Dan Abbeele. Minneapolis: University of Minnesota Press.

———. 1989. *The Lyotard Reader.* Ed. Andrew Benjamin. Oxford: Blackwell.

———. 1990. *Heidegger and "the jews."* Trans. Andreas Michel and Mark Roberts. Minneapolis: University of Minnesota Press.

————. 1991. *The Inhuman.* Trans. Geoffrey Bennington and Rachel Bowlby. Stanford, Calif.: Stanford University Press.

————. 1992. "*Sensus Communis.*" In *Judging Lyotard,* ed. Andrew Benjamin, 1–25. New York: Routledge.

————. 1993. *Political Writings.* Trans. Bill Readings and Kevin Paul Geiman. Minneapolis: University of Minnesota Press.

————. 1994. *Lessons on the Analytic of the Sublime.* Trans. Elizabeth Rottenberg. Stanford, Calif.: Stanford University Press.

Lyotard, Jean-François, and Christine Pries. 1989. "Das Undarstellbare—Wider das Vergessen: Ein Gespräch zwischen Jean-François Lyotard und Christine Pries." In *Das Erhabene: Zwischen Grenzerfahrung und Größenwahn,* ed. Christine Pries, 319–47. Weinheim: VCH, Acta Humaniora.

Lyotard, Jean-François, and Jean-Loup Thébaud. 1985. *Just Gaming.* Trans. Wlad Godzich. Minneapolis: University of Minnesota Press.

McCormick, John P. 1997. *Carl Schmitt's Critique of Liberalism: Against Politics as Technology.* Cambridge, Eng.: Cambridge University Press.

McGowan, John. 1991. *Postmodernism and Its Critics.* Ithaca, N.Y.: Cornell University Press.

McGuinness, Brian. 1988. *Wittgenstein: A Life. Young Ludwig, 1889–1921.* Berkeley: University of California Press.

Marquard, Odo. 1989. *Aesthetica und Anaesthetica: Philosophische Überlegungen.* Paderborn: Friedrich Schöningh.

Marquard, Odo, et al. 1995. *Menschliche Endlichkeit und Kompensation.* Bamberg: Verlag Fränkischer Tag.

Marsh, James L. 1989. "Strategies of Evasion: The Paradox of Self-Referentiality and the Post-Modern Critique of Rationality." *International Philosophical Quarterly* 29: 339–49.

Maturana, Humberto R. 1981. "Autopoiesis." In *Autopoiesis: A Theory of Living Organization,* ed. Milan Zeleny, 21–33. New York: North Holland.

————. 1990. "The Biological Foundations of Self Consciousness and the Physical Domain of Existence." In Niklas Luhmann, et al., *Beobachter: Konvergenz der Erkenninistheorien?,* 47–117. Munich: Wilhelm Fink.

————. 1991. "Science and Daily Life: The Ontology of Scientific Explanation." In *Research and Reflexivity,* ed. Frederick Steier, 30–52. London: Sage.

Maturana, Humberto R., and Francisco J. Varela. 1980. *Autopoiesis and Cognition: The Realization of the Living.* Dordrecht: Riedel.

————. 1992. *The Tree of Knowledge: The Biological Roots of Human Understanding.* Revised Edition. Trans. Robert Paolucci. Boston: Shambhala.

Meier, Heinrich. 1995. *Carl Schmitt and Leo Strauss: The Hidden Dialogue.* Chicago: University of Chicago Press.

————. 1998. *The Lesson of Carl Schmitt: Four Chapters on the Distinction Between Political Theology and Political Theology.* Trans. Marcus Brainard. Chicago: University of Chicago Press.

Mouffe, Chantal. 1993. *The Return of the Political*. London: Verso.

Müller, Harro. 1994. "Luhmann's Systems Theory as Theory of Modernity." *New German Critique* 61: 39–54.

Neumann, John von. 1966. *Theory of Self-Reproducing Automata*. Ed. Arthur W. Burks. Urbana: University of Illinois Press.

Oakes, Guy. 1988. *Weber and Rickert: Concept Formation in the Cultural Sciences*. Cambridge, Mass.: MIT Press.

Pagels, Heinz. 1989. *The Dreams of Reason: The Computer and the Rise of the Sciences of Complexity*. New York: Bantam.

Pippin, Robert B. 1989. *Hegel's Idealism: The Satisfactions of Self-Consciousness*. Cambridge, Eng.: Cambridge University Press.

Platt, Robert. 1989. "Reflexivity, Recursion and Social Life: Elements for a Postmodern Sociology." *Sociological Review* 37: 636–67.

Popper, Karl L. 1965. *Conjectures and Refutations: The Growth of Scientific Knowledge*. 2d ed. New York: Basic.

———. 1994. *The Myth of the Framework: In Defence of Science and Rationality*. Ed. M. A. Notturno. London: Routledge.

Prigogine, Ilya, and Isabelle Stengers. 1982. "Postface: Dynamics from Leibniz to Lucretius." In Michel Serres, *Hermes: Literature, Science, Philosophy*, 137–55. Baltimore: Johns Hopkins University Press.

Quine, Willard Van Orman. 1964. *From a Logical Point of View: 9 Logico-Philosophical Essays*. 2d ed. Cambridge, Mass.: Harvard University Press.

———. 1969. *"Ontological Relativity" and Other Essays*. New York: Columbia University Press.

———. 1981. *Theories and Things*. Cambridge, Mass.: Harvard University Press.

Riegas, Volker. 1990. "Das Nervensystem-offenes oder geschlossenes System?" In *Zur Biologie der Kognition: Ein Gespräch mit Humberto R. Maturana und Beiträge zur Diskussion seines Werkes*, ed. Volker Riegas and Christian Vetter, 99–115. Frankfurt: Suhrkamp.

Riegas, Volker, and Christian Vetter. 1990. "Gespräch mit Humberto R. Maturana." In *Zur Biologie der Kognition: Ein Gespräch mit Humberto R. Maturana und Beiträge zur Diskussion seines Werkes*, ed. Volker Riegas and Christian Vetter, 11–90. Frankfurt: Suhrkamp.

Ritter, Joachim, ed. 1971–98. *Historisches Wörterbuch der Philosophie*. 10 volumes to date. Darmstadt: Wissenschaftliche Buchgesellschaft.

Rorty, Richard. 1989. *Contingency, Irony, and Solidarity*. Cambridge, Eng.: Cambridge University Press.

Rose, Gillian. 1981. *Hegel Contra Sociology*. London: Athlone.

Rosen, Robert. 1977. "Complexity as a System Property." *International Journal of General Systems* 3: 227–32.

———. 1985. *Anticipatory Systems: Philosophical, Mathematical and Methodological Foundations*. Oxford: Pergamon.

———. 1986. "The Physics of Complexity." In *Power, Autonomy, Utopia: New Approaches Toward Complex Systems,* ed. Robert Trappl, 35–42. New York: Plenum.

Rosen, Stanley. 1969. *Nihilism: A Philosophical Essay.* New Haven, Conn.: Yale University Press.

Scheuerman, William. 1999. *Carl Schmitt: The End of Law.* Lanham, Md.: Rowman and Littlefield.

Schlegel, Friedrich. 1971. "On Incomprehensibility." In Friedrich Schlegel, *"Lucinde" and the "Fragments,"* trans. Peter Firchow, 259–71. Minneapolis: University of Minnesota Press.

Schleiermacher, Friedrich. 1977. *Hermeneutics: The Handwritten Manuscripts.* Ed. Heinz Kimmerle. Trans. James Duke and Jack Forstman. Missoula, Mont.: Scholars.

Schleifer, Ronald; Robert Con Davis; and Nancy Mergler. 1992. *Culture and Cognition: The Boundaries of Literary and Scientific Inquiry.* Ithaca, N.Y.: Cornell, University Press.

Schmidt, Siegfried J., ed. 1987. *Der Diskurs des Radikalen Konstruktivismus.* Frankfurt: Suhrkamp.

Schmitt, Carl. 1976. *The Concept of the Political.* Trans. George Schwab. New Brunswick, N.J.: Rutgers University Press.

———. 1985. *The Crisis of Parliamentary Democracy.* Cambridge, Mass.: MIT Press.

———. 1988. *Der Nomos der Erde im Völkerrecht des Jus Publicum Europaeum.* Berlin: Duncker und Humblot.

Schwab, George. 1989. *The Challenge of the Exception: An Introduction to the Political Ideas of Carl Schmitt Between 1921 and 1936.* New York: Greenwood.

Schwanitz, Dietrich. 1995. "Systems Theory According to Niklas Luhmann—Its Environment and Conceptual Strategies." *Cultural Critique* 30: 137–70.

Serres, Michel. 1982a. *Hermes: Literature, Science, Philosophy.* Baltimore: Johns Hopkins University Press.

———. 1982b. *The Parasite.* Trans. Lawrence R. Schehr. Baltimore: Johns Hopkins University Press.

Shannon, Claude E., and Warren Weaver. 1949. *The Mathematical Theory of Communication.* Urbana: University of Illinois Press.

Simon, Josef. 1989. "Good Will to Understand and the Will to Power: Remarks on an 'Improbable Debate.'" In *Dialogue and Deconstruction: The Gadamer/Derrida Encounter,* ed. Diane P. Michelfelder and Richard E. Palmer, 162–75. SUNY Series in Contemporary Continental Philosophy. Albany, New York: SUNY Press.

Smith, Barbara Herrnstein. 1997. *Belief and Resistance: Dynamics of Contemporary Intellectual Controversy.* Cambridge, Mass.: Harvard University Press.

Spencer Brown, George. 1979. *Laws of Form.* New York: Dutton.

Stäheli, Urs. 1996. "From Victimology Towards Parasitology: A Systems Theoretical Reading of the Function of Exclusion." *Recherches Sociologiques* 27, no. 2: 59–80.

Stepan, Nancy Leys. 1986. "Race and Gender: The Role of Analogy in Science." *Isis* 77: 261–77.

Strauss, Leo. 1953. *Natural Right and History.* Chicago: University of Chicago Press.

———. 1976. "Comments on Carl Schmitt's *Der Begriff des Politischen.*" In Carl Schmitt, *The Concept of the Political,* trans. George Schwab, 81–105. New Brunswick, N.J.: Rutgers University Press.

———. 1988. *"What Is Political Philosophy?" and Other Studies.* Chicago: University of Chicago Press.

Thompson, John B. 1982. "Universal Pragmatics." In *Habermas: Critical Debates,* ed. John B. Thompson and David Held, 116–33. Cambridge, Mass.: MIT Press.

Varela, Francisco; Evan Thompson; and Eleanor Rosch. 1993. *The Embodied Mind: Cognitive Science and Human Understanding.* Cambridge, Mass.: MIT Press, 1993.

Waismann, Friedrich. 1965. "Notes on Talks with Wittgenstein." *Philosophical Review* 74: 12–16.

Weaver, Warren. 1948. "Science and Complexity." *American Scientist* 36: 536–44.

Weber, Max. 1946. *From Max Weber: Essays in Sociology.* Ed. H. H. Geerth and C. Wright Mills. New York: Oxford.

Weber, Samuel. 1985. "Afterword: Literature—Just Making It." In Jean-François Lyotard and Jean-Loup Thébaud, *Just Gaming,* trans. Wlad Godzich, 101–20. Minneapolis: University of Minnesota Press.

Wellmer, Albrecht. 1991. *The Persistence of Modernity: Essays on Aesthetics, Ethics, and Postmodernism.* Cambridge, Mass.: MIT Press.

White, Stephen K. 1988. *The Recent Work of Jürgen Habermas: Reason, Justice and Modernity.* Cambridge, Eng.: Cambridge University Press.

Wilson, Harlan. 1975. "Complexity as a Theoretical Problem: Wider Perspectives in Political Theory." In *Organized Social Complexity: Challenge to Politics and Policy,* ed. Todd LaPorta, 281–331. Princeton, N.J.: Princeton University Press.

Wittgenstein, Ludwig. 1961. *Tractatus Logico-Philosophicus.* Trans. D. F. Pears and B. F. McGuinness. London: Routledge.

———. 1965. "A Lecture on Ethics." *Philosophical Review* 74: 3–12.

Wolfe, Cary. 1994. "Making Contingency Safe for Liberalism: The Pragmatics of Epistemology in Rorty and Luhmann." *New German Critique* 61: 101–27.

———. 1998. *Critical Environments: Postmodern Theory and the Pragmatics of the "Outside."* Minneapolis: University of Minnesota Press.

Wolin, Richard. 1992. *The Terms of Cultural Criticism: The Frankfurt School, Existentialism Poststructuralism.* New York: Columbia University Press.

# Index

Abraham, 70f

Adorno, Theodor W., 30, 110, 127, 130, 144, 168

Antinomy, 3, 5, 9–14 *passim*, 27, 92, 116, 119

Apel, Karl Otto, 32

Archimedean standpoint, 31, 105, 112

Arendt, Hannah, 228

Aristotle, 21, 90, 198

Atlan, Henri, 61, 227n2

Auschwitz, 230n6

Autopoesis, 128–30, 144–49 *passim*, 172–74, 193, 206, 216–19, 226n13, 231n8

Baecker, Dirk, 231n8

Bartley, W. W., III, 37, 229n3

Bateson, Gregory, 172

Baudelaire, Charles-Pierre, 111

Beardsworth, Richard, 230n4

Benhabib, Seyla, 6, 126

Bentham, Jeremy, 147

Berlin, Isaiah, 151

Blackmun, Harry Andrew, 141, 143

Bohm, David, 80

Bohr, Niels, 80–81, 86–87

Butler, Judith, 27, 125–26

Cantor, Georg, 189

Cartesianism, 14, 44, 78–84 *passim*

Causality, 5, 13–19 *passim*, 38, 76–82, 99, 129, 178, 192, 208, 218

Chomsky, Noam, 6, 44

Clinton, Bill, 147, 213

Code/Encode, 39, 60–62, 66, 68, 108, 122, 145–49, 161, 167, 184–89 *passim*, 206–16 *passim*, 227n4, 231n7

Cohen, Jean, 165

Cole, G. D. H., 157f

Communication, 22, 26f, 31–33, 40–45 *passim*, 50–65 *passim*, 69, 71, 76–81 *passim*, 103–9 *passim*, 116–21 *passim*, 129, 131, 144–48 *passim*, 161, 167, 172, 183, 186, 195, 198, 201, 227n4

Complexity, 18, 26f, 32–55 *passim*, 63–68 *passim*, 81, 88, 100, 104, 111–14 *passim*, 121, 144–49, 184, 189, 202, 208, 226, 227n16

Comte, Auguste, 111

Constructivism, 26ff, 73–82 *passim*, 104, 179, 184, 192

Contingency, 2–12 *passim*, 18–33 *passim*, 39, 50–55 *passim*, 62–66 *passim*, 77–78, 97, 104–8 *passim*, 126, 131–35 *passim*, 142, 147, 171, 225n9

Copernicus, Nicolaus, 73

Cornell, Drucilla, 27f, 138–43

Critical Theory, 30–31, 102, 112, 127. *See also* Frankfurt School

De Man, Paul, 229n10

Derrida, Jacques, 13, 26, 55–62 *passim*, 88, 136–41 *passim*, 230, 231n8

Differend, 27, 92–97, 106, 115–20, 142, 230n4

Differentiation, 9–12 *passim*, 23–30

*Cultural Memory* | *in the Present*

Didier Maleuvre, *Museum Memories: History, Technology, Art*

Jacques Derrida, *Monolingualism of the Other; or, The Prosthesis of Origin*

Andrew Baruch Wachtel, *Making a Nation, Breaking a Nation: Literature and Cultural Politics in Yugoslavia*

Niklas Luhmann, *Love as Passion: The Codification of Intimacy*

Mieke Bal, ed., *The Practice of Cultural Analysis: Exposing Interdisciplinary Interpretation*

Jacques Derrida and Gianni Vattimo, eds., *Religion*